Wise Management in Organisational Complexity

Wise Management in Organisational Complexity

Edited by

Mike J. Thompson
China Europe International Business School, China

and

David Bevan
China Europe International Business School, China

First published 2013 by
PALGRAVE MACMILLAN

Palgrave Macmillan in the UK is an imprint of Macmillan Publishers Limited, registered in England, company number 785998, of Houndmills, Basingstoke, Hampshire RG21 6XS.

Palgrave Macmillan in the US is a division of St Martin's Press LLC, 175 Fifth Avenue, New York, NY 10010.

Palgrave Macmillan is the global academic imprint of the above companies and has companies and representatives throughout the world.

Palgrave® and Macmillan® are registered trademarks in the United States, the United Kingdom, Europe and other countries.

ISBN 978–1–137–00264–8

This book is printed on paper suitable for recycling and made from fully managed and sustained forest sources. Logging, pulping and manufacturing processes are expected to conform to the environmental regulations of the country of origin.

A catalogue record for this book is available from the British Library.

A catalog record for this book is available from the Library of Congress.

10   9   8   7   6   5   4   3   2   1
22 21 20 19 18 17 16 15 14 13

Printed and bound in the United States of America

This volume is dedicated to Henri-Claude de Bettignies, Distinguished Emeritus Professor of Globally Responsible Leadership, China Europe International Business School (CEIBS) and Emeritus Professor of Asian Business, the Aviva Chair in Leadership and Responsibility, INSEAD, who has given his career in humility and wisdom to the development of responsible leadership in business schools across the world. Prof. de Bettignies is founder of the Euro–China Centre for Responsibility and Leadership (ECCLAR) at CEIBS in 2006.

Contents

List of Illustrations

Notes on Contributors

David Bevan is Senior Research Fellow at the Euro–China Centre for Responsibility and Leadership at the China Europe International Business School in Shanghai. David has a PhD in Management from the School of Accounting at King's College London, he is a Fellow of the Higher Education Academy (UK) and holds advanced degrees in Managing Change (Sheffield) and Academic Practice (King's College London). He is Professor of Applied Ethics at Grenoble Ecole de Management (France) and Senior Wicklander Fellow at the Institute for Professional and Business Ethics at DePaul University (Chicago). In outreach work David has held the office of Academic Director of EABIS from 2008–12. David is a visiting professor at EDHEC Lille and at the Université Libre de Bruxelles. David's research interests operate around a critical management perspective on the role of business in society.

Robert Chia is Research Professor of Management at the Adam Smith Business School, University of Glasgow. He received his PhD from Lancaster University. He has authored/edited five books and published extensively in the top international management journals including *Academy of Management Journal, Organization Science, Organization Studies, Human Relations, Journal of Management Studies, Journal of Management Inquiry* and *Long Range Planning*. His research interests include: the application of process thinking to human actions, decisions and change; the logic of practice in strategy making; East–West philosophies and wisdom and their implications for the conduct of business; and the aims of management education.

Mary C. Gentile is director of an innovative curriculum, Giving Voice to Values, launched by Aspen Institute and Yale SOM, now supported by Babson College. This pioneering approach to values-driven leadership has been featured in the *Financial Times, Harvard Business Review, McKinsey Quarterly* online, *Stanford Social Innovation Review, Strategy + Businesss* and is being piloted in 250 business schools and organisations globally. She is the author of numerous books and articles, including *Giving Voice to Values: How to Speak Your Mind When You Know What's Right* (2010). Currently on the faculty at Babson College and an educational consultant, she was previously at Harvard Business School. She obtained her PhD from State University of New York-Buffalo.

Jay Hays has been at Swinburne University of Technology, Melbourne, Australia, since 2010, developing the university's Industry Engaged Learning curriculum and community engagement frameworks, including new service learning, internship, and workplace learning units. Jay previously taught management and leadership courses at the Australian National University (ANU) in Canberra, Australia. It was at ANU where Jay realised that the management curriculum lacked depth, nuance, meaningfulness and twenty-first-century relevance. He began to redress this lacuna by introducing experiential components and aspects of wisdom into his seminars and courses. His efforts to enrich and make higher education more relevant have been recognised by nominations for numerous international honours, including the American Order of Merit, International Educator of the Year and Gold Medal for Australia. He received his PhD from Boston University.

Robin Holt is a professor at the University of Liverpool Management School, UK. With Robert Chia he published *Strategy without Design*, which, if nothing else, is a good description of an academic career that has seen him hold down various jobs in UK universities, mainly as a researcher. Having studied government, economics and philosophy at the London School of Economics, his work addresses questions of organisational form configured by experiences of judgment, sympathy and imagination. He is senior editor of the journal *Organization Studies* and is co-editor of the *Oxford Handbook of Process Philosophy and Organization Studies*.

Po-Keung Ip is Distinguished Professor and Director of the Center for Applied Ethics, the Graduate Institute of Philosophy, National Central University, Taiwan. He graduated from the Chinese University of Hong Kong, studying philosophy and sociology, and received his doctoral degree in philosophy from the University of Western Ontario, Canada. He is a member of the editorial board of the *Journal of Business Ethics* and *Asian Journal of Business Ethics*. He is editor of the 'Eastern Cultural, Philosophical and Religious Foundations of Business Ethics' section of the *Handbook of Philosophical Foundations of Business Ethics*, edited by C. Lütge (2012). His research interests include business ethics, applied ethics and wellbeing studies. He is currently working on the ethical and cultural foundation of Chinese business systems.

François Lépineux is a professor at ESC Rennes School of Business, where he is in charge of the CANON Chair 'Foresight and the Common Good' and head of the Centre for Responsible Business. Recent publications as co-editor include *Social Responsibility, Entrepreneurship and the Common Good – International and Interdisciplinary Perspectives* (with C. Bonanni and J. Roloff, 2012), *Business, Globalization and the Common Good* (with H.-C. De Bettignies, 2009) and *Finance for a Better World: The Shift toward Sustainability* (with H.-C. De Bettignies, 2009). He is co-founder and past president (2002–05) of ADERSE, the French academic association for the development of education and interdisciplinary research on CSR.

John Little runs a Melbourne-based consultancy in governance, strategy and organisational change. An abiding interest in evoking clear and courageous thinking and in accessing the inner wisdom of the deeper self for creative and sustainable decision-making and managerial practice has been the guiding inspiration of his professional work. Alongside his consultancy he was the founding director of CREDO (Centre for Research into Ethics and Decision-making in Organizations) at the Australian Catholic University, prior to which he was an associate director of the Mt Eliza Executive Education Centre of the Melbourne Business School. In his early career, John worked for Peat Marwick consultants in Montreal, International Computers in London and numerous Australian companies in engineering and computer systems. He received his PhD from Australian Catholic University.

Bernard McKenna is an associate professor at the University of Queensland Business School where he primarily teaches communication. He researches in wisdom studies and critical discourse theory, publishing in such journals as *Leadership Quarterly, Public Administration Review* and *Applied Linguistics*. He has written four books, the most recent being *Wisdom and Management in the Knowledge Economy* (2010). Bernard is on the editorial board of four journals. He is also a national assessor for Australian Research Council (ARC) grant applications and has won two nationally competitive ARC grants. He regularly provides consultancies to industry and government as well. His wisdom research over the past ten years has moved from the conceptual and theoretical phase to a more recent interest in empirical research.

Simon Robinson, FRSA, is Professor of Applied and Professional Ethics, Leeds Metropolitan University. Educated at Oxford and Edinburgh Universities, he became a psychiatric social worker before entering the Church of England priesthood in 1978. He entered university chaplaincy in Edinburgh and Leeds, developing research and lecturing in areas of applied ethics and business ethics. He has written and researched extensively in business ethics, corporate social responsibility, the nature and dynamics of responsibility, equality, ethics and culture, and ethics and care. His books include: *Case Histories in Business Ethics*; *Values in Higher Education*; *The Teaching and Practice of Professional Ethics*; *Engineering, Business and Professional Ethics*; *Spirituality, Ethics and Care*; *Ethics for Living and Working*; *Ethics and the Alcohol Industry*; *Leadership Responsibility*; *Business Ethics in Practice*; and *Islam in the West*. He is co-general editor of the Peter Lang book series on International Studies in Applied Ethics.

David Rooney is an associate professor at the University of Queensland Business School and is recognised internationally as a leading thinker about knowledge-related matters. David Rooney's principle teaching interests are knowledge management and change management. He supervises research students with interests in creative industries, knowledge management and change management. His PhD was based on historical studies of the relationship between technology and various levels of organisation in the Australian music industry. David has published extensively in relation to knowledge-based economies, knowledge management, change management and creative industries. He is currently co-director of the Australian Creative Resources Online (ACRO) research centre and formerly director of the Business School's Business Communication Program and associate director of the Centre for Social Research in Communication.

Jean-Jacques Rosé is a researcher at the Norbert Elias Centre, EHESS–CNRS, Marseille and Research Affiliate, ESC Rennes School of Business, France. He is interested in the application of lexical analysis methods to Business Ethics, CSR and Sustainable Development literatures. Recent publications include *La RSE entre globalisation et développement durable* (co-edited with N. Barthe, 2011), *La RSE – La Responsabilité sociale des entreprises: Théories et pratiques* (with F. Lépineux, C. Bonanni and S. Hudson, 2010) and the essay, 'Corporate Responsibility and Global Social Contract: New Constructivist, Personalist and Dialectical Perspectives' (in *Business, Globalization and the Common Good*, 2009). Jean-Jacques Rosé is vice president of the Association for the Development of Education and Research on Corporate Social Responsibility (ADERSE).

Mark Strom is an adviser to corporate, government and community leaders and organisations on leadership, learning, innovation, and engagement. Among the many roles of his working career, Mark counts himself privileged to have led the turnaround of an 85-year-old cherished undergraduate and postgraduate academy in Aotearoa New Zealand. He received his PhD in the history of ideas from the University of Western

Sydney. Drawing on his diverse experiences as CEO, adviser and intellectual, Mark has spoken to groups as diverse as the McKinsey & Company global partners' conference, the Harvard Club, the Australian Young Leaders Forum and many corporate events.

Mike Thompson is Professor of Management Practice and Director of the Centre for Leadership and Responsibility at the China Europe International Business School. Mike was formerly CEO of GoodBrand which works with a number of multinational clients in sustainable enterprise strategies. Mike speaks and writes on wise leadership, corporate governance and sustainable brand strategy. He received his PhD from the University of Kent, UK in 1997.

Peter Verhezen is Practitioner Professor in Strategy and Risk Management at the Vlerick Business School and at the University of Antwerp, a Visiting Associate Professor for Global Corporate Governance at the University of Melbourne, and he occasionally teaches business ethics at IPMI and ITB business schools in Jakarta. He has been a Fellow at and still collaborates with the Ash Institute for Governance and Asian Studies of the Harvard Kennedy School (USA). During the Asian crisis (1997–2001), he was a senior financial advisor for IBRA, the bad-debt bank of the Ministry of Finance of Indonesia. He currently advises boards and executives on risk management, strategy and governance.

Li Yuan is a lecturer of Management Philosophy in the School of Philosophy at the Renmin University of China. She received her PhD in management from University of Aberdeen, UK in 2011. She received both her Master's and BA in Philosophy from Beijing Normal University. Her research interests include human resource management, comparison of East–West thinking, the impact of contrasting East–West thinking on HRM practices, philosophy of management and leadership ethics.

1
Wise Management in Organisational Complexity: An Introduction

Mike Thompson and David Bevan

The mission of the China Europe International Business School (CEIBS) is to educate responsible leaders versed in 'China Depth, Global Breadth'. The CEIBS Euro-China Centre for Leadership and Responsibility (ECCLAR) supports that mission by creating and disseminating knowledge on the practice and development of wise and responsible leadership especially in the corporate context. This collection of essays furthers that mission in providing a resource of wise praxis and reflection in the context of organisational complexity for managers, researchers and teachers in management education.

Interest in wisdom as a topic for research has been growing across the disciplines of organisational studies, leadership studies, philosophy, psychology and ethics. Blanchard-Fields and Norris (1995, p. 105) note that 'wisdom has been legitimised in the science of psychology by operationalising it into a knowledge system framework, i.e., borrowing from an established scientific approach'. Psychological theorists have posited that wisdom is a multidimensional construct characterised by cognitive, affective and behavioural dimensions that develop increasing integration over time; included in this latter process is the often pains-taking effort at integrating opposing self-schemes and reflecting on the experiences of self and other (Kramer, 2000).

Scholarly attention to wisdom in management is, according to Mick, Bateman and Lutz (2009), either strictly conceptual, oriented solely toward the management field or focused on organisational level analysis (not individuals and their decision-making or behaviours). In the field of leadership studies, McKenna, Rooney and Kimberley (2009) have led the way in arguing for an augmentation of existing leadership models with the wisdom dimension. They argue that

1

wisdom is critically dependent on ethics, judgment, insight, creativity, and other transcendent forms of human intellection. Wisdom is concerned less with how much we know and more with what we do and how we act. Wisdom is a way of being and is fundamentally practical in a complex and uncertain world. (McKenna, Rooney and Kimberley, 2009, p. 187)

The authors of *Wise Management in Organisational Complexity* underpin their perspectives of wise management in business with the ideal of balancing the requirements of profit while wisely managing the implicit and explicit responsibilities of companies towards wider society. This dynamic balance is what Mary Gentile calls the higher purpose of business, or what may be regarded as the renovated ideal of the common good. Robert Chia, Robin Holt and Li Yuan give the example of Konusuke Matsushita as one person who exemplifies the dispositions of experienced 'wise' business people. Such individuals, they say, offer a service that reflects a 'vocational opportunity to perfect oneself and at the same time contribute to the common good' (p. 63). Jay Hays expresses this simply: 'A wise act is a deliberate one that concerns the common good; it serves interests greater than the self' (p. 138), and, as Li Yuan observes, 'wise and virtuous business leadership in modern society not only benefits organisation, but also serves the wellbeing and harmony of society as a whole' (p. 108). Their findings concur with the conclusions of Birren and Svensson (2005), who find that the promotion of the common good and rising above self-interest is one of the most consistent subcomponents of wisdom from both ancient and modern literature.

A distinctive feature of this volume is the various explications and applications of Aristotle's notion of *phronèsis* (practical wisdom) described by Bernard McKenna as 'the ability to act virtuously in difficult situations' (p. 15). Jean-Jacques Rosé and François Lépineux provide a semantic analysis of *phronèsis* as a means of addressing the disruption caused by agents 'forgetting all elementary principles of prudence, and playing a game as if it had no limits' (p. 70). In such times of crises, short-termism and the dysfunctions of hubris challenge the effectiveness of quantitative management and 'call for wise management so as to safeguard management itself' (p. 69). For Rosé and Lépineux the antidote to this hubris is Aristotelian *phronèsis* which is 'the spring that enables the definition of wise management for the twenty-first century' (p. 76). They re-articulate the *phronèsis* of *Nicomachean Ethics* and *Politics*, nuanced by extensive and original references to postmodern, or continental, authors.

Peter Verhezen and Bernard McKenna each express a concern that instrumental rationality, such as formalistic corporate governance rules and pecuniary corporate incentives, should be adequately balanced with value rationality which, McKenna says, is becoming increasingly difficult if not impossible. He points to often well-intended but ultimately disabling regulations and laws that take agency from those who then follow safe legally endorsed courses rather than the wise course. The conflicts between wise decision-making and the quality of independence in corporate governance structures is addressed by Verhezen, who argues that boards that are genuinely guided by practical wisdom perceive *independence as a state of mind*, not as a legal compliance issue. For Verhezen, a wisdom approach to corporate governance is now required for managers, so that the prospect of pecuniary gain does not affect their decisions and actions adversely. Verhezen's view of managers is informed by readings of MacIntyre, for whom managers too easily operate 'outside of ethics' and seek only to fulfil actions. On this basis, corporate governance founded on managerial responsibility and accountability can only arise under wise leaders with the necessary integrity, knowledge and experience. This is a continuously emergent and reconstitutive process, or activity, involving integrity, knowledge and professional experience.

Phronèsis is one of three words that Aristotle uses in his discourses on wisdom and virtue. McKenna gives an overview of *technē*, the expert knowledge of a trade or profession); *nous*, an intuitive capacity, and *sophia*, a metaphysical capacity. Wisdom is thus presented as ultimately being concerned to enhance social *eudaimonia*, or human flourishing and living the virtuous life, specifically: humility, courage, temperance and justice. For Aristotle, McKenna says, 'the wise person acts virtuously when dealing with the shifting contingencies of life and situations. They do this by being reflexively intuitive and possessing human(e) instincts' (p. 15). His chapter also draws from philosophical and psychological paradigms to apply wisdom to an organisational context, suggesting that a tri-level framework (macro, meso and micro) is useful. McKenna then considers whether wisdom should be measured, and evaluates the measures used by the 'Berlin School', Sternberg and US empiricists. From this analysis, five core elements of wisdom are derived. However, he further argues that an ethical foundation and conation are necessary other components of wisdom and proposes a list of wisdom criteria as the foundation of 'social practice wisdom'. He summarises wise thinking as being 'rational, based on sound knowledge, but is also intuitive, ethical, and capable of metaphysical reflexivity. It is the explicit combination of intuition and science, values and truth, intuition and transcendent cognitions to solve real-world problems' (p. 15).

In his chapter, 'Empirical Wisdom Research: A Community Approach', David Rooney puts forward the case for wisdom as an alternative research approach. He is critical of a hegemonic tendency he perceives in the rigid approach to research excellence predicated on a disciplinary silo approach to management. This, he suggests, has emphasised the tendency for business schools to become marginalised from management practice. Rooney challenges us to accept organisational complexity as a twenty-first-century 'given', and to extend our practice of wisdom to find new interdisciplinary, methodological and pedagogical approaches. He observes that contemporary empirical research about wisdom has been done by psychologists and that this research has added significantly to our knowledge of wisdom, but sociology (broadly defined) and business research is missing. Rooney wants to broaden the methodological spectrum beyond what psychologists have used with phronetic research which requires the integration of methodologies: ontology (ways of being and becoming), axiology (values and value), epistemology (knowledge creation), praxeology (enactment or application of knowledge) and *eudaimonia* (wellbeing or human flourishing). It is the integration of each of these into the foundations of a coherent methodology that matters.

Rooney's radical suggestion is to approach wisdom research through action, convened in community-of-practice type settings. He proposes that wisdom is the means, or at least a metaphorical lens, through which twenty-first-century academe may be reinvigorated through a complex systems approach. Rosé and Lépineux are likely to be in such a community-of-practice with their commitment to demonstrate how *phronèsis* can be the means that renders possible the integration of moderation into governance, so that economic transition and paradigm shift do not remain utopias but actually become the finalities of business praxis. Their approach will rely on an attempted synthesis of paradigms combined with the systemic integration of the empirical contribution of humanities and social science to management practice and education delivered by business schools according to the three levels of application of practical wisdom: micro, meso and macro.

Yuan explains why Chinese leadership research cannot be isolated from the Chinese cultural context, especially as defined in philosophical Confucianism in which ethics is inseparable from the practice of leadership. In her chapter, Yuan proposes a 'Confucian meritocracy' as a leadership standard which fully values knowledge/ability/skill and ethics. Confucian meritocracy requires leadership by the *wise*, those who possess both virtue and ability in the Confucian sense.

Po-Keung Ip also finds meritocracy to be a central value in the practice of Wang Dao (the 'Kingly Way') management in the case of Stan Shih of the Acer Group and his commitment to the practice of Wangdao management. Both Mencius and Xunzi explained the nature of the Wang Dao/Kingly Way by contrasting it with a competing way of ruling – the Hegemonly Way (Ba Dao), which was the dominant ruling philosophy and practice of the Warring States Period in Ancient China. Wang Dao is rule by moral rightness and benevolence in contrast to Ba Dao, meaning rule by brute force and conquest. The content of the classical idea of Wang Dao, which is political in nature, is reconstructed with respect to the core of the Confucian moral element – *ren* (benevolence), *yi* (rightness), *li* (ritual-following), *zhi* (wisdom) and *xin* (trustworthiness). Its organisation and corporate version is worked out as Kingly (Corporate) Governance. Ip explores the extent to which Kingly Governance is wise management based on recent conceptualisations of wisdom in the literature.

Mark Strom's chapter, '"To Know as We Are Known": Locating an Ancient Alternative to Virtues', presents a contrary view to Aristotle and the Hellenistic moral philosophers. Aristotle's schema, he argues, is elitist, not egalitarian and geared to the status quo and not to transformation. He explores the legacy of Paul of Tarsus which he asserts is obscured by anachronistic, Christian readings. But when Paul is read in terms of the history of ideas, several major innovations appear, and Strom focuses on three. First, grace inverted the Greco-Roman social pyramid. Second, 'transformation' entered Western vocabulary as a positive term. Third, a relational epistemology was outlined – 'to know as I am known' – that challenged the detached and elitist rationalisations of classical philosophy. The mode of this relational epistemology was faith, hope and love. Yuan also identifies love as a guiding virtue in Confucian thought. However, unlike the love espoused by Paul, based on grace, Confucian love is graded according to the proximity and distance of each relationship. Yuan explains that to deny the graded relationship is to obstruct the path of humanity and righteousness and even destroy the harmony of all things, as the hierarchy of everything that exists in the universe. Strom concludes that the innovation of grace reframed *phronèsis* from Aristotelian conventionality to a mindset that opened the way to the modern ideas of equality and fraternity. Transformation became a universal hope and knowledge was reframed as relational: 'to know as I am known', animated by faith, hope and love.

Chia, Holt and Yuan in their chapter, 'In Praise of Strategic Indirection: Towards a Non-instrumental Understanding of *Phronèsis* as Practical Wisdom', draw on Western (Aristotle) and Eastern (Lao Tzu) concepts of wisdom to approach organisational complexity. They suggest that we abandon the established, dichotomy-laden thinking that leads to all strategy being based on pre-determined outcomes. In place of this purely rational approach, Chia, Holt and Yuan invite us to be less Western (seen as *direct*) and more Eastern (seen as *indirect*): not either/or, but both/and. Here they neologise the concept of *strategic indirection* as a means to non-deliberative change.

In addressing the context of organisational complexity the authors are, as with the focus of wise management, equally polyphonic and complementary. McKenna establishes complexity as an inherent contextual given of both organisational and social interaction, to the extent that any plausible exercise of wise management must be able to survive its paradoxical and incommensurable uncertainties. Complexity is a naturally occurring context that undermines 'the natural human desire for linearity, predictability, and equilibrium' (p. 27) and which, perhaps, suggests that some wise resilience is the optimal reaction. For Rooney this organisational complexity is also paradoxical as well as systemic. Complexity here is effectively globalised and – perhaps following such globalisation scholars as Scholte (2005), Beck (2000) and Giddens (1999) – it is a structural agent of multiple, unintended consequences, and must be considered in any reactions to paradoxical challenges. In many ways explicitly following McKenna, Simon Robinson, too, finds structural pragmatic links between complexity and globalisation. Robinson focuses on the trait of massification: 'the increased numbers of students, partly realised because of the social narrative of equality of access, sets up another complex narrative around providing customers with the best possible experience, given increasingly limited human and material resources' (p. 184).

On a similar tack, Rooney scopes and constructs his communitarian approach to social practice wisdom around the concept of

> a complex, multidimensional integration that creates clarity and decisiveness through equanimity and corresponding dispositions that generate the insight, composure and motivation to deploy the resources needed to act excellently and successfully in the best interests of oneself, others and the planet. (p. 36)

The chapter most focused on complexity is that of Hays, who opens with dramatic urgency on this point:

> The challenges confronting humanity today are many, stubborn, competing and tangled. They may be more complex and far-reaching than challenges posed at any time in the past. The modern age is turbulent and fraught with uncertainty and unpredictability. To make matters worse, the pace of change is relentless and accelerating. (p. 134)

This emergent hyperbole is justified by Hays's concern that in as much as complexity is one of the discernible causes, or features, of the contemporary global crisis, then higher education must do more to teach people/managers how to deal with it. For Hays this complexity revolves around a concern for rationally wicked problems (a theme signalled also in McKenna), which he elaborates with care. In consequence, 'the thinking requisite to solve wicked problems ... is characterised dialogically and dialectically; the former involving fair consideration of multiple perspectives, and the latter integrating or synthesising multiple and opposing views' (p. 137). The relationship between wisdom and complexity has to be symbiotic and inherently systemic.

In her chapter, Gentile echoes this symbiotic turn and suggests that one practical means of dislodging the wicked problems, foregrounded by Hays, may come from engagement in the vocalising of wise leadership values. Gentile nuances her well-established 'giving voice to values' (GVV) approach to teaching to explore how such an engaging process could be applied to leadership training and education while dealing with the complexities inherent in applying pure rationalism to values and ethics.

This apparent symbiosis is also a feature in the complexity of Verhezen, who suggests with a quasi-pragmatic rationale that

> wisdom may be understood as a way of being that is fundamentally practical in a complex and uncertain world: the praxis to act rightly, depending on our ability to perceive the situation accurately, to have the appropriate intuition about such a situation or trend, to discern and reflect about what is appropriate in this particular situational context and to act upon it. (p. 201)

He shows complexity as being fraught with ambiguity and uncertainty; a complexity which evokes and elicits wisdom.

The hyperbole of Hays is echoed in a number of other chapters. Chia, Holt and Yuan take complexity as a tacit but structural subtext. Here complexity is inscribed in the following terms: 'The social, economic and political world is currently experiencing an unprecedented level of nervousness and uncertainty characterised by instability, volatility and unexpected and disruptive change' (p. 55). In their case this uncertainty becomes the foundation for a symbiotic, if potentially counter-intuitive, and innovative practice of wise management. For John Little, the complexity of organisational life is also a foundation of action: a given requiring a reinterpretation of intentionality in the practice of management.

For Rosé and Lépineux the complexity is more explicit and potentially destructive. Evoking postmodern – in the sense of critical and post-Kantian – authors, like Ricoeur and Serres, their worldview is one of complexity as the result, perhaps more than the cause, of 'current crises and foreseeable perils'. In Yuan we see this argument offered from an alternate perspective in which organisational complexity is again structural: it arises as a consequence of the 'dynamic interaction between the leader, follower and situation'. For Strom, complexity is an urgent contemporary danger:

> The ambiguity, contradictions, and anomalies that accompany organisational complexity require ways of knowing that do not mask, but embrace, uncertainty. Complexity is more than complication: more than the sum of many puzzles amenable to logic. Complexity is fuzzy, ambiguous and uncertain. (p. 95)

Complexity is, at the same time, a mirror of humanness – and so something which we do not need to fear, but which we may need to deal with through 'ways of knowing that are relational' (p. 95).

Ip takes a constructive approach and formulates the common good as predicated on a harmonious balance which embraces or comprehends complexity:

> the achievement of a common good through a balance among intrapersonal, interpersonal and extra-personal interests, over short and long terms, in order to achieve a balance among adaptation to existing environments, shaping of existing environments and the selection of new environments. (p. 125)

Without attempting to explore the complexity of the multiple overlaps across all the ideas developed in the chapters that follow, we draw this introductory chapter to a close with a discussion of what appear to us to be the strands of an organising principle which we have conceptualised reflexively, after the event. It is clear that the works of Aristotle suggest one significant, unifying feature. Each chapter develops its own trace, but the whole work seems to rest on the foundation of questions that do not go away; or at least have not been resolved consensually in more than two millennia. For some readers – and perhaps simplistically at that – questions that take such a time to resolve might indicate that either we (academics) are dumb, or that there is not really a problem. Eschewing that simple dichotomy, we prefer to suggest that this says something important about the nature of knowledge and practice (at least in the field of management), which is elaborated succinctly but iteratively in this volume. Let us first consider some of the specific strands from Aristotle.

We have passed through a time when serious concerns about management education have evolved. Many of these concerns are reflected among our contributors, some of whom refer to a seminal article in the journal *Academy of Management Learning and Education* (Ghoshal, 2005). In this problematic context, wisdom, with its tacit understanding of and commitment to a good life, offers a different ontological lens and thus, we suggest tentatively, a different epistemology Such a non-instrumental understanding of practical wisdom echoes Aristotle's most highly valued achievement of the good life in his conceptualisation of *eudaimonia* (the flourishing life):

> It is held to be the mark of a prudent man to be able to deliberate well about what is good and advantageous for himself, not in some one department, for instance what is good for his health or strength, but what is advantageous as a means to the good life in general. (Aristotle, 1934: 6.5)

Our authors challenge us to think about wisdom afresh. Here, we suggest wisdom as a practice – perhaps a practice which is never completed, nor finished, never a totality of wise management as such, in the way that reason might force us to consider. In light of the wisdom captured in these pages lies an opportunity for personal self-discovery rather than an abstract concept for academic discussion, or a scientific reality which can be examined under a microscope.

Phronèsis is intrinsically about the *practice* of life and, in both Aristotelian and Confucian thought, is inseparable from practising the virtues which, in turn, become the axioms of wisdom, and potentially, for wise management in organisational complexity. Malan and Kriger (1998, p. 249) reflect the view of many organisational researchers that 'managerial wisdom is the ability to detect those fine nuances between what is right and what is not'. Nonaka and Takeuchi (2011, p. 60) argue that CEOs must draw on practical wisdom that 'enables people to make prudent judgments and take actions based on the actual situation, guided by values and morals'. Such practical wisdom is, however, resistant to purely rational knowledge based on scientific certainties. As we have noted above in our comments on Aristotle's incomplete, infinite practice, it cannot be reduced to a totality:

> Dependence only on explicit knowledge prevents leaders from coping with change. The scientific, deductive, theory-first approach assumes a world independent of context and seeks answers that are universal and predictive. However, all social phenomena – including business – are context dependent, and analyzing them is meaningless unless you consider people's goals, values, and interests. (Aristotle, 1934, 6.5)

To make prudent judgments people need a 'mechanism' or a routine to enable them to 'transcend their egocentric viewpoint as they reason about self-relevant issues' (Kross and Grossman, 2012, p. 43).

Additionally, and in recent years, there has been a significant body of psychological theory-informed research into the nature and experience of wisdom including conceptual constructions of a psychology of wisdom. Many of these studies in organisational behaviour, leadership and general management have also relied upon, included references to, and contemporary applications of an Aristotelian concept of wisdom. Among these we can identify not least the contributions of: Kunzmann and Baltes (2005); Melé (2010); Meynhardt (2010); Nikitin (2011); Nonaka and Takeuchi (2011).

Staudinger, Lopez and Baltes (1997) have proposed that creativity, social intelligence and cognitive styles offer the closest in measuring 'wisdom related performance' (pp. 1201–2). McKenna, in his reference to the work of the 'Berlin School', notes two basic criteria: rich self-knowledge based on deep insight and the heuristics of growth and self-regulation, particularly in relation to emotions and deep social relations. Wisdom, then, may be conceived as a human faculty of a perception of the self and the other/or others, held together in a way that provides an ability to make fine judgments which may be recognised as distinctively wise. But in describing an epistemological path in wisdom with such terms we stray into almost unknown, phenomenological territories. Rooney argues that these concepts need to be integrated into the foundations of a coherent methodology in order to contribute to wise practice research. Rooney is not alone in challenging the contemporary limitations of positivism and the notion of certainties. McKenna, Gentile, Hays, Robinson, Rosé and Lépineux, Chia, Holt and Yuan, Strom, Little and Verhezen, each in their clear way, repudiate the certainties of positivism almost as if these themselves have an almost structurally negative effect on management and business. Along with Aristotle they rather encourage us away from digital either/or thinking to a continuous analogue of both/and practice.

The multiple crises facing the world call for attention to wise decision-making and for the development of wise managers who exemplify the characteristics of wisdom narrated extensively by the authors of this volume. Wisdom, as we, they and others have discussed, does not fit the pure and simple logical-positivist paradigm, nor the self-serving model of *homo economicus*; but at the same time it is entirely consistent with Drucker's (2001, p. 13) and Hamel's (2012, p. 354) description of management as a 'liberal art' and not just a scientific practice. The complexity of managing large-scale operations has reinforced the reality that 'right answers' are not always clear. Further, the demands for the 'right decisions' vary according to the agenda and priorities asserted by a range of sometimes contending, internal and external powerbrokers. At a macro level, the postmodern paradigm of business and society prevailing here leads to doubts about the scientific/rational choice-theory approach as the optimal means to arrive at decisions in an objective way. 'Since the Enlightenment, thinkers have progressively differentiated humanity from the rest of nature and have separated objective truth from subjective morality. The greatest challenge of postmodern society may reside in their reintegration' (Gladwin, Kennelly and Krause, 1995, p. 896). In this analogue way we suggest that a revival of wisdom in management practice is one of humankind's pressing and pragmatic antidotes.

References

Aristotle (1934). *Nicomachean Ethics*, vol. 19, trans. H. Rackham. Harvard University Press, Cambridge, MA.

Beck, U. (2000). *World Risk Society*. Polity Press, Cambridge.

Birren, J.E., and C.M. Svensson (2005). 'Wisdom in History'. In R.J. Sternberg and J. Jordan (eds), *A Handbook of Wisdom: Psychological Perspectives*, pp. 3–31. Cambridge University Press, New York.

Blanchard-Fields, F., and L. Norris (1995). 'The Development of Wisdom'. In M.A. Kimble, S.H. McFadden, J.W. Ellor and J.J. Seeber (eds), *Aging, Spirituality, and Religion: A Handbook*, pp. 102–18, Fortress Press, Minneapolis, MN.

Drucker, P.F. (2001). *The Essential Drucker*. Collins, New York.

Ghoshal, S. (2005). 'Bad Management Theories Are Destroying Good Management Practices'. *Academy of Management Learning and Education*, 4(1): 75–91.

Giddens, A. (1999). *Runaway World: How Globalisation Is Shaping Our Lives*. Profile Books, London.

Gladwin, T.N., J. Kennelly and T.-S. Krause (1995). 'Shifting Paradigms for Sustainable Development: Implications for Management Theory and Research'. *Academy of Management Review*, 20(4): 874–907.

Hamel, G. (2012). *What Matters Now*. Jossey-Bass, San Francisco.

Kramer, D. (2000). 'Wisdom as a Classical Source of Human Strength: Conceptualization and Empirical Enquiry'. *Journal of Social and Clinical Psychology*, 19(1): 83–101.

Kross, E., and I. Grossmann (2012). 'Boosting Wisdom: Distance from the Self Enhances Wise Reasoning, Attitudes, and Behavior'. *Journal of Experimental Psychology*, 141(1): 43–8.

Kunzmann, U., and P.B. Baltes (2005). 'The Psychology of Wisdom: Theoretical and Empirical Challenges'. In R.J. Sternberg and J. Jordan (eds), *Handbook of Wisdom: Psychological Perspectives*. Cambridge University Press, New York.

Malan, L.C., and M.P. Kriger (1998). 'Making Sense of Managerial Wisdom'. *Journal of Management Inquiry*, 7(3): 242–51.

McKenna B., D. Rooney and B. Kimberley (2009). 'Wisdom Principles as a Meta-theoretical Basis for Evaluating Leadership'. *Leadership Quarterly*, 20: 171–90.

Melé, D. (2010). 'Practical Wisdom in Managerial Decision Making'. *Journal of Management Development*, 29 (7/8): 637–45.

Meynhardt, T. (2010). 'The Practical Wisdom of Peter Drucker: Roots in the Christian Tradition'. *Journal of Management Development*, 29(7/8): 616–25.

Mick, D.G.T., T.S. Bateman and R.J. Lutz (2009). 'Wisdom: Exploring the Pinnacle of Human Virtues as a Central Link from Micromarketing to Macromarketing'. *Journal of Macromarketing*, 29(2): 98–118.

Nikitin, M. (2011). 'Can Aristotle Help Us Specify the Very Nature of Management Problems?' 29 January. Available at SSRN: http://ssrn.com/abstract=1750971.

Nonaka, I., and H. Takeuchi (2011). 'The Wise Leader'. *Harvard Business Review* (May): 59–67.

Scholte, J.A. (2005). *Globalization: A Critical Introduction*. Palgrave, Basingstoke.

Staudinger, U.M., D.F. Lopez and P.B. Baltes (1997). 'The Psychometric Location of Wisdom-related Performance: Intelligence, Personality, and More'. *Personality & Social Psychology Bulletin*, 23: 1200–14.

2
The Multi-dimensional Character of Wisdom

Bernard McKenna

Introduction

Human life is most meaningful and happy when we create the conditions of our happiness by living the virtuous life. This Aristotelian notion of *eudaimonia*, or to use Nussbaum's (1994) term, 'human flourishing' or 'wellbeing', lies at the core of my theoretical approach to wisdom. It is also the foundation of the ongoing wisdom research project in which I and my colleagues are involved. This project took as its starting point, and continues to be driven by, my conviction that wisdom should underlie the management of people and the organisations in which they work and/or live (McKenna, Rooney and Boal, 2009; Rooney, McKenna and Liesch, 2010). This chapter is in five parts: (1) The characteristics of wisdom; (2) Wisdom within a tri-level framework; (3) Can or should wisdom be measured?; (4) Core elements of wisdom; and (5) Wisdom in the face of dealing with paradox, complexity and incommensurability.

1. The Characteristics of Wisdom

To put it simply, happiness (or better still, contentment) requires two things, physical comfort and psychological balance: to use psychological terms, Subjective Well Being (SWB) and Psychological Well Being (PWB). Subjective Well Being (Ryff and Keyes, 1995; Ryff and Singer, 2000, 2008), or hedonic interests, means life satisfaction measured as 'individuals' perceived distance from their aspirations' and also happiness as measured by the balance of positive and negative affect (Keyes, Shmotkin and Ryff, 2002, p. 1008). However, physical satisfaction and comfort are insufficient to achieve full humanity and to contribute to the common weal of the society or the planet we share. Psychological

Well Being is necessary to fulfil our human potential. From psychology, Ryff and Singer (2008) identify *eudaimonia* as comprising: self-acceptance; positive relations with others; personal growth; purpose in life; environmental mastery; and autonomy.

Given this psychological endorsement of Aristotle's philosophy (and the much-welcomed appropriation of his term, *eudaimonia*), I now elaborate another Aristotelian principle as it applies to organisations. Aristotle (1960) distinguished between three actions performed by people in the completion of their tasks. The first of these, *technē*, is understood as expert competence guided by rational accounts of organisational activity. *Sophia* is a metaphysical (or philosophical) capability. Finally, *phronèsis* is wise action, or 'the ability to find some action in particular circumstances which the agent can see as the virtuous thing to do' (Hughes, 2001, p. 105).

To put this into a contemporary context, *technē* is the expert knowledge of a trade or profession. It is essential that doctors, engineers, aircraft mechanics, financial analysts and the like should competently perform their craft and give rational accounts of their activity based on foundational principles. Thus *technē* is based on an *episteme*, or underlying knowledge base (Aristotle, 1960). However, Aristotle differentiates infallible *episteme* from fallible *doxa* and *logismos*, which include *technē* (Barker, 2005). I understand *doxa* in Bourdieu's terms: 'spontaneous belief or opinion [that] ... would seem unquestionable and natural' (Bourdieu and Eagleton, 1992, p. 112) or 'things people accept without knowing' (p. 114). Furthermore, people have the capacity for *nous*, an intuitive capacity that should act to check actions based purely on the processes of *technē*. *Nous*, says Aristotle, 'is concerned with the ultimate particular ... [It is] of definitions, for which there is no reasoning' (Aristotle, 1984, Bk 6, 1142b: 25–8). It can also be defined as 'the insightfulness that makes up for the imprecision of rationality' (Dunne, 1997, p. 15). In organisations, it might be seen as 'invisible ... soft data' (Kriger and Malan, 1993, p. 393).

Aristotle not only identified the need for intuition, but also proposed that the transcendent was crucial in wise decision-making. This transcendent capacity is largely contained in the concept of *sophia*, a difficult and – although he calls it 'the most precise of the sciences' – still unclear notion (Aristotle, 1984, Bks VI, 1145a: 7–12 and X, 7–9). Its transcendent nature is implied in identifying *sophia* as concerned with that which remains 'always the same' (Aristotle, 1984, Bk VI.7, 1141a: 24–5). The application of *sophia* thus allows us to go beyond the physical confines of *technē*, 'to transcend the world of transient finitude'

(Long, 2002, p. 39). Finally, *phronèsis*, to paraphrase my previous definition, is the ability to act virtuously in difficult situations. My deep concern, however, is that the opportunity to balance instrumental rationality with value rationality (Flyvbjerg, 2004, p. 285) in contemporary organisations is becoming increasingly difficult if not impossible. This is because of often well-intended, but ultimately disabling regulations and laws that take agency from those who then follow the safe legally endorsed course rather than the wise course. This is not an argument for industry self-regulation that has proved to be disingenuous and self-serving. Rather it is a plea for organisational members to be allowed the space to make wise decisions and for organisations to remember above all else why the regulation is there in the first place.

Also central to an Aristotelian orientation is the importance of living the virtuous life. That is, ethical behaviour is central to wise practice. Aristotle argues that, to contribute to community wellbeing, one must acquire and practise intellectual and moral excellence. To act prudently, Aristotle says, one must be infused with virtues such as humility, courage, temperance and justice: one should do 'what one does just because one sees those actions as noble and worthwhile' (Hughes, 2001, p. 89). Thus, for Aristotle, the wise person acts virtuously when dealing with the shifting contingencies of life and situations. They do this by being reflexively intuitive and possessing human(e) instincts. Because emotions are so instinctive, we must not set them aside as 'irrational', but open our emotions to scrutiny. Wise people identify the source of emotions of exhilaration, anger and so on (Kekes, 1995, p. 10) resulting from, say, a sense of injustice. Thus, judgment should be balanced, but not necessarily dispassionate (Eflin, 2003; see also Sherman, 1997, ch. 2).

To sum up, wise thinking is rational, based on sound knowledge, but is also intuitive, ethical and capable of metaphysical reflexivity. It is the explicit combination of intuition and science, values and truth, intuition and transcendent cognitions that solve real-world problems. I propose that wise people can be identified, and outline potential indicators in the third section below.

Linking these wisdom characteristics to management and organisation, the eighteenth-century Aristotelian, Giambattista Vico, provided a timeless taxonomy of four managerial types. At the top, the wise person (*sapientes*) has practical and theoretical wisdom: 'through all the obliquities and uncertainties of human actions, [they] aim for eternal truth, follow roundabout ways ... and execute plans which in the long run are for the best, as far as the nature of things allows' (Miner, 1998, p. 56). A level below this is the astute ignoramus (*illiterates astutus*) who knows how to succeed in worldly affairs, but lacks *phronèsis* (reflexive humane wisdom). Because they are ignorant of the most important things, as evidenced by constantly preferring utility over what is right, they ensure failure in the most important matters. The second lowest level is the fool (*stultus*) who 'lacks knowledge of either the general or the particular', and so 'constantly pays for his [or her] rashness'. The lowest order is the imprudent savant (*doctus imprudentis*), who 'approaches ethics as though it were a manual of propositions to be memorised; makes decisions slowly, is arrogant; and lacks persuasive communication'. The savant moves 'in a straight line from general to particular truths' in order to 'burst through the tortuous curves of life' (Miner, 1998, p. 57). Sometimes successful, they more often fail. Vico was challenging the 'New Science' emphasis on reason and fact alone (Benedict, 2001, p. 27). Because contemporary technocratic rationality has its provenance in the positivist features of this New Science, Vico's imprudent savant and astute ignoramus are too often evident in managers who fail to negotiate the 'tortuous curves of life'.

2.   Wisdom within a Tri-level Framework

In applying wisdom to organisations, I propose that this should be understood in the context of organisational location and practice. I propose a tri-level context: individuals (micro) operate within organisational contexts (meso), which themselves operate within social, political, geographic and economic frameworks (macro). The case for using a multi-level framework is well established. For example, Rousseau and House (1994) proposed that meso-organisational research integrates micro-perspectives, which focus on psychological phenomena, and macro-perspectives, which focus on socioeconomic phenomena. Meso-research, they argue, assumes that micro- and macro-perspectives cannot be treated separately, and I agree. Research at the meso-level concerns organisational processes, rather than individual experiences (micro) or the macro-level concerns of contextual social structures (see also House, Rousseau, and Thomas-Hunt, 1995). Similarly, Bligh, Pearce and Kohles (2006) and Kozlowski and Klein (2000) describe meso theories as providing a cross-level or multi-level perspective on organisational research. In sociology, Biggart and Beamish (2003) see a meso orientation as bridging a gap between structural, macroeconomic explanations and microeconomic theories that typically assume individual, rational actors. Organisational meso-research, therefore, refers to something in between macro- and micro-levels, and can enhance our understanding of relationships between individual experience and broader, social phenomena. In my three-level analysis, then, the micro-level refers to individual organisational members; the meso-level refers to organisations; and the macro-level refers to environmental, societal, national or transnational conditions.

Unfortunately, some of the most contemporary multi-level research theory in management and organisation studies lacks two vital elements: political economy and historical location. Surely, even if we disagreed with everything else that Foucault said, his identification of the spatio-temporal location of discourse and practice is something that cannot be discounted in theorising about the phenomena of our social existence. Discourses, Foucault (1978) tells us, are 'transformable units of history' (p. 19), allowing us to ascribe meaning to the phenomena we encounter, but which differ according to the different geographical, cultural and temporal dimensions (Foucault, 1967, p. 7). Thus, particular space-time phenomena have their own 'regime of truth' constituted by their own discursive rules, values and supporting institutions and networks (Foucault, 1980, pp. 131ff.). A recent paper in the prestigious *Journal of Management* by Mathieu and Chen (2011), entitled 'The Etiology of the Multilevel Paradigm in Management Research', is typical of the concern I have. In reviewing the literature about multi-level paradigms, this otherwise erudite paper gave no account whatsoever of the historical, cultural, economic or political situatedness of the management phenomenon being researched.

This multi-level framework for understanding wisdom as a social phenomenon can be applied to organisational and management studies. At the micro-level, individual characteristics such as core traits and dispositions could be considered: that is, the characteristics of individual organisational members, particularly leaders, are fundamental to the potential for wisdom in an organisation (McKenna, Rooney and Boal, 2009). At an interpersonal level, this capability refers to wise people's 'ability to grasp and reconcile the paradoxes, changes, and contradictions of human nature' (Bigelow, 1992, p. 146). The meso-level accounts for organisational structure, climate and culture. Assuming Giddens's (1984) structuration notion of a recursive relationship between individual and organisation, I propose that distributed wisdom feeds back into the organisation. At the meso-level, organisational performance is primarily considered: productivity, profit, social benefit, and employee satisfaction and wellbeing. But wise practice would be particularly evident in the organisation's ability 'to detect the changing patterns ... occurring in the internal and external environments of the organisation' (Malan

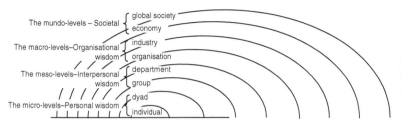

Figure 2.1   Mark Edwards's multi-levels of wisdom model

and Kriger, 1998, p. 247). The macro-level takes into account the potential effect of national and international variables that impact on how organisations operate, including the prevailing dominant ideology, government, national culture and economic conditions. To evaluate wisdom at the macro-level, longer-term societal and global outcomes are considered.

If we were to evaluate organisational wisdom at the three levels, then the following measures could be considered. At the micro-level, measures could include organisational performance, but, just as importantly, Psychological Well Being (PWB). Such measures would include self-acceptance; positive relations with others; personal growth; purpose in life; environmental mastery; and autonomy. Personal happiness, contentment and personal performance might be considered. At the meso-level, measurable indicators of organisations meeting goals such as output, productivity and client satisfaction might be considered. At the macro-level, measures of social *eudaimonia* or social wellbeing that fulfil life-affirming and socially just values could include sustainability and community engagement variables.

Multi-level analysis could also be developed at four levels, as has been proposed by Edwards (2010). He presents micro-meso-macro-mundo levels each with their own ecology as a way to understand the contexts in which wise practices can take place (see Fig. 2.1).

3.   Can or Should Wisdom Be Measured?

Since Clayton and Birren (1980) introduced the concept of wisdom into psychology studies, there has been a considerable development in wisdom research. Thirty years later, a number of clear 'schools' have emerged. I will briefly identify these schools and then look at how they measure wisdom: the Berlin School; Robert Sternberg; and the US Positivists.

The Berlin School

The Berlin School developed from work in the 1980s at the Max Planck Institute for Human Development, headed by Baltes (1939–2006). Originally concerned, like Clayton and Birren (1980), with life-span development, Baltes became increasingly interested in the notion of wisdom. In fact, he took a six-month sabbatical from his intense research programme to study the philosophy of wisdom in different cultures. Adopting an explicit theory of wisdom, the Berlin School understands wisdom as it is devised by expert theorists and researchers rather than by laypeople, and emphasises advanced cognitive functioning. This has laid the Berlin School open to treating wisdom as 'cold cognition', as suggested by Ardelt (2004). Baltes and Kunzmann (2004) counter that context-related, expertise-related and person-related factors are 'distal factors' in defining wisdom as 'excellence in mind and virtue and ... excellence in the conduct and meaning of life' (pp. 294–5). While there is little doubt that the Berlin School is committed to virtuous outcomes, it remains the case that their model lacks virtuous and moral development in its variables. They define wisdom as 'expert knowledge in the fundamental pragmatics of life that permits exceptional insight, judgement, and advice about complex and uncertain matters' (Baltes and Staudinger, 2000, p. 125). These pragmatics include insight into the social nature and incompleteness of human existence, the variability of life goals, knowledge about oneself and the limits of one's knowledge and insight into how knowledge is translated into behaviour.

The Berlin School also differentiates between cognitive mechanics and cognitive pragmatics of the mind. This distinction is built on the distinction between fluid intelligence (cognitive mechanics) and crystallised intelligence (cognitive pragmatics) devised by Horn and Cattell (1967). The issue of intelligence is an important one in wisdom research, with the US researcher, Robert Sternberg, adamant that knowledge must be accompanied by other attributes to constitute wisdom. While acknowledging that intelligence is manifested in multiple forms, I want to concentrate on fluid and crystallised intelligence.

Fluid intelligence involves abstract reasoning that is independent of learning, experience and education. By contrast, crystallised intelligence is expressed in abilities of a 'judgmental, discriminatory, and reasoning nature' built on experience and/or learning. Highly intelligent people deploy both intelligences. It is thought that fluid intelligence peaks between 30 and 40 years of age, whereas crystallised intelligence grows with age provided people reflexively consider their experience. Cognitive mechanics is based on the 'neurophysiological architecture of the brain' (Baltes, 1993, p. 582). By contrast, cognitive pragmatics involves cultural knowledge about the nature of the world and processes. It can be enhanced with age depending on the degree of reflexivity. Fluid intelligence is relatively easy to measure; crystallised intelligence much less so.

One important cautionary point needs to be made about high levels of fluid intelligence. Mickler and Staudinger (2008) found that, although the cognitive variables were significantly correlated with the Personal Wisdom (PW) construct, those with higher levels of fluid intelligence presented an inverted U-shaped relationship between PW and fluid intelligence. This finding and another finding, that the top 15 per cent scored lower in the universalism value domain, caution us that very high intellectual skill as indicated by fluid intelligence (e.g. finance brokers) is not a good predictor of wisdom.

To be wise, the Berlin School propose that people need to have high aptitude in two basic criteria and three metacriteria (Baltes and Staudinger, 2000; Staudinger and Glück, 2011). The two basic criteria are rich self-knowledge based on deep insight and heuristics of growth and self-regulation, particularly in relation to emotions and deep social relations. The three metacriteria focus on ways of processing information to make judgments about one's life: being aware of 'the contextual embeddedness of one's behaviour, feelings, or both' (Mickler and Staudinger, 2008, p. 788); the capacity to honestly appraise one's own behaviour without losing self-esteem and also to tolerate divergent values; and tolerance of ambiguity, manifested in managing life's uncertainty (e.g. accidents, illnesses) and developing from experience.

Robert Sternberg

The most prolific wisdom researcher, Sternberg (1998), developed a Balance Theory of Wisdom. Central to this is the role of values. He argues that clever people (i.e. people with high fluid intelligence) can be foolish and unethical (Sternberg, 2005). Smarter and better-educated businesspeople and politicians are not necessarily wiser. Humility and concern for others are vital characteristics of wisdom: these manifest as concern for others, being thoughtful and fair, admitting mistakes, and also learning from them (Sternberg, 1990).

Notwithstanding his leading scholarship, Sternberg, has a most inelegant definition of wisdom:

> the application of intelligence and experience as mediated by values toward the achievement of a common good through a balance among

(1) intrapersonal, (2) interpersonal, and (3) extrapersonal interests, over the (1) short and (2) long terms, to achieve a balance among (1) adaptation to existing environments, (2) shaping of existing environments, and (3) selection of new environments. (Sternberg, 2004a, p. 165)

Another problem with Sternberg's vast and impressive work is that his measures are not clearly identified or are only partly revealed in his work. His WICS model best summarises the nature of the wisdom that he measures: 'to use one's intelligence, creativity, and experience for a common good' (Sternberg, 2003, p. 397). Thus an ethical dimension is essential to Sternberg's model. While assuming that intelligence is crucial to wisdom, Sternberg is wary of the ways in which this construct is operationalised. While wisdom requires the capacity to think in the abstract, Sternberg argues that wisdom requires practical intelligence, 'the ability to solve everyday problems by utilising knowledge gained from experience in order to purposefully adapt to, shape, and select environments' (Sternberg, 2003, p. 388). Such a construct of wisdom would at once eliminate the cultural bias that so often renders certain ethnic types as perennially inferior.

Another way to construe practical intelligence in an organisational context is to understand it as tacit knowledge (Polanyi, 1967), which is procedural knowledge and understanding, relevant to attaining goals that people value, and is acquired with little help from others. Organisational wisdom, then, would at least apply tacit knowledge intelligently and creatively, and mediated by values, direct such knowledge towards achieving a common good such that intrapersonal, interpersonal and extrapersonal (institutional or other larger) interests are balanced along with long- and short-term perspectives (Sternberg, 2004b). Significantly, both the Berlin School and Sternberg (1996) share a belief that a 'progressive style' that 'implies moving beyond existing rules and being tolerant of ambiguous situations' is one of the most salient predictors of wisdom (Baltes and Staudinger, 2000, p. 129).

US Positivists[1]

Three other US researchers have developed important empirical tests of wisdom. Ardelt (2004) operationalises wisdom as a three-dimensional construct incorporating the cognitive, reflective and affective dimensions first devised by Clayton and Birren (1980). Wise people have 'an understanding of life, and a desire to know the truth' (Ardelt, 2004, p. 275). Ardelt shares the Berlin School's belief that acceptance of life's dialectical and uncertain nature is fundamental to wisdom, as is the understanding that knowledge has inherent limits. Wise people, she says, must also have 'sympathetic and compassionate love for others' (p. 275). Although all three dimensions need to be present, the reflective dimension is regarded as 'crucial' (Ardelt, 2003, p. 279). Ardelt's Three-Dimensional Wisdom Scale (3D-WS) measurement instrument comprises 39 items for the three dimensions: cognitive, reflective and affective (Ardelt, 2003, pp. 316–18).

Webster (2003) provides a parsimonious account of wisdom as 'competence in, intention to, and application of, critical life experiences to facilitate the optimal development of self and others' (p. 71). He identifies five dimensions (Webster, 2003, 2007, 2010): critical life experiences; reminiscence/reflectiveness; openness to experience; emotional regulation; and humour. His Self-Assessed Wisdom Scale (SAWS) contains 40 items. Webster has also shown in other research that there is a positive relationship between wisdom and three types of positive psychosocial variables: ego-integrity, life attitudes and values.

Brown's (Brown, 2004; Greene and Brown, 2009) Wisdom Development Scale understands wisdom as comprising eight dimensions measured by 79 items: self-knowledge; altruism; leadership; judgment; life knowledge; life skills; emotional management; and willingness to learn.

4.   Core Elements of Wisdom

From this brief overview of the wisdom literature, it is possible to distil five core elements of wisdom: values tolerance; self-insight; balance of three intelligences; emotional understanding and regulation; and tolerance of ambiguity and uncertainty.

Values Tolerance

Values tolerance is understood as 'openness to experience that challenges [one] to think differently about issues' (Webster, 2010, p. 73). It is vital in judgment that the decision-maker understand that there are different ways of looking at an issue when making key decisions. The Berlin School sees judgment as the outcome of personal attributes, expertise, and experience: the realisation of reflexive practice.

Self-insight

Self-insight is a fundamental criterion of the Berlin School, who define it as rich self-knowledge manifested by a 'deep insight into oneself and one's own life' (Mickler and Staudinger, 2008, p. 788). Most US theorists agree. For example, Sternberg (1998) talks about growing intellectually throughout one's life. Bergsma and Ardelt (2012) see it as 'an under-standing of life' (p. 484). Webster (2007, 2010) goes further to suggest that people must experience pain in critical life experiences. Greene and Brown (2009) extend the Berlin definition of 'self-knowledge' to include a sense of interconnectedness with the natural world. A person with self-insight reviews the past to help gain perspective on current concerns. Associated with this is self-relativism: the capacity to honestly appraise one's own behaviour without losing self-esteem.

The Balance of Three Intelligences

The balance of three intelligences entails fluid, crystallised and practi-cal contextual intelligence. Whereas cognition refers to all the mental processes related to knowledge acquisition and understanding that are used when we make judgments, intelligence is the capacity for us to be able to do those things. I have already outlined the differences between fluid and crystallised intelligence, or cognitive mechanics and cognitive pragmatics. In discussing organisational wisdom, I would propose that a third form of intelligence is necessary: Practical Contextual Intelligence. This is a form of practical political acumen that is founded on knowledge about an organisation's strengths, weaknesses, real priorities and the nature of internal politics, power and status. Research has shown that older organisational members who rated higher in wisdom performed better on the factor Practical Political Acumen (Limas and Hansson, 2004) which incorporates evaluating a problem or situation without imposing one's own values as well as understanding the environment and priorities of an organisation, including its group norms.

From an organisational aspect, it is also important to note that crucial to cognitive pragmatics (Crystallised and Practical Contextual Intelligence) are three dispositions: the humility and willingness to learn; using trial and error, or 'heuristics of growth' that reflects on prior experience; and a metaphysical capacity or 'a desire to know the truth' and to understand the 'significance and deeper meaning of phenomena and events'.

Emotional Understanding and Emotional Regulation

Emotional understanding involves a deep understanding of a wide vari-ety of people in varying contexts. It also requires advanced communi-cation skills that articulate thoughts meaningfully to others. Emotional regulation, the capacity to understand and regulate one's own emo-tions, is important because emotions are whole-body phenomena that cause changes in our subjective experience, behaviour and central and peripheral physiology that lead us toward some action. Emotional regulation helps us to refrain from inappropriate responses.

Tolerating Ambiguity and Uncertainty

The capacity to tolerate ambiguity and uncertainty is agreed upon by all wisdom theorists. Tolerating ambiguity is a characteristic of life skills: the ability to manage one's daily multiple roles and responsibilities effectively; and a practical competence, an ability to understand systems and anticipate problems, with tools and strategies for dealing with multiple contexts in life. Also inherent in this core element is an attitude to knowledge. This means accepting the inherent limit of knowledge (Ardelt, 2004) or possessing ontological acuity, which is the ability to question the assumptions upon which 'facts' are arrived at (McKenna and Rooney, 2008).

While these five core elements provide excellent predictors of wise action, I believe that two other elements are vital: moral commitment and conation. Although all the theorists surveyed imply that wise people have appropriate moral qualities and act ethically within an organisational context, it concerns me that this is not explicit in any major extant model of wisdom. The second element that may be missing from the five core elements of wisdom is conation. Moral conation is 'the capacity to generate responsibility and motivation to take moral action in the face of adversity and persevere through challenges' (Hannah, Avolio and May, 2011, p. 664). Because conation involves moral maturation, this implies judgment, which in turn implies advanced cognition (meta-cognition). However, conation also involves human agency, psychological ownership, self-efficacy, means efficacy and courage. Thus the process from the moral cognition needed to form moral judgment through to moral action involves moral motivation. The gap between moral judgment and moral motivation is the essence of conation. The impulse to act, or moral conation, will depend on a sense of moral identity that incorporates high levels of moral ownership, moral efficacy and moral courage (ibid., p. 666). Conation, therefore, is vital to morally wise action. It is significant that strongly conative people use three reflective techniques (Eccles and Wigfield, 2002): self-observation to monitor their own activity; self-assessment to compare the results of their own activities with the standard norm, or with the results achieved by other individuals in the environment; and positive self-reaction: that is, reacting to the results of their activities, and even when results are negative, still striving to attain the goal. This reflexive aspect is consistent with the other wisdom principles.

Social Practice Wisdom Principles

Taking all these elements into account, I present a list of wisdom criteria as the foundation of Social Practice Wisdom (based on Rooney, McKenna and Liesch, 2010: 56–8):

Wise people make careful observations to establish 'facts' from which they draw sound inferences and logical deductive explanations. However, they understand that 'facts' have various levels of salience and rest on, often, tacit ontological assumptions that must sometimes be tested. Rather than being immobilised by epistemological and ontological uncertainty, wise people ultimately accept certitude, even if temporarily. Through self-critique, wise people allow their own assumptions to be tested.

Wise people acknowledge the limitations of reason and 'fact' and allow a place for the metaphysical and the non-rational. That is, they acknowledge that the visceral and emotional aspects of our humanity need to be understood in ourselves and others. Wise people also draw upon their own and others' experience (*praxis*) to provide insight into similar cases and situations. Wise people understand the contingency of life, that it is never a predictable or linear narrative. They also understand the constructedness of phenomena that occur in different times and places. In short, wisdom is not reducible to method. Wise people use insights from the past, but they can also *see* (imagine) possibilities in the future.

Because wisdom is directed to *eudaimonia* (human flourishing), it is humane, virtuous, tolerant, and empathetic. Wise people manifest good character because they desire the social good. They value the long-term and communitarian good over short-term expediency. In this respect, it is vital that wise people are open-minded, open to critique, and open to new experiences.

Wise people must be able to articulate their judgments and opinions aesthetically and creatively, using imagination, style, and appropriate genres. They are contemplative and reflect on their role in bringing about harmony and happiness.

Wisdom must be both prudent and practical. This means that wise people must be sensibly worldly enough to understand their own community, society and other cultures. They are capable of independent thought and action to change the conditions of life.

There is an inevitable impulse to measure a concept once it becomes a construct in any realm of human study. Although natural and understandable, this impulse needs to be curbed in the case of wisdom. My argument would be that, if we seek to develop wisdom in people and to create wise organisations, it is important that we subject the concept to rigorous study from multiple disciplines: philosophy, psychology, sociology, political economy and discourse theory are five disciplines that I have drawn upon in wisdom research.

I made a strong commitment when I began such research to do all I could to ensure that, when wisdom research in management and organisational studies became popular, it would not be reduced to faddism given that management fads impelled our research. Similarly, I feared the prospect of organisational psychologists adding yet another battery of 'wisdom' tests to their psychometric assessment of staff, an ugly and contradictory idea. Thus, I want to briefly outline and comment on the dominant wisdom tests that exist.

The Berlin School's 'think aloud' technique asks participants to think aloud for 20 minutes about a hypothetical problem or a personal reflection. The transcribed recorded responses are then assessed by trained raters according to five general (GW) or five personal (PW) wisdom criteria[2] respectively.

The US positivists use self-report scales that measure different dimensions. As stated, Ardelt measures three dimensions with 39 items (cognitive, reflective and affective). Webster measures five dimensions comprising 40 items. Brown measures six dimensions using 79 items. While I believe that measuring some dimensions such as cognition and affect can provide useful information about the potential for wisdom, the self-report scale has limitations. This is because people have biased, typically inflated self-perceptions of their knowledge, skills and abilities (Staudinger and Glück, 2011) and also because of common method bias (Avolio, Walumbwa and Weber, 2009; Podsakoff et al., 2003). For those seeking to measure wisdom, a multi-method approach using qualitative, quantitative and textual analysis is essential. But above all, researchers must always acknowledge and respect the ineffable nature of wisdom: it appears in multiple ways in multiple contexts and is enacted by the most powerful and the meekest of people.

5.   Dealing with Paradox, Complexity and Incommensurability

Lest I give the impression that wisdom is the panacea of our human existence, I want to conclude by asking those who are interested in developing wisdom to acknowledge the boundedness of our human potential.

Not only are we bounded by the physical and mental capability we inherit and develop, but also by circumstance. It is not true as some contemporary individualist ideologies proclaim that we can do any-thing if we want, which begs the question even if that were true, But should we? And this brings me back to the tri-level model. In an organi-sational context, at the micro-level we are bounded by our interpersonal and formal relations, at the meso-level we are bounded by the nature of the organisation and at the macro-level we are bounded by the space, time and ideological frameworks in which we live.

Contemporary thinkers know of complex emergent systems, com-plexity theory (Snowden and Boone, 2007) and chaos theory, but wise people always knew that these undermine the natural human desire for linearity, predictability and equilibrium (Lansing, 2003). We should be empowered by the knowledge that cooperation, communication and intuition have produced better results than rational choice in complex, unpredictable and uncertain situations (Axelrod, 1997; Frank, 1988). We are also aware of wicked problems, which are mostly addressed in public administration theory and practice (Australian Public Service Commission, 2007; Head 2008). These are problems that are difficult to clearly define, are unstable and evolving, socially complex, have many stakeholders, have no clear and correct solution, and will often involve some stakeholder losing out. Let me briefly refer to one wicked problem within Australia where I live.

This is the relationship between Australia's indigenous people, the Aborigines – one of the world's oldest peoples – and non-indigenous Australians. Not dissimilarly to many other indigenous peoples in advanced technological societies, they have been murdered, marginal-ised, raped and exploited. Australian law took 91 years to remove the legal fiction of *terra nullius* – literally empty land – by a judgment of the Australian High Court in 1992. And it took a brave prime minister, in the face of considerable racist reaction by Australians and vested inter-ests, particularly mining companies, to produce the enabling legislation to guarantee those Aboriginal land rights. Twenty years prior to that, another brave prime minister introduced a vast range of legislation that tried to remedy the 200 years of neglect and exploitation. But the cur-rent reality is that: in 2011, Aborigines born between 2005 and 2007 can expect to live about ten years less than any other Australian child (Australian Medical Association, 2011); Aborigines are 13 times more likely to be imprisoned than non-Aboriginal people (Korff, 2012); and the indigenous unemployment rate is three and a half times the non-indigenous (Whittaker, 2011).

In summary, in the face of 200 years of losing their land and much of their culture and traditions, of rampant discrimination and exploitation, and having to choose between assimilation or tradition and the various points in-between, and in spite of well-intentioned efforts by whites to redress this, the situation is diabolical. What is the wise choice for this wicked problem?

Unsurprisingly, it seems to be coming from the ranks of indigenous peoples themselves who recognise that the paradox of good white intentions has been to produce lassitude in many communities; who recognise the incommensurability of communal cultures of hunter-gatherers dealing with the massively overwhelming individualist culture of market society and capitalism and urban nuclear families; who recognise the sad reality of lateral violence that happens in the most oppressed communities; and the vested interests of those running government-funded agencies to maintain power. Indigenous leaders such as Noel Pearson[3] have shown enormous wisdom and courage to confront these issues knowing that he is not going to see considerable improvement in his own lifetime. In other words, in the face of wicked problems, wise people will act in the knowledge that, in the short term, good outcomes will be limited, and that the longer-term good may well be destroyed by the despair of victims and the evil wrought by ignorant and malevolent forces.

Thus at a global and organisational level, wisdom is needed as much as it ever has been in human history. I share Isaiah Berlin's (2000) belief that perfection is both unattainable and inconceivable, but I do very much believe in pursuing the ideal. While I strongly encourage the scholarly address of wisdom, I warn against the hubris of believing that the mystery of wisdom can truly be understood by anyone entering the fray.

Notes

1. See Indick (2002) for a good explanation of what I understand by psychological positivism.
2. The Berlin School uses the following criteria for the GW task where participants are asked to write about 300 words in response to the question, 'In reflecting over their lives, people sometimes realise that they have not achieved what they had once planned to achieve. What should one/they do and consider?'

   1. Rich factual knowledge about the fundamental pragmatics of life;
   2. Rich procedural knowledge about dealing with the fundamental pragmatics of life;

3. Life span contextualism: Understanding of life contexts and their temporal (developmental) relations;
4. Relativism of values and life priorities: Knowledge about the differences in values and life goals; and
5. Recognition and management of uncertainty: Knowledge about the relative uncertainty of life and its management.

The Berlin School uses five other criteria to evaluate PW where participants write in response to a question such as 'Please think about yourself as a friend. What are your typical behaviours as a friend? How do you act in difficult situations? Can you think of examples? Can you think of reasons for your behaviour? What are your strengths and weaknesses as a friend? What would you like to change?':

1. Rich self-knowledge;
2. Heuristics of growth and self-regulation;
3. Interrelating the self;
4. Self-relativism;
5. Tolerance of ambiguity/uncertainty.

3. See, for example Noel Pearson's two pieces for *The Australian*, 'Individualism versus communalism' (Pearson, 2011a) and 'Job-service parasites get rich living off the unemployed' (2011b).

References

Ardelt, M. (2003). 'Empirical Assessment of a Three-dimensional Wisdom Scale'. *Research on Aging*, 25 (3): 275–324.

Ardelt, M. (2004). 'Wisdom as Expert Knowledge System: A Critical Review of a Contemporary Operationalization of an Ancient Concept'. *Human Development*, 47(5): 257–85.

Aristotle (1960). *Posterior Analytics*. Harvard University Press, London.

Aristotle (1984). *Nicomachean Ethics*, trans. H.G. Apostle. The Peripatetic Press, Grinnell, IO.

Australian Medical Association (2011). '2010–11 AMA Indigenous health report card – Best practice in primary health care for Aboriginal peoples and Torres Strait Islanders' (May). Available at http://ama.com.au/node/6629#anchorthree.

Australian Public Service Commission (2007). 'Tackling wicked problems: A public policy perspective'. APSC, Canberra.

Avolio, B.J., F.O. Walumbwa and T.J. Weber (2009). 'Leadership: Current Theories, Research, and Future Directions'. *Annual Review of Psychology*, 60: 421–49.

Axelrod, R. (1997). *The Complexity of Cooperation: Agent-based Models of Cooperation and Collaboration*. Princeton University Press.

Baltes, P.B. (1993). 'The Aging Mind: Potential and Limits'. *The Gerontologist*, 33(5): 580–94.

Baltes, P.B., and U. Kunzmann (2004). 'The Two Faces of Wisdom: Wisdom as a Gneral Theory of Knowledge and Judgment about Excellence in Mind and

Virtue vs. Wisdom as Everyday Realization in People and Products'. *Human Development*, 47(5): 290–9.

Baltes, P.B., and U.M. Staudinger (2000). 'A Metaheuristic (Pragmatic) to Orchestrate Mind and Virtue toward Excellence'. *American Psychologist*, 55(1): 122–36.

Barker, E.M. (2005). 'Aristotle's Reform of *Paideia*'. Available at www.bu.edu/wcp/Papers/Anci/AnciBark.htm.

Benedict, B.M. (2001). *Curiosity: A Cultural History of Early Modern Inquiry*. University of Chicago Press.

Bergsma, A., and M. Ardelt (2012). 'Self-reported Wisdom and Happiness: An Empirical Investigation'. *Journal of Happiness Studies*, 13(3): 481–99.

Berlin, I. (2000). *The Power of Ideas*. Princeton University Press.

Bigelow, J. (1992). 'Developing Managerial Wisdom'. *Journal of Management Inquiry*, 1(2): 143–53.

Biggart, N.W., and T.D. Beamish (2003). 'The Economic Sociology of Conventions: Habit, Custom, Practice, and Routine in Market Order'. *Annual Review of Sociology*, 29: 443–64.

Bligh, M.C., C.L. Pearce and J.C. Kohles (2006). 'The Importance of Self- and Shared Leadership in Team-based Knowledge Work: A Meso-level Model of Leadership Dynamics'. *Journal of Managerial Psychology*, 21(4): 296–318.

Bourdieu, P., and T. Eagleton (1992). 'Doxa and Common Life: In Conversation'. *New Left Review*, 191: 111–21.

Brown, S.C. (2004). 'Learning across the Campus: How College Facilitates the Development of Wisdom'. *Journal of College Student Development*, 45(2): 134–48.

Clayton, V.P., and J.E. Birren (1980). 'The Development of Wisdom across the Life-span: A Reexamination of an Ancient Topic'. In P.B. Baltes and O.G. Grim Jr (eds), *Life-span Development and Behavior*, vol. 3, pp. 103–35. Academic Press, New York.

Dunne, J. (1997). *Back to the Rough Ground: Practical Judgement and the Lure of Technique*. University of Notre Dame Press.

Eccles, J.S., and A. Wigfield (2002). 'Motivational Beliefs, Values, and Goals'. *Annual Review of Psychology*, 53: 109–33.

Edwards, M.G. (2010). *Organisational Transformation for Sustainability: An Integral Metatheory*. Routledge, London.

Eflin, J. (2003). 'Epistemic Presuppositions and Their Consequences'. *Metaphilosophy*, 34(1/2): 48–67.

Flyvbjerg, B. (2004). 'Phronetic Planning Research: Theoretical and Methodological Reflections'. *Planning Theory and Practice*, 5(3): 283–306.

Foucault, M. (1967). *Madness and Civilization: A History of Insanity in the Age of Reason*. Tavistock Publications, London.

Foucault, M. (1978). 'Politics and the Study of Discourse'. *Ideology and Consciousness*, 3: 7–26.

Foucault, M. (1980). 'Truth and Power'. In C. Gordon (ed.), *Power/knowledge: Selected Interviews and Other Writings, 1972–1977*, pp. 107–33. Pantheon Books, New York.

Frank, R.H. (1988). *Passions without Reason*. Norton, New York.

Giddens, A. (1984). *The Constitution of Society: Outline of a Theory of Structuration*. Polity Press, Cambridge.

Greene, J.A., and S.C. Brown (2009). 'The Wisdom Development Scale: Further Validity Investigations'. *International Journal of Aging and Human Development*, 68(4): 289–320.

Hannah, S.T., B.J. Avolio and D.R. May (2011). 'Moral Maturation and Moral Conation: A Capacity Approach to Explaining Moral Thought and Action'. *Academy of Management Review* 36(4): 663–85.

Head, B. (2008). 'Wicked Problems in Public Policy'. *Public Policy*, 3(2): 101–18.

Horn, J.L., and R.B. Cattell (1967). 'Age Differences in Fluid and Crystallized Intelligence'. *Acta Psychologica*, 26: 107–29.

House, R., D.M. Rousseau and M. Thomas-Hunt (1995). 'The Meso Paradigm: A Framework for the Integration of Micro and Macro Organizational Behavior'. *Research in Organizational Behavior*, 17(1): 71–114.

Hughes, G.J. (2001). *Aristotle on Ethics*. Routledge, London.

Indick, W. (2002). 'Fight the Power: The Limits of Empiricism and the Costs of Positivistic Rigor'. *Journal of Psychology*, 136(1): 21–36.

Kekes, J. (1995). *Moral Wisdom and Good Lives*. Cornell University Press, Ithaca and London.

Keyes, C.L., D. Shmotkin and C.D. Ryff (2002). 'Optimizing Well-being: The Empirical Encounter of Two Traditions'. *Journal of Personality and Social Psychology*, 82(6): 1007–22.

Korff, J. (2012). 'Aboriginal Prison Rates'. Sydney, Australia: Creative Spirits. Available at www.creativespirits.info/aboriginalculture/law.

Kozlowski, S.W.J., and K.J. Klein (2000). 'A Multi-level Approach to Theory and Research in Organizations: Contextual, Temporal, and Emergent Processes'. In idem (eds), *Multilevel Theory, Research, and Methods in Organizations*, pp. 3–90. Jossey-Bass, San Francisco.

Kriger, M.P., and L.-C. Malan (1993). 'Shifting Paradigms: The Valuing of Personal Knowledge, Wisdom, and Other Invisible Processes in Organizations'. *Journal of Management Inquiry*, 2(4): 391–8.

Lansing, J.S. (2003). 'Complex Adaptive Systems'. *Annual Review of Anthropology*, 32: 183–204.

Limas, M.J., and R.O. Hansson (2004). 'Organizational Wisdom'. *International Journal of Aging and Human Development*, 59(2): 85–103.

Long, C.P. (2002). 'The Ontological Reappropriation of *Phronèsis*'. *Continental Philosophy*, 35(1): 35–60.

Malan, L.-C., and M.P. Kriger (1998). 'Making Sense of Managerial Wisdom'. *Journal of Management Inquiry*, 7(3): 242–51.

Mathieu, J.E., and G. Chen (2011). 'The Etiology of the Multilevel Paradigm in Management Research'. *Journal of Management*, 37(2): 610–41.

McKenna, B., and D. Rooney (2008). 'Wise Leadership and the Capacity for Ontological Acuity'. *Management Communication Quarterly*, 21(4): 537–46.

McKenna, B., D. Rooney and K.B. Boal (2009). 'Wisdom Principles as a Meta-theoretical Basis for Evaluating Leadership'. *Leadership Quarterly*, 20(2): 177–90.

Mickler, C., and U.M. Staudinger (2008). 'Personal Wisdom: Validation and Age-related Differences of a Performance Measure'. *Psychology and Aging*, 23(4): 787–99.

Miner, R.C. (1998). 'Verum-Factum and Practical Pisdom in the Early Writings of Giambattista Vico'. *Journal of the History of Ideas*, 59(1): 53–73.

Nussbaum, M. (1994). *The Therapy of Desire: Theory and Practice in Hellenistic Ethics*. Princeton University Press.

Pearson, Noel (2011a). 'Individualism versus communalism'. *The Australian* (6 August). Available at www.theaustralian.com.au/national-affairs.

Pearson, Noel (2011b). 'Job-service parasites get rich living off the unemployed'. *The Australian* (3 September). Available at www.theaustralian.com.au/news/opinion.

Podsakoff, P.M., S.B. MacKenzie, J.-Y. Lee and N.P. Podsakoff (2003). 'Common Method Biases in Behavioral Research: A Critical Review of the Literature and Recommended Remedies'. *Journal of Applied Psychology*, 88(5): 879–903.

Polanyi, M. (1967). *The Tacit Dimension*. Doubleday, Garden City.

Rooney, D., B. McKenna and P. Liesch (2010). *Wisdom and Management in the Knowledge Economy*. Routledge, New York.

Rousseau, D.M., and R.J. House (1994). 'Meso Organizational Behavior: Avoiding Three Fundamental Biases'. In C.L. Cooper and D.M. Rousseau (eds), *Trends in Organizational Behavior*, pp. 13–30. Wiley, Chichester, UK.

Ryff, C.D., and C.L.M. Keyes (1995). 'The Structure of Psychological Wellbeing Revisited'. *Journal of Personality and Social Psychology*, 69(1): 719–27.

Ryff, C.D., and B.H. Singer (2000). 'Interpersonal Flourishing: A Positive Health Agenda for the New Millenium'. *Personality and Social Psychology Review*, 4: 30–44.

Ryff, C.D., and B.H. Singer (2008). 'Know Thyself and Become What You Are: A Eudaimonic Approach to Psychological Well-being'. *Journal of Happiness Studies*, 9(1): 13–39.

Sherman, N. (1997). *Making a Necessity of Virtue: Aristotle and Kant on Virtue*. Cambridge University Press, Cambridge and New York.

Snowden, D.J., and M. Boone (2007). 'A Leader's Framework for Decision Making'. *Harvard Business Review* (November): 69–76.

Staudinger, U.M., and L. Glück (2011). 'Psychological Wisdom Research: Commonalities and Differences in a Growing Field'. *Annual Review of Psychology*, 62: 215–41.

Sternberg, R.J. (1990). *Wisdom: Its Nature, Origins and Development*. Cambridge University Press.

Sternberg, R.J. (1996). 'Styles of Thinking'. In P.B. Baltes and U.M. Staudinger (eds), *Interactive Minds: Life-span Perspectives on the Social Foundation of Cognition*, pp. 347–65. Cambridge University Press, New York.

Sternberg, R.J. (1998). 'A Balance Theory of Wisdom'. *Review of General Psychology*, 2(4): 347–65.

Sternberg, R.J. (2003). 'WICS: A Model of Leadership in Organizations'. *Academy of Management Learning and Education*, 2(4): 386–401.

Sternberg, R.J. (2004a). 'What Is Wisdom and How Can We Develop It?' *Annals of the American Academy of Political and Social Science*, 591(1): 164–74.

Sternberg, R.J. (2004b). 'Words to the Wise about Wisdom? A Commentary on Ardelt's Critique of Baltes'. *Human Development*, 47(5): 286–89.

Sternberg, R.J. (2005). 'Foolishness'. In R.J. Sternberg and J. Jordan (eds), *A Handbook of Wisdom: Psychological Perspectives*, pp. 331–52. Cambridge University Press, New York.

Webster, J.D. (2003). 'An Exploratory Analysis of a Self-assessed Wisdom Scale'. *Journal of Adult Development*, 10(1): 13–22.

Webster, J.D. (2007). 'Measuring the Character Strength of Wisdom'. *International Journal of Aging and Human Development*, 65(2): 163–83.

Webster, J.D. (2010). 'Wisdom and Positive Psychosocial Values in Young Adulthood'. *Journal of Adult Development*, 17(2): 70–80.

Whittaker, J. (2011). 'The massive indigenous employment gap stagnates'. Melbourne, Australia: Crikey.dot.com. Available at www.crikey.com.au/2011/07/01.

3
Empirical Wisdom Research: A Community Approach

David Rooney

Researching organisational wisdom presents a unique challenge and it is not altogether certain that the broader management and organisational studies research community is ready for it. This chapter therefore considers the future of wisdom research, including wisdom-based research methods for doing wise research. In doing this I first discuss what might be called the classical view of developing wise understandings of reality, then extend that discussion by considering research as an art and craft, including approaching research as a creative and aesthetic process that includes emotions. The discussion will then cover issues connected to creating a community of organisational wisdom researchers before considering important elements of the institutional framework in which such a community might work. This institutional framework discussion includes arguing for changes in universities and related research institutions such as the academic journal system; changes in university management style; and changes in the social architecture that links universities, the community and business. The underlying argument I present is about integration and that a community approach to organisational wisdom research is foundational to an effective global research programme.

Why Organisational Wisdom Research Is Important

Organisational wisdom research is important because it can address the problem of the lack of integration across a number of important areas of organisational life and between organisations and the rest of reality. Wisdom research is also important because wisdom brings a focus to larger issues that go beyond the narrow, short-term interests of managers and shareholders. Wisdom is about human flourishing and therefore must have an interest in climate change, global conflict, global poverty, water and food security, and other great challenges facing humanity today. Wisdom research can help business to understand its roles in dealing with such issues, to significantly improve business practice and, I hope, therefore stimulate more wisdom. It is clear that bringing more knowledge, technology and expertise to bear on organisational life is not enough to materially improve businesses contribution to the planet. Never has there been such an abundance of business knowledge, technology and expertise, yet major problems persist despite the many benefits these things bring. Intelligence, innovation and creativity are not enough on their own either. Average IQ continues to increase (Sternberg, 2003) and there has never been a greater focus on innovation and creativity in business than there is now. Intelligence, innovation and business creativity are as much a part of the problem as they can be part of the solution. Similarly, ethics on its own is not enough. Most people can discern right from wrong and most business school graduates have studied ethics, but that did not prevent the global financial crisis. Each of these aspects of reality plus, for example, judgment theory, decision-making theory and other related areas of research have clearly made their contributions to practice, but the reality of the world we experience is nevertheless poised in a state of stark precariousness and promises to remain so in the foreseeable future, despite the best efforts of contemporary research. I argue in this context that pursuing wisdom as an alternative research approach makes good sense.

The work Bernard McKenna and I have done in our Social Practice Wisdom (SPW) research (McKenna and Rooney, 2008; McKenna, Rooney and Boal, 2009; Rooney, 2010; Rooney and McKenna, 2008; Rooney, McKenna and Liesch, 2010), and others such as Mark Edwards (in press), Wendelin Küpers and Matt Statler (Küpers, 2007; Küpers and Statler, 2008) who have developed specific foci on integration and integral wise practice, have taken the lead. Wisdom research rises above silos of knowledge, judgment, decision-making, innovation, ethics and other literatures when standing on their own because they do not share the inclusive focus on integration (among other things) in the way that wisdom theory usually does. An important question a community of organisational wisdom researchers needs to answer is, What is it that we can do with our wisdom perspectives that cannot already be easily done? Using our SPW approach, the answer is to do things better because we can integrate by:

- Being clear about the roles and relevance of one's dispositions and their recursive relationship with *habitus*, including cultural artefacts like knowledge and values;

- Explaining the importance of culture and institutions in facilitating the integration of equanimity, virtue, transcendence and reason, leading to ontological commitment through clear thinking, and then on to deep understandings and insight that foster SPW;
- Showing how self-insight, intellectual virtues, reason and transcendence require equanimity to create ontological acuity and commitment that underpin deep understanding and insight and wise dispositions;
- Giving due emphasis to the aesthetics, social practice and relational aspects of being wise, particularly applying knowledge/theory through social practice and dialogue (including eloquence and the art of communication);
- Finally, SPW's integration results in wellbeing or human flourishing and rises above narrow interests.

The central dynamic in SPW is therefore a complex, multidimensional integration that creates clarity and decisiveness through equanimity and corresponding dispositions that generate the insight, composure and motivation to deploy the resources needed to act excellently and successfully in the best interests of oneself, others and the planet.

There is a second dimension to my argument in support of organisational wisdom research. Business, management and leaders matter too much to be left unguided by wisdom research. Business, management and leadership have to play their roles in achieving sustainable excellence in the world. To do this, a new and dependable research and practice paradigm has to be found, and wisdom-based approaches hold much hope for this endeavour.

Wise Research

Wisdom research can speak to perplexing global issues. However, beyond this I argue that there is also merit in using wisdom theory for pursuing basic change in our approach to social research itself. Wisdom is a challenge for standard approaches to management and organisational studies research, making visible some fundamental problems in mainstream approaches. It is timely to note here that some scholars have suggested that management research has run out of ideas (Alvesson and Sandberg, in press; Buckley, 2002). As a research construct wisdom is complicated in ways that make standard social science uncomfortable, even threatened. A decade's worth of sometimes bizarre journal and conference reviewers' reports on our work testifies to this. When considering wisdom as a research subject, it is safe to say that nothing else is quite like it, but wisdom's potential is profound as a research focus, as a research methodology and as business practice. I specifically turn to wise research methodology now.

My battle cry in relation to methodology is 'phronesiology not epistemology'. The central shift here is to move away from epistemology and its theory of knowledge (Hearn, Rooney and Mandeville, 2003) to a theory of *phronèsis* or practical wisdom as a conceptual foundation for wise research. *Phronèsis* integrates and employs knowledge and other resources well to create excellent practice and human flourishing. Flyvbjerg (2001, 2011) has used this logic to argue for the merits of using ethnomethodology, discourse analysis and case studies to produce wise social research outcomes. Similarly, Eikeland (2008) shows that a core element of practical wisdom is dialogue, and therefore he says that research should be dialogical. Action research, he argues, is the best way to achieve his aims. Another important method in use in wisdom research is the 'thinking out loud' exercise used in the Berlin wisdom research paradigm (Baltes and Staudinger, 2000) where research participants are asked to think out loud about a perplexing or difficult life-matter or decision. This technique provides insight into the range of resources individuals can gather and integrate in real time to address a difficult problem. The thinking out loud technique can easily be used in field research and even adapted to role-play scenarios. If wisdom's central dynamic is integration (which is assisted by dialogue and analyses of action and discourse in the field), then how research evaluates integration and what is integrated should be important questions for developing new phronetic research designs. However, these difficult integration questions have not yet been adequately answered in methodological terms in the wisdom-based research methods literature, although as I mention above some have started working through these issues.

It is safe to assume we can extend the range of phronetic methods beyond what Flyvbjerg and Eikeland have presented for phronesiology, particularly if we more carefully consider integration and all the many facets of *phronèsis* as well as other multi-method research designs (Rooney and McKenna, 2008). It is important to acknowledge that the bulk of contemporary empirical research about wisdom has been done by psychologists and that this research has added significantly to our knowledge of wisdom (Staudinger and Glück, 2011). However, sociology (broadly defined) is largely missing and so too is business missing as a research participant and collaborator. What is important here is that by adding sociology we broaden the methodological spectrum beyond what psychologists have used, which includes expanding the role of qualitative methods. Furthermore, adding business as research partners (not just participants), we are taking research into the field and expanding the size and diversity of our community of research practice. Before I continue to explore what methods could be used within the phronetic approach I want to go back to some classical Greek fundamentals.

From Classical Knowing to Phronesiology

Ontology (ways of being and becoming), axiology (values and value), epistemology (knowledge creation), praxeology (enactment or application of knowledge) and *eudaimonia* (wellbeing or human flourishing) are all relevant to social research methodology and all provide intellectual and practical foundations for wisdom that the classical philosophers provided for us (Rooney, 2013; Rooney et al., 2003). Epistemology is familiar to most (although not all) management and organisational studies researchers, and ontology is understood by some. But axiology, praxeology and *eudaimonia* are almost unknown. I argue that the absence of any of these concepts from methodologies puts those methodologies at a disadvantage if they are to contribute to wise social research. More specifically, it is the integration of each of these into the foundations of a coherent methodology that matters.

In this spirit of classical integration, Flyvbjerg (2001, pp. 129–40) argues that phronetic research works by balancing instrumental rationality with value rationality. The central focus is values (axiology), but creating knowledge (epistemology) and carefully discerning the way things are (ontology) are part of this approach. Flyvbjerg's focus on values guides research to ask: (1) Where are we going? (2) Is this desirable? (3) What should be done? Along with values, Flyvbjerg places power at the core of analysis. The fundamental questions here are, Who gains and who loses and by which mechanisms of power relations? With these additions, *praxis* and *eudaimonia* are also entrained in the research process. At a procedural level, Flyvbjerg says researchers must get close to reality. One must be a close observer but without what Flyvbjerg calls 'going native'. In adopting this close observer role, a researcher can, and should, emphasise the little things, local micropractices in the research site. An important part of this aspect of research is that it is important to look at practice before discourse. This is because Flyvbjerg maintains that what people do carries more detail than what is eventually filtered through to their words. Flyvbjerg urges us to study cases and contexts because practice is always influenced by situation and context-dependent judgment. It is imperative in this view to ask 'how' and to do narrative analysis. An important theoretical element of this approach is that it joins structure and agency and is concerned about *habitus*. The really important dynamic in doing this kind of research is developing dialogue with a polyphony of voices.

Phronèsis and *praxis* are intrinsically dialogical and empathetic for Eikeland (2008) and these are central to his views on wise social research. Eikeland (2008) seamlessly integrates epistemology, ontology, axiology, praxeology and *eudaimonia*. *Phronèsis* is the executive virtue that coherently integrates intellectual and ethical virtues to create deliberative excellence. The knowledge that feeds practical wisdom consists of *logos* (reasoning) and tacit elements in emotions/passions, habits, desires and skills, and, of course, action (Eikeland, 2008, p. 68). For Aristotle, knowledge is not so much a possession (in memory), knowledge is performative. Going further, facts only have value if they are deeply incorporated in ways of knowing. This is a process view, but also points to structure, indeed structural integration, by virtue of its acknowledgement of the importance of ways of organising ideas and attitudes/ dispositions that make up habitus and that orient action. All knowledge's forms are therefore relational and socially constructed (Rooney et al., 2003). When knowledge forms are enacted, 'there is an intrinsic connection between (a) relational knowledge forms and ways of knowing ... (b) constitutional political forms regulating relations between citizens, and (c) justice, considered to be the highest ethical virtue because it concerns relations to others' (Eikeland, 2008, p. 81).

The situated nature of knowledge is important to acknowledge because it points to how wisdom integrates values and knowledge in practice in particular situations through connections and relations (structure). Places are particular in their physical make up and also in how people react to them emotionally (Rooney et al., 2003; Rooney, McKenna and Liesch, 2010).

Phronèsis and *praxis* are intrinsically communicative (and in particular, dialogical) because both assume empathy, or understanding that there are other minds (sentient people) with other views and that connecting those minds through eloquence, persuasion, explanation, justification, conviction, trust, social cohesion and so forth is part of the process of *phronèsis*. Taking counsel, consultation, learning and teaching are all parts of the *habitus* of practical wisdom (Eikeland, 2008, pp. 102–3). If only for the sake of argument, we can take *habitus* as a kind of environment, and then note Sternberg's (2003) definition of wisdom that includes knowing when and how to change one's environment and when and how to adapt to one's environment. Empathy can also be seen in this light as empathy with the natural environment. Of course, the natural environment cannot be understood as just physical places because the natural environment is always impacted by human activity.

In discourse analysis, values, knowledge and other ideas are formulated as 'texts' and various actors may attempt to embed these ideas as taken-for-granted assumptions about reality in social groups (Fairclough, 2003). Texts are linguistic or visual images and other representations that are critical to the social construction of knowledge, beliefs and ideologies that in turn feed back to shape and create social behaviour. Texts that are convincingly presented are more likely to be accepted or institutionalised as shared values.

To be embedded and institutionalised a new idea must be presented as a compelling text and one that people feel they want to consider as an alternative. Novel texts may be threatening to elites who may want to dismiss them and in doing so create tension with those who do want to consider them. Power and values are therefore central to this process and so are communication skills. Wise communication needs to overcome tensions caused by new texts and win the attention of those who are threatened by them. Wise communication is more than an inherently compelling text; new texts need to be artfully and skilfully carried into discourse. For this to happen texts (and communicators) have to make sense, have legitimacy, be coherent and be presented in an appropriate and effective genre. This is a large part of what we call aesthetics in the SPW principles.

The art of wise communication is complex. One must consider the genre, structure and coherence of new ideas and creatively integrate them as relevant and usable ideas that are shown to be meaningfully linked to existing assumptions, values, goals and knowledge. A wise communicator must earn legitimacy in the eyes of others, and must show that they can deal with existing circumstances in the process of delivering an alternative. A simple reality is that new ideas that are commensurate with broader macro discourses appear persuasive and legitimate in ways that novel ideas are not (Phillips, Lawrence and Hardy, 2004).

Communicating wisely requires (Barge and Little, 2002; Rooney, McKenna and Liesch, 2010, p. 80):

1. Understanding the usually tacit ontological foundations of any discourse.

2. Understanding how non-language phenomena also communicate. These include paralinguistic features, corporeal aspects including *habitus*, and artefacts.
3. Understanding that the time and place in which texts or utterances occur are crucial in constructing meaning.
4. Allowing effective communication to take us unselfishly into the world of the other.
5. Having the capacity to articulate wise judgments aesthetically, imaginatively and appropriately is also a feature of wise people.

Communication processes founded on these tenets are important because they facilitate, for example, the processes of integration of learning, empathy, agency, social engagement, sense of place and the negotiation of intellectual, social and cultural change. Moreover, communication like this creates a humanising impulse. In *Politics* (252a24–1253a40), Aristotle sees a commonwealth as an emergent property of social relations and shared understandings, if those relations and understandings are presupposed by virtuous dispositions. Organisational wisdom and phronetic research must rest heavily on communication and the skills needed to navigate within a discursive context, and to achieve the level of integration that wisdom needs. Theoretical reasoning, practical reason, emotional regulation and ethical imagination must integrate coherently and this integration is critical to practical wisdom and to *praxis*. Practical wisdom is nothing without engagement, dialogue and sociality (Eikeland, 2008, p. 457). Wisdom is learning to live, see, experience, value, participate and create (Maxwell, 1984) and that is what research should contribute to.

> Granted that enquiry has as its basic aim to help enhance the quality of human life, it is actually profoundly and damagingly irrational and unrigorous for enquiry to give intellectual priority to the task of improving knowledge. Rather, intellectual priority needs to be given to the task of articulating our problems of living, and proposing and criticising possible solutions, namely possible human actions. (Maxwell, 1984, pp. 2–3)

This statement has resonance with the view of wisdom as expert knowledge in the pragmatics of life (Baltes and Staudinger, 2000), and the imperative of engaging directly in the everyday life of civic reality. Wise research therefore is a dialogical and empathetic process that is concerned with micro practices and values: it creates actionable knowledge as a relational process using the fullness of situations being researched. It is not research done only for the sake of creating or testing theory, and it does not valorise abstraction above all else.

Taking this line of argument a step further we can also say that truly expert phronetic researchers must necessarily go creatively and insightfully beyond mechanical rules of social scientific methods, just as all kinds of exemplary experts do (Dreyfus and Dreyfus, 1986). Practically wise research cannot simply be confined to following a prescribed, rigid, formulaic method, because to do so limits unnecessarily the extent to which some of the most powerful capacities of wisdom can be used. Wise research must engage with insight, imagination, judgment, empathetic feeling and values.

Keep in mind that when Aristotle uses the word 'reason' (*logos*) its meaning is not the same as the modern words 'logic' and 'rational' and has no direct relationship to the failing modern ideology of logical positivism. For Aristotle reason is the process that discerns what is harmful and what is helpful for humanity, what is just and unjust, and what is good and evil. Values are an inescapable part of such reasoning. Such discernment is not based solely on mechanical logic, it also includes (at the very least) emotional and social intelligence and moral character as well as open-mindedness (Cooper, 2012). Aristotle sees at least two types of reason. The first is the ability simply to think things out to make reasoned judgments of value. We might call this practical thinking. The second is theorising (or philosophical thinking and contemplative wisdom – *sophia*), which is needed to discern ultimate truths (Cooper, 2012, pp. 84–9). This is not values-free positivism, which Aristotle would likely reject out of hand as an aspect of practical wisdom.

Sociological imagination (Mills, 1959) as a component of social research is not a new idea, but it is one that resonates with new calls for phronetic research. Phronetic researchers are researchers who can improvise in the field without compromising rigour and quality (cf. Dreyfus and Dreyfus, 1986). This kind of improvisational plasticity and openness is reflected in Flyvbjerg and Eikeland when they identify methodologies that fit within the family of open research approaches (Charmaz, 2006) like grounded theory, ethnography, ethnomethodology, case study and so on, that are iterative, procedurally adaptive and explicitly conducive to improvisation. Wise social research is strongly reliant on the art and craft of creating actionable knowledge.

One of the five core principles of SPW is aesthetics. Emotions are now understood by scientists to be a critical component of reasoned thinking and all kinds of problem solving and decision-making (Damasio, 2000;

Hall, 2010; Rolls, 2012), and I argue that emotion is central to the aesthetic practices of wisdom. Rationality and emotions are better seen as two sides of the same coin, much like Aristotle understood reason to be. Equanimity is part of the aesthetic dimension of wisdom and it allows values and judgment to be part of phronetic research because it includes the dispositions that enable social and emotional intelligence to replace values-free and unemotional research mindsets in mainstream social research methods. Bernard McKenna and I use the term 'aesthetics' in a particular SPW way. We do not use it in the normal philosophical sense it has today of being about informed or sophisticated consumption or appreciation of art and beauty. We use it in a communicative and social practice sense that identifies satisfying qualities like expressivity, equanimity, pleasure and reward as important to wisdom. The interpretation of Aristotle's use of the term aesthetics in relation to practical wisdom that we (Rooney, McKenna and Liesch, 2010) make is that it is the creative art of living with special reference to communicating difficult-to-convey ideas in everyday social practice, and communicative excellence that creates value for oneself and others.

How do you express a wise idea so that it inspires or persuades others to undertake difficult actions to bring about positive change in the world? It is undeniable that satisfaction/pleasure, beauty, emotions, love and creativity are important components of Aristotle's aesthetics, but aesthetic activities also teach, elicit reflection, create a sense of psychological safety and enhance emotional intelligence that is critical to practical wisdom. Thus, intrinsically rewarding practices, like mindfulness meditation, that access and re-evaluate subconscious schemas, are also part of wisdom's aesthetics because they create equanimity and because they can renovate difficult to scrutinise and dysfunctional subconscious processes that detract from wise practice. These are the foundations of the critical micro social skills needed for SPW.

Communication is essential to social practice: there is no such thing as society if there is no communication. In SPW, aesthetics is a central part of what weaves or integrates reason, transcendence and virtue together to be deployed or expressed as wise social practice. Collins (1998, pp. 379–81) says that networks of personal contacts that pass 'emotional energy (passion, motivation) and cultural capital from generation to generation' are critical features of intellectual evolution. Elaborating this point, Collins says that what is also important within these networks is that there are always tensions between competing ideas or explanations of reality. He argues that 'interaction rituals' are important processes in sustainable intellectual change if they keep intellectual networks open to new ideas and, more to the point, open to genuine debate about competing ideas as they engage with those tensions. Communicative excellence in SPW therefore brings a focus to discourse and its role in opening admission of new ideas. This focus explicitly includes the expressive, including the presentational and rhetorical processes that are at play. Socrates, Aristotle and Buddha were excellent communicators and teachers who understood something about the theatre and art of an open pedagogy.

Empathy, altruism, compassion and love, for example, are central to western and eastern explanations of wisdom and they are impossible without emotion and mean little if they are unexpressed. If wisdom's emotions are virtuous, then emotional regulation is a vital part of it. Indeed, as I have already suggested, there is a growing consensus among scientists that emotional regulation is one of the most foundational components of moral reasoning and discernment (Hauser, 2008). In important ways, wisdom is irreducibly a product of human hearts and micro-level social action. Passion and emotion are researchable in wisdom-based research, but they are also important and positive elements of a researcher's motivations and his or her moral compass. It is also important that the research itself is aesthetic; that it effectively communicates difficult-to-communicate ideas that create valuable change, and that contribute to equanimity, to compassion and to positive emotional energy.

A Research Community

Researching wisdom and doing phronetic research requires more wisdom than any of us have as individuals (Sternberg, 1990). The challenges of wisdom research and wisdom theory itself seem to call out for an interdisciplinary community-of-practitioners approach. More specifically, it is time to establish a creative dialogue and collaboration across research, the community, business and teaching by making porous the boundaries between each, which is what wisdom theory suggests we do.

What might the social practices of a community for phronetic research be (cf. Hearn, Rooney and Mandeville, 2003)? The short answer is that the practices of this community are those described in wisdom theory. At the macro level is an engaged, integrated and virtuous community of practitioners that as a collective is expert in the art, craft and science of research that produces excellence through creating actionable research that is valuable for the planet.

Micro social practices deployed in the field for doing phronetic research are also important. The dialogical and discursive elements of phronetic research have already been pointed out above, along with the need for empathy and the capacity to be able to articulate the values, micro practices, emotions and other tacit elements of reality in situations being researched. It is also noted above that getting close to the situation without going native is important. For me, this is not simply being a passive-objective observer but being an open-minded and empathetic one who interacts to test observations by, for example, asking questions, or simply participating in the conversations of everyday life there. But researchers can undertake other kinds of interventions such as those that help people to unpack how to voice their values (Gentile, 2010); working through processes that aid individual reflection and reflexivity (Cunliffe, 2002; Cunliffe and Jun, 2005); practising ethical reasoning using devices like the Potter Box (Backus and Ferraris, 2004); developing emotional intelligence and action regulation (Ciarrochi and Blackledge, 2005); evaluating integration (Edwards, in press); assessing openness (McCrae and Costa, 1997; Staudinger and Glück, 2011); and understanding the impact of place on identity and cognition (Rooney et al., 2010). In terms of overarching principles what matters for phronetic research is (1) empathetic and open-minded interaction in the field; (2) how you understand wisdom working as a construct (balance, expert knowledge, *phronèsis*, SPW); and (3) integral practice of the art and craft of research as an expert researcher.

At the level of data and analysis, mixed methods research in an interdisciplinary framework understands not just all the relevant data and ontological features of the research site but also the axiological, praxeological and eudaimonic, and the extent to which they integrate (or not). Given the participatory and observational nature of these designs, I have already pointed to action research, grounded theory, ethnography and case study as relevant research design models. However, the openness and plasticity of these designs can only be as wise as the researchers' dispositions, because

> Phronesis must take into consideration where ... others are, emotionally, intellectually, and in their skills and attitudes, in trying to find the right thing to do, but it cannot use these circumstances manipulatively ... It must know how to deal with egotistical, strategic, manipulative behaviour in others without itself becoming like this, but also without simply being subdued by it and letting such behaviour prevail in others and in general. (Eikeland, 2008, p. 149)

Institutional or Organisational Wisdom

In line with what has already been suggested, what embeds the long-term intellectual change I am asking for is cultural/institutional/organisational change. Collins (1998) provides a sociological explanation of the structures and modes of organisation of intellectual communities in their quests for further understanding, to develop deep insights, and to enlighten humanity about life. His explanation of global intellectual change since ancient times also suggests what the modes of social organisation are that will most likely foster the discovery of profound knowledge. First, Collins (1998, p. 324) describes a three-phase process for shaping intellectual creativity: (1) appropriate economic-political structures, that shape (2) the organisations which support intellectual life; and these in turn allow a build up of (3) networks among participants in centres of intellectual controversies, which constitute the idea-substance of intellectual life. Second, it is change to this organisational base that is most important: 'innovative practices come from a long-term change in the organisational base, the full ideological ramifications of what has transpired do not emerge for many decades' (Collins, 1998, p. 333). His argument is that organisational changes cause the relationships between competing schools of thought to change, which promotes creative outputs. On top of all this, networks of personal contacts that pass passion, motivation and cultural capital from generation to generation within contemporaneous social networks are crucial. This explanation is broadly compatible with Phillips, Lawrence and Hardy (2004). Collins (1998, pp. 379–81) though is more particular about rivalry between points of view. Third, the absence of an imposed single orthodoxy, the presence of a culture of tolerant scepticism, and having the leading thinkers directly involved in creating the organisational transformations of the modes of intellectual production are essential to positive intellectual change. Collins (1998) clearly identifies the role of networks and shows that within these networks tensions between competing ideas or explanations of reality are critical in the history of intellectual change. He also argues that interaction rituals are important processes in sustainable intellectual change if they keep intellectual networks open to new ideas and, very importantly, open to debate about competing ideas. Rituals are important aspects of any culture, including research culture. Rituals that for example maintain tolerant scepticism are important for wise research.

The other side of intellectual history is that there have been periods of serious stagnation. A climate of intellectual stagnation is created through (1) loss of cultural capital, where important ideas are lost or forgotten; (2) dominance of the classics, where a limited range of dominant ideas overshadow everything else and are seen as unchallengeable; and (3) technical refinement, where intellectual focus falls to the level of being concerned with pedantry for its own sake, doctrinal orthodoxy and making small incremental technical advances (Collins, 1998, pp. 502–4; Landes, 1998). Stagnation is therefore also associated with rote learning as central to the education system, routinisation and bureaucratisation of intellectual modes of production, and vulgar careerism through credentialism (Collins, 1998, p. 509). If some of this has a familiar ring to it today, and it does to me, then considering change to the current social research culture and climate will appear more urgent to you. In this vein Maxwell (1984, 2009, 2012) argues that universities should move from contributing to knowledge to contributing to wisdom.

Institutions, organisational structures, organisational climate and organisational culture all matter when it comes to wise practice, including wise research. With these organisational features in mind, Bernard McKenna and I argue that organisations need to create the space for people to be wise in. Now is probably a good time for universities to revisit what it means to be a university in the twenty-first century and this should include revisiting their organisational climate, culture and structure. Given the timeless nature of core aspects of wisdom and its ability to make itself relevant to changed circumstances, a wisdom approach could inform a process of re-imagining the university.

A starting point is to ask what values are essential to a wise university, or a university that creates the space for wisdom. Second is to ask what power relations are needed to make universities work to honour those values. Third is to ask what kinds of dialogues need to take place and with whom. Fourth is to ask what kinds of dispositions are needed to motivate appropriate action. Fifth is to ask what practices are needed to translate all of this into positive outcomes for the planet. The other side of all this is to consider if some of what we privilege now does not honour these imperatives. Managerialism, the intense focus on quantifiable competition, and obsession for remote abstraction appear to not readily honour the value of wise universities (Rooney and Hearn, 2000). Misconceived Key Performance Indicators that drive institutional and researcher behaviour, research that universities value primarily as a PR opportunity, and a conservative, even reactionary, scholarly journal system that is not working are also symptomatic of problems in need of a wisdom-based solution. Similarly, a long-term failure to understand that commercialisation is not the only way to appreciate practical outcomes of research is also questionable. Finally, that work-place mental health (psychological distress) in universities appears to be sliding a long way from anything that is describable as acceptable and that enables wellbeing is also problematic (Biron, Brun, and Ivers, 2008; Hilton et al., 2008).

We Need to Embrace the New Three Rs

To complete this chapter I make three points to motivate thinking about the five steps outlined above to rethink the institutional and cultural context that creates the space for wise research and wise researchers in universities. I argue that we must

1. Reimagine academia as a global twenty-first century system (new vision);
2. Reinvigorate the twenty-first-century academy through the wisdom lens (reinvigorated motivation/dispositions);
3. Reinvent research practices as a twenty-first-century activity that has wisdom values (creatively identify appropriate micro practices in research and university work generally).

An important assumption I make here is that there is no golden age back to which academia should return. The twenty-first century brings its own unique challenges for research and its own unique contextual features, all of which need to be addressed in their own rights. What I am suggesting though is that we should work from first principles, as it were, to answer the questions that arise from the three points set out above. A starting point is to begin with something like Flyvbjerg's values rationality. The question is, What are the basic intellectual, social and organisational values needed in the twenty-first century for academic research to continue to matter and that honour how creativity, knowledge and wisdom work? The intellectual values that honour creativity, knowledge and wisdom are well established and have endured over time. Openness, collegiality, freedom to question authority, creating wellbeing for the many and so on are already known and have been shown time and again to be important in all periods of civilisations (Benedict, 2001; Burke, 2000; Collins, 1998; Landes, 1998; Mokyr, 2002; Shapin, 1994). The difficult question is how to enact in creative new ways those values in the twenty-first century. This is where we cannot rely solely on historical practices in universities and must be creative and insightful ourselves.

University College London (UCL) provides an interesting case study. UCL's Grand Challenges wisdom-based research strategy is an example of how changes to the organisational base of the academy are already happening. At its core is a change from an epistemic model of research strategy to wisdom inquiry. Nicholas Maxwell (2012) interviewed David Price, Vice Provost, Research at UCL, and the person responsible for introducing the change. UCL's research strategy says,

> The world is in crisis. Billions of us suffer from illness and disease, despite applicable preventions and cures. Life in our cities is under threat from dysfunctionality and climate change. The prospect of global peace and cooperation remains under assault from tensions between our nations, faiths and cultures. Our quality of life – actual and perceived – diminishes despite technological advances. These are global problems, and we must resolve them if future generations are to be provided with the opportunity to flourish. (in Maxwell, 2012, p. 171)

UCL wants its researchers to face up to the biggest practical challenges of living. UCL then takes the challenge of translating research into practice. David Price provides this example of doing just that:

> Next September, we will be leading our public policy campaign whereby we will take the knowledge and wisdom we have developed at UCL, and try to translate them into examples of public policy, and try to influence government action for the better. So that's, if you like, the research through from specialised research, via wisdom, to public policy. (in Maxwell, 2012, p. 175)

Nothing I have written in this chapter is beyond our capabilities to do. I do not suggest for a moment that there are not major challenges and that it is not very difficult, but it is all doable and there is nothing strange about taking this line of thinking through to implementation.

References

Alvesson, M., and J. Sandberg (in press). 'Has Management Research Lost Its Way? Ideas for More Imaginative and Innovative Research'. *Academy of Management Review*.

Backus, N., and C. Ferraris (2004). 'Theory meets practice: Using the Potter Box to teach business communication ethics'. Paper presented at the Association for Business Communication Annual Convention, Cambridge, Massachusetts (25–9 October).

Baltes, P.B., and U.M. Staudinger (2000). 'A Metaheuristic (Pragmatic) to Orchestrate Mind and Virtue towards Excellence'. *American Psychologist*, 55(1): 122–36.

Barge, J.K., and M. Little (2002). 'Dialogical Wisdom, Communicative Practice, and Organisational Life'. *Communication Theory*, 12(4): 375–97.

Benedict, B.M. (2001). *Curiosity: A Cultural History of Early Modern Inquiry*. University of Chicago Press.

Biron, C., J.P. Brun and H. Ivers (2008). 'Extent and Sources of Occupational Stress in University Staff'. *Work*, 30(4): 511–22.

Buckley, P. (2002). 'Is the International Business Research Agenda Running Out of Steam?' *Journal of International Business Studies*, 33(2): 365–73.

Burke, P. (2000). *A Social History of Knowledge: From Gutenberg to Diderot*. Polity, Cambridge.

Charmaz, K. (2006). *Constructing Grounded Theory: A Practical Guide through Qualitative Analysis*. Sage, London.

Ciarrochi, J., and J.T. Blackledge (2005). 'Mindfulness-based Emotional Intelligence Training: A New Approach to Reducing Human Suffering and Promoting Effectiveness'. In J. Ciarrochi and M.D. Forgas (eds), *Emotional Intelligence in Everyday Life: A Scientific Inquiry*, 2nd edn, pp. 206–28. Lavoisier, Cachan.

Collins, R. (1998). *The Sociology of Philosophies: A Global Theory of Intellectual Change*. Belknap, Cambridge, MA.

Cooper, J.M. (2012). *Pursuits of Wisdom: Six Ways of Life in Ancient Philosophy from Socrates to Plotinus*. Princeton Univeristy Press.

Cunliffe, A.L. (2002). 'Reflexive Dialogical Practice in Management Learning'. *Management Learning*, 33(1): 35–61.

Cunliffe, A.L., and J.S. Jun (2005). 'The Need for Reflexivity in Public Administration'. *Administration and Society*, 37(2): 225–42.

Damasio, A. (2000). *The Feeling of What Happens: Body, Emotion and the Making of Consciousness*. Vintage Books, London.

Dreyfus, H., and S. Dreyfus (1986). *Mind Over Machine: The Power of Human Intuition and Expertise in the Era of the Computer*. Free Press, New York.

Edwards, M.G. (in press). 'Wisdom and Integrity: On Being Wise in an Age of Turbulence'. In D. Pauleen and W. Küpers (eds), *A Handbook of Practical Wisdom: Leadership, Organisation and Integral Business Practice*. Gower, London.

Eikeland, O. (2008). *The Ways of Aristotle: Aristotelian Phronesis, Aristotelian Philosophy of Dialogue, and Action Research*. Peter Lang, Berne.

Fairclough, N. (2003). *Analysing Discourse: Textual Analysis for Social Research*. Routledge, London.

Flyvbjerg, B. (2001). *Making Social Science Matter: Why Social Inquiry Fails and How It Can Succeed Again*, trans. S. Sampson. Cambridge University Press.

Flyvbjerg, B. (2011). 'Case Study'. In N.K. Denzin and Y.S. Lincoln (eds), *The Sage Handbook of Qualitative Research*, 4th edn, pp. 301–16. Sage, Thousand Oaks.

Gentile, M. (2010). *Giving Voice to Values: How to Speak Your Mind When You Know What's Right*. Yale University Press, New Haven.

Hall, S.S. (2010). *Wisdom: From Philosophy to Neuroscience*. University of Queensland Press, Brisbane.

Hauser, M.D. (2008). *Moral Minds: How Nature Designed Our Universal Sense of Right and Wrong.* Abacus, London.

Hearn, G., D. Rooney and T. Mandeville (2003). 'Phenomenological Turbulence and Innovation in Knowledge Systems'. *Prometheus,* 21(2): 231–46.

Hilton, M.F., H.A. Whiteford, J. Sheridan, C.M. Cleary, D.C. Chant, P.S. Wang and R.C. Kessler (2008). 'The Prevalence of Psychological Distress in Employees and Associated Occupational Risk Factors'. *Journal of Occupational and Environmental Medicine,* 50(7): 746–57.

Küpers, W. (2007). 'Phenomenology and Integral Pheno-practice of Wisdom in Leadership and Organisation'. *Social Epistemology,* 21(2): 169–93.

Küpers, W., and M. Statler (2008). 'Practically Wise Leadership: Toward an Integral Understanding'. *Culture and Organisation,* 14(4): 379–400.

Landes, D.S. (1998). *The Wealth and Poverty of Nations: Why Some Nations Are So Rich and Some So Poor.* Little, Brown and Company, London.

Maxwell, N. (1984). *From Knowledge to Wisdom: A Revolution in the Aims and Methods of Science.* Blackwell, Oxford.

Maxwell, N. (2009). 'Are universities undergoing an intellectual revolution?' *Oxford Magazine,* 290: 13–16.

Maxwell, N. (2012). 'How Universities Can Help Humanity Learn How to Resolve the Crises of Our Times – From Knowledge to Wisdom: The University College London Experience'. In D. Rooney, G. Hearn and T. Kastelle (eds), *Handbook on the Knowledge Economy,* vol. II, pp. 158–79. Edward Elgar, Cheltenham.

McCrae, R.R., and P.T. Costa (1997). 'Conceptions and Correlates of Openness to Experience'. In R. Hogan, J.A. Johnson and S.R. Briggs (eds), *Handbook of Personality Psychology,* pp. 825–47. Academic Press, San Diego, CA.

McKenna, B., and D. Rooney (2008). 'Wise Leadership and the Capacity for Ontological Acuity'. *Management Communication Quarterly,* 21(4): 537–46.

McKenna, B., D. Rooney and K. Boal (2009). 'Wisdom Principles as a Meta-theoretical Basis for Evaluating Leadership'. *Leadership Quarterly,* 20(2): 177–90.

Mills, C.W. (1959). *The Sociological Imagination.* Oxford University Press, New York.

Mokyr, J. (2002). *The Gifts of Athena: Historical Origins of the Knowledge Economy.* Princeton University Press.

Phillips, N., T.B. Lawrence and C. Hardy (2004). 'Discourse and Institutions'. *Academy of Management Review,* 29(4): 635–52.

Rolls, E.T. (2012). *Neuroculture: On the Implications of Brain Science.* Oxford University Press.

Rooney, D. (2010). 'Creatively Wise Education in a Knowledge Economy'. In D. Araya and M.A. Peters (eds), *Education in the Creative Economy: Knowledge and Learning in the Age of Innovation,* pp. 177–97. Peter Lang, New York.

Rooney, D. (2013). 'Grounding Organisational Wisdom Theory: Ontology, Epistemology, and Methodology'. In D. Pauleen and W. Küpers (eds), *A Handbook of Practical Wisdom: Leadership, Organisation and Integral Business Practice.* Gower, London.

Rooney, D., and G. Hearn (2000). 'Of Minds, Markets and Machines: How Universities Might Transcend the Ideology of Commodification'. In S. Inayatullah and J. Gidley (eds), *The University in Transformation: Global Perspective on the Futures of the University.* Bervin and Garvey, Westport.

Rooney, D., G. Hearn, T. Mandeville and R. Joseph (2003). *Public Policy in Knowledge-based Economies: Foundations and Frameworks*. Edward Elgar, Cheltenham.

Rooney, D., and B. McKenna (2008). 'Wisdom in Public Administration: Looking for a Sociology of Wise Practice'. *Public Administration Review*, 68(4): 707–19.

Rooney, D., B. McKenna and P. Liesch (2010). *Wisdom and Management in the Knowledge Economy*. Routledge, London.

Rooney, D., N. Paulsen, V.J. Callan, M. Brabant, C. Gallois and E. Jones (2010). 'A New Role for Place Identity in Managing Organisational Change'. *Management Communication Quarterly*, 24(1): 44–73.

Shapin, S. (1994). *A Social History of Truth: Civility and Science in Seventeenth-Century England*. University of Chicago Press.

Staudinger, U.M., and J. Glück (2011). 'Psychological Wisdom Research: Commonalities and Differences in a Growing Field'. *Annual Review of Psychology*, 62: 215–41.

Sternberg, R.J. (1990). 'Understanding Wisdom'. In R.J. Sternberg (ed.), *Wisdom: Its Nature, Origins and Development*, pp. 3–9. Cambridge University Press.

Sternberg, R.J. (2003). *Wisdom, Intelligence and Creativity Synthesized*. Cambridge University Press.

4
In Praise of Strategic Indirection: Towards a Non-instrumental Understanding of *Phronèsis* as Practical Wisdom

Robert Chia, Robin Holt and Li Yuan

Introduction

Practical wisdom (*phronèsis*) is an ancient, enigmatic and intractable notion that fascinates, yet the manner of its workings and its influence on public life, professional practice and civil society remains ever elusive. At times it is reminiscent of that proverbial enigmatic, shadowy and elusive nocturnal creature that appears only fleetingly for us to catch a glimpse of before it disappears mysteriously back into the darkness and beyond. Despite its profound effect on virtually every aspect of modern life, full understanding and comprehension of practical wisdom eludes us at every turn. Its reticence in revealing itself fully to our scholastic gaze may have something to do with our academic temperament, our motivations and the overly deliberate nature of our method of inquiry. In this chapter we propose a more oblique and circuitous approach for understanding practical wisdom and its inner workings. We call it *strategic indirection*. We maintain that true practical wisdom cannot be grasped directly but must be approached elliptically so that its hidden nature, its inner workings and its indirect influence on our lives can be fully appreciated. Instead of associating practical wisdom with the high-profile, spectacular and heroic actions of significant individuals, we should look elsewhere to the mundane and the everyday to find that which we seek. Practical wisdom finds quiet expression in the inconspicuous and seemingly inconsequential acts and spontaneous gestures of ordinary individuals that unexpectedly produce extraordinary outcomes. It is rarely to be found in formal learning or in the 'books of the wise'. Instead, it appears intaglioed, something that is etched into and filled through lives as they are lived, arising more as an unintended, *positive* consequence of human action (Merton, 1936) than through deliberate, calculative action. It finds expression in circumstances where 'great enthusiasms, commitments, and actions' are displayed without any expectation for 'great outcomes' but as a response to the 'arbitrary and unconditional claims of a proper life' (March, 2003, p. 206).

The implication of this understanding is that instead of viewing *phronèsis* in instrumental-rational terms as a 'resource' or even as a form of 'useful' knowledge that can be purposefully deployed in output-oriented, productive action (*poièsis*) and/or for personal gain, we need to view it more fundamentally in *praxeological* terms as a self-cultivating form of action (Dunne, 1993, pp. 244–6). *Phronetic* action does not flow from a desire for external rewards or recognition but from an existential desire to perfect self and to attain the ultimate 'good' of pure unmediated experience (Nishida, 1990; Suzuki, in Herrigel, 1985, p. 5). Yet, despite this lack of instrumentality, actions that flow from such a cultivated disposition can nevertheless surprisingly produce tangible and substantial achievements, albeit as a by-product of the extensive investment of effort involved. Practical wisdom, then, is not associated with acquiring ever-more knowledge (*episteme*) or even skill (*technè*) but rather is about learning through practical experience the *limits* and *limitations* of such forms of knowledge. It is more associated with *unlearning* than it is with *learning*; 'letting go' is a prerequisite for learning anew. As an ancient Chinese sage puts it well, 'In order to grasp, it is necessary first to release'[1] (Lao Tzu in Chan, 1963, p. 157). So also, to truly grasp practical wisdom we must return to that 'waning candlelight' of pristine, raw experience 'unwarped by the sophistication of theory' (Whitehead, 1929, p. 295) to seek that for which we are looking. Intellectual naivety, or *learned ignorance*, more than theoretical sophistication is what brings us nearer to practical wisdom. Such an intellectual meekness (or what the Japanese industrialist Konusuke Matsushita calls a *sunao mind* [Matsushita, 1978, p. 65]) precipitates a heightened sensitivity to real-world happenings that is qualitatively different from the confident, assertive and acquisitive mentality associated with the 'consequentialist theology' (March, 2003, p. 205) taught in most business schools.

The Global Context of Business

The motive of success is not enough. It produces a short-sighted world which destroys the sources of its own prosperity ... A great society is a society in which its men of business think greatly about its function.

Low thoughts mean low behaviour, and after a brief orgy of exploitation, low behaviour means a descending standard of life.
– Alfred North Whitehead (1933, p. 120)

The social, economic and political world is currently experiencing an
unprecedented level of nervousness and uncertainty characterised by
instability, volatility and unexpected and disruptive change. It is a
world in which the improbable, the unanticipated and the downright
catastrophic seem to occur with alarming regularity. The recent global
financial crisis of 2008 caused by the collapse of the sub-prime mortgage
sector in the United States, the unexpected events of the 'Arab Spring',
the escalating sovereign debt crisis in Europe and especially in Greece
that is threatening to undo the entire Eurozone, and the dramatic rise of
China and possibly India as major global economic forces, all point to
the influence of the unlikely or even the completely unpredictable – the
latter the subject of Nicholas Nassem Taleb's 'black swans' in which
the former financier and essayist investigates our epistemological pre-
sumptiveness in always assuming the future is something that can be
envisaged through forecasts or scenarios. What appeared as seemingly
outlier events and peripheral occurrences have unexpectedly turned
out to have dramatic consequences for the global economy and for
governments and businesses throughout the world. Who, for instance,
three decades ago would have thought that the Chinese obsession with
saving would create a global 'savings glut' that helped fuel America's
unsustainable spending extravagance so that it has produced the most
bizarre of situations where China has effectively 'become banker to
the United States of America' (Ferguson, 2008, p. 334)? This and many
other recent examples show that what we *least expect* seems intent on
thwarting our business aspirations and our best-laid plans in innumerable ways. Such a global quagmire reflects, not so much a lack of knowledge and/or information, a failure of accountability and regulation,
the deficiencies of a free market economy, or the failure of capitalism,
or even a supposed lack of morals per se. Rather these are symptomatic
of deeper and more fundamental epistemological inadequacies associated with an overly instrumentalised predisposition towards the world
as being somehow a 'resource' that is readily available for us to exploit
to the best of our ability. It is an overall attitude that gives rise to what
Robert Merton (1936, p. 901) called 'the imperious immediacy of interests' in which the wider unanticipated global consequences of government policies and business decisions are systematically overlooked in
the interest of attaining an expedient resolution of immediate concerns.

Such an overzealous preoccupation with achieving short-term results is what generates the unintended consequences that end up eventually thwarting the very efficacy of the actions taken.

A heightened awareness of the ever-present possibility of the unexpected and the unintended constitutes an entry into the realms of a complex and *oblique* form of thinking in which initiating causes are recognised as irretrievably indirect, multiple, mutually interactive and emergent. This is what *strategic indirection* entails and this is what allows us a better appreciation of what *phronèsis* is and how it affects our predisposition to life and business performance. Strategic indirection reflects a kind of thinking that: strives to touch base with the pristine immediacy of pure lived experience (Morin, 1992, pp. 392–3; Ruskin, 1927, XV, p. 27; James, 1996b, p. 23; Nishida, 1921/1990, p. 3); recognises and embraces the inherent messiness, contradictions and puzzling character of social reality (Morin, 2008, p. 6; James, 1996a, p. 50); and resists or overflows our familiar categories of thought (Bergson, 1992, pp. 161–2; James, 1996a, pp. 78–9; Whitehead, 1985, p. 64; Morin, 1992, p. 393). Our thought, says Edgar Morin, 'must lay siege to the unthought which commands and controls it' (Morin, 1992, p. 16). In directing our attention to the as yet unthought and unattended to, *strategic indirection* heightens awareness of our ignorance of ignorance. It forces us to realise that all forms of seeing and knowing involve the simultaneous act of foregrounding and back-grounding: that there is an inevitable blindness in our seeing and an unac*knowledge*d 'owing' in our 'kn-*owing*'. Ignorance then becomes not just a 'gap' in knowledge, but also a gnawing imperative that 'changes the very nature of what I think I know' (Johnson, 1989, p. 16). And it is only through this intellectual modesty and 'meekness' that we can then begin to glimpse that illusive realm called practical wisdom.

Strategic Indirection: An Indirect Way of Knowing

> The indirect approach is as fundamental to the realm of politics as it is to the realm of sex.
> – Basil Liddell-Hart, *Strategy: The Indirect Approach* (1967, p. xix)

> To point at a chicken to insult the dog.[2]
> – Chinese proverb (in Jullien, 2000, p. 49)

We learn to know in two distinct and different ways. In the first instance when, for instance, we observe one swan to be white in colour and subsequently notice other swans to be also white, we then gradually gravitate to the generalisation that 'all swans are white'. Elevating the value of *sameness*, we begin to develop an expectation for swans to be white in colour thereby falling into the conceptual trap that Taleb (2007) calls a 'confirmation bias' (p. 50). Knowledge acquired through this process of registering *sameness* is convergent, cumulative and confirmatory. We know what a thing is because the coagulation of *sameness* leads to the identity of things. This form of learning is not to be denigrated for it facilitates instrumental manipulation and productive action. Achieving skill, competence and expertise are a direct consequence of this form of learning and knowing that is associated with what James March (1991) calls a strategy of 'exploitation'; knowledge/skills are used to exploit 'resources' to generate wealth and surplus. Many of the unquestioned achievements of modern society are based upon this principle of efficient exploitation of limited resources.

Knowing through *difference*, on the other hand, takes place when an anomaly such as a 'black' swan is observed. This contradicts and 'falsifies' (Popper, 1959) our generalised understanding forcing us to radically revise and reconsider what we think we know about the colour of swans. What the sighting of a black swan does is to register a difference that jolts us into a heightened awareness of the vulnerability of our understanding and upsets the apparent coherence of things, thereby forcing us to revise our initial paradigm of understanding. We now learn *indirectly* on a rebound, so to speak, that *not all swans are white*. It is the *differences registered that make a difference* (Bateson, 1972). Indirect learning heightens perceptual sensitivity rather than increases knowledge.

Indirect knowing occurs, when, for example, we visit another country or experience a different culture where the traditions, attitudes and practices are vastly alien to that of our own. The culture shock that we then experience forces us to reassess our own, often idiosyncratic ways of understanding and dealing with the world. Difference, in this instance, jolts our hitherto established ways of thinking and behaving; it makes our dispositions apparent. Paradoxically, therefore, it is only by immersing ourselves in another alien world that we can come to truly be aware of our own. This awareness is more than being knowledgeable. To know something is to make a claim in relation to questions (Do you know?), whereas this heightened awareness entails registering differences that make a difference. It is what prompted the poet T.S. Eliot to observe that the purpose of venturing out into the unknown, away from the familiar and secure ground of our heritage, will be to 'arrive at where we started; / And know the place for the first time' ('Little

Gidding', in Eliot 2001: 15). It is this exposure to radical differences that make a difference that characterises the approach adopted by *strategic indirection*.

Such a form of *strategic indirection* is familiar to those brought up in the traditional East. While 'Westerners find it natural and normal to meet the world head-on' (Jullien, 2000, p. 7) and pride themselves on 'going directly to the marrow of a subject', it is virtually impossible 'from merely hearing what a Chinese says, to tell what he means' (Smith, 1894, p. 63). Smith was exasperated. His role as a nineteenth-century American missionary was to convert and he was failing to find any grip on those over whom he sought to influence, but there are others in the West who fully appreciate the efficacy and subtlety of the 'indirect approach' (Liddell-Hart, 1967) in dealing with human affairs. There is recognition that in many social life situations, a direct approach can be unproductive. Sentiments must sometimes be expressed obliquely. We need to 'test the ground', feel the mood, let our proposition drift suggestively remaining 'instigatory, and thus inchoate, instead of insistent or imposing' (Jullien, 2000, p. 129). It must resemble a form of 'wind power' which despite being imperceptible and not capable of being directly apprehended nevertheless still 'insinuates itself into the heart of things' so that its 'immaterial presence never ceases to invade and animate' (Jullien, 2000, pp. 63–4). Such a subtle and suggestive strategy vastly contrasts with the more direct and frontal approach to business, to human relations and to academic inquiry widely practiced around the world. It is an approach that is crucial to our attempts to understand the phenomenon of *phronèsis* as practical wisdom and how it orients business practice.

Starting from What *Phronèsis Is Not*! Detouring to Gain Access

The Tao (Way) that can be told of is not the Eternal Tao;
The name that can be named is not the eternal name.[3]
— Lao Tzu (in Chan, 1963, p. 139)

Regarding *practical wisdom* we shall get at the truth by considering who are the people we credit with it.
— Aristotle, *Nicomachean Ethics* (6.5.1140a25)

Language limits our capacity to think (Wittgenstein, 1961, 6.54), for without language our raw experience 'is only a shapeless and indistinct mass' (Saussure, 1966, p. 111); a 'big blooming buzzing confusion'

(James, 1996a, p. 50). Yet this limit is not a restriction, it is what gives a boundary to sense whereby we become aware of a beginning and opening out. *In the limits of words and sentences comes the possibility of thinking.* Words and concepts are not simply external 'wrappings in which things are packed for the commerce of those who write and speak' (Heidegger, 1971, p. 134). Instead, 'it is in words and language that things come to be and are' (Heidegger, 1959, p. 13). Language makes possible what is thinkable but it also simultaneously produces the unthinkable and the *unthought.* In order to begin to access this excluded realm of unthought experience, language must be metaphorically made to stretch and 'groan' (Serres, 1982), to find in its limits opportunities to investigate, to work and play with meaning. Immediate comprehension of a phenomenon must be resisted and an oblique, circumnavigational approach to enquiry adopted so that a more nuanced and richer comprehension of the object of investigation can be arrived at beyond the realms of intellection. Words must be treated like the nets we use to catch fish: 'Only those who can take the fish and forget the net are worthy to seek the truth' (Kao-seng Chuan, in Chang, 1963, p. 43). In the light of this understanding of the distorting role of language, a more delicate and circuitous approach for grasping the phenomenon of *phronèsis* seems eminently appropriate.

Perhaps a starting point is to consider what *phronèsis* is *patently not.* Aristotle's *Nicomachean Ethics* (NE), which discusses the various types of knowledge together with *phronèsis* (NE 1139a27–28), albeit in a variety of ways that continues to challenge and divide contemporary Aristotelian scholars (Gadamer, 2004; MacIntyre, 1984), provides us with the initiating backdrop for our inquiry. For Aristotle, there are five forms of knowledge: art, scientific knowledge, practical wisdom, philosophic wisdom and intuitive reason, with philosophic wisdom (*sophia*) being unquestionably the highest form of knowledge arrived at through the integration of scientific knowledge (*episteme*) with intuitive reason (*logos*). Yet *sophia* is described by Aristotle as 'remarkable, admirable, difficult and divine, *but useless*' (NE, 1141b6–7, emphasis added) because it is only attained with the benefit of leisure. Art (*techné*) on the other hand is practical and associated with craft and productive action and it is Aristotle's exploration of the distinction between *techné* and the more 'deviant' notion of *phronèsis* (Dunne, 1993, p. 245) that helps us to get a better sense of what the latter might mean. While both *techné* and *phronèsis* are 'practical' and deal with the world of affairs, the status of *phronèsis* as a form of knowing/doing/disposition is by no means uncontroversial since Aristotle himself seems to vacillate between different emphases of the latter. Sometimes he seems to suggest that *phronèsis* is a form of knowledge not unlike that of *techné*. At other times he seems to suggest that we can only know of *phronèsis* by only 'considering who are the persons we credit with it' (NE 6.5.1140a25), thereby implying that it is more a characteristic of a person than a form of knowledge. *Phronèsis* is associated with what a *phronimos* does. For instance, he writes, 'we think Pericles and men like him have practical wisdom ... because they can see what is good for themselves and what is good for men in general' (NE 6.5.1140b5–10). Sometimes he seems to relate *phronèsis* to *techné* when he says,

> The man who is truly good and wise, we think, bears all the chances of life becomingly and always makes the best of circumstances, as a good general makes the best military use of the army he commands and a shoemaker makes the best shoes out of the hides that are given to him; and so with all the other *technitai*. (NE 1.10. 1100b35–1101a6)

Yet, further on he writes, '*phronèsis* cannot be ... *techné* because action and making are different kinds of things' (NE 6.5.1140b–4).

These are just some instances of how Aristotle seems to display an ambivalence about how *phronèsis* qualitatively differs from *techné*. On occasions he seem to see *phronèsis* as a 'type' of *techné* by comparing *phronèsis* to it, on others he is much more insistent on *phronèsis* being entirely different from *techné*, maintaining that 'Plainly ... practical wisdom is a virtue and not an art' (NE 6.5.1140b–24).

In this account we lean towards an interpretation that accentuates the difference as proffered by contemporary writers such as MacIntyre (1984), Dunne (1993) and Eikeland, (2008). Their starting point is Aristotle's clear assertion that '*phronèsis* cannot be ... *techné* ... because action and making are different kinds of things' (NE 6.1140b–4). And again, 'while making has an end other than itself, action cannot, *for good action itself is its end*' (NE 6.1140b6–7, emphasis added). *Techné* describes the kind of knowledge possessed by an expert in a specific craft; a person who is able to produce an object or a desired outcome (e.g. a chair, a car, a safe journey, a successful and profitable venture) in a professional and competent manner. *Techné* is a generative source of useful things and desirable outcomes. It resides in an instrumental means–ends framework in which materials, tools, knowledge, 'human resources' and so forth can be used by the expert to produce a desired end. Dunne (1993, p. 254) points out that *techné* is not to be just identified with 'making things' but also with producing intangible outcomes that are more 'state-of-affairs than durable products'. What defines *techné* and differentiates it from the 'other' that is *phronèsis* is the predominance of a calculative means–ends mentality that characterises the kind of 'consequentialist theology' March (2003, p. 205) speaks of, whereby alternative courses of action are evaluated 'in terms of expected consequences' and strategies are implemented 'with expected outcomes that appear attractive'. It is this *instrumental* mindset that quintessentially defines *techné* and its not insubstantial modern-world achievements.

Phronèsis, on the other hand, is something else; it is almost a 'deviant' concept that seems to be described by its *difference* from *techné* and that 'represents a characteristic strain in his [Aristotle's] philosophic anthropology' (Dunne, 1993, p. 245). *Phronèsis* is something that characterises a *phronimos*, someone who knows how to live well. *Phronèsis* only makes sense in reference to the attitude, behaviour and predispositions displayed (often unselfconsciously) by a specific individual in a specific set of circumstances. Elaborating on this Aristotelian distinction between *techné* and *phronèsis*, Dunne and others such as Eikeland (2008) argue that whilst *techné* is the knowledge that guides the activity of making (*poiêsis*) in which means and ends are distinguishable from one another, *phronèsis* is the practical wisdom that guides *praxis*, such that the 'doing' that is carried out constitutes an end in itself. As Eikeland (2008, p. 122, emphasis in original) puts it well, 'Poiêsis *Makes Things*, Praxis *Makes Perfect*'. While *poiêsis* is intimately linked to a means–ends orientation, *praxis* issues from *phronèsis* as action that contains both its means and its end. As Dunne (1993, p. 244) writes, '*Praxis* has to do with the conduct of one's life and affairs primarily as a citizen of the *polis*; it is activity whose end is realised in the very doing of the activity itself'. *Praxis* is 'perfecting actualization … *praxis* never stops before it is perfect' (Eikeland, 2008, p. 124). Whilst *techné* is a craft skill that is employed to produce an artefact that once completed is identifiable and separable from the producer, *phronèsis* produces no such tangible output. Whereas the quality of output produced by *techné* can be evaluated without reference to its producer, a *phronetic* act 'can never be identified as such without reference to the tendencies and dispositions of the agent who performs it' (Dunne, 1993, p. 247). While *techné* does not speak to the object it uses, manipulates or influences, '*Phronèsis* does, since what it influences are minds like itself' (Eikeland, 2008, p. 100). Moreover, *phronèsis* expresses the kind of person one *is*, not the kind of knowledge one *has*. It 'comes into its own only in situations that draw the self into action' (Dunne, 1993, p. 268). While *techné* can be conceptualised in terms of its 'possession' (being) and its 'application' (use), *phronèsis* cannot. *Phronèsis* 'cannot be instrumentalized' because 'whatever issues from it by way of action, already has the full weight of ourselves behind it' (ibid.). This means that while in the arts and sciences a voluntary error is not as bad as an involuntary error, in *phronetic* action where there is often ethical import, a voluntary mistake is worse than an involuntary mistake' because it would imply 'a premeditated injustice' and this would be 'worse than doing the same 'not-on-purpose' (Eikeland, 2008, p. 63). After an extensive exploration of the differences between *techné* and *phronèsis*, Dunne (1993, p. 272) comes to the conclusion that '*Phronèsis* ... is not a knowledge of ethical ideas as such, but rather a *resourcefulness of mind* that is called into play' when circumstances demand such an intervention. It is a habituated disposition that has 'developed an "eye"... or a "nose" for what is salient in concrete situations' (Dunne, 1993, p. 368) thereby enabling the practitioner to 'see aright' (NE 1143b13). Thus, virtuous acts cannot be done simply because we are 'told to do them, forced to, seduced to, tempted to, persuaded to, etc., nor as mere passionate reactions ... nor because of some prospective extraneous gain or reward' (Eikeland, 2008, p. 122). Virtuous acts are non-instrumental in character, and closely bound up with the kind of person one is; a cultivated disposition born of experience rather than of knowledge.

Phronèsis as Cultivated Disposition: Wise Management as a 'Calling' to Serve the Common Good

> ... it is only by being an apprentice to one's parents and teachers that one gains ... practical wisdom.
>
> – H.L. Dreyfus (2001, p. 48)

Our brief exploration of *techné* and *phronèsis* and the difference between the two has led us to move away from the more common understanding of *phronèsis* as a kind of practical knowledge, not unlike that of *techné*, that can be 'applied' meaningfully to attain desired ends, to a gradual realisation that it is more about an internalised predisposition than it is a form of cognition. Practical wisdom is more associated with who we are and how we act rather than the knowledge we possess. Our *phronetic* acts arise from 'within the terrestrial magnetism of our past acts which lie *sedimented in our habits* ... And this is an important reason why it *cannot be instrumentalized*' (Dunne, 1993, p. 268, our emphasis). *Phronetic* action is habituated action, the origins of which lie 'neither in the "decisions" of reason understood as rational calculation nor in the determinations of mechanisms external to and superior to the agents' (Bourdieu, 1990, p. 50). It is not a 'resource' or even a mental schema that we can consciously draw from at subjective will. Rather, it reflects a modus operandi – a stylistic configuration of tendencies inscribed onto material bodies – that expresses itself unthinkingly in everyday practices in the conduct of a proper life. This is the real reason why Aristotle finds it necessary to look to Pericles as an exemplar of a practically wise individual; what *phronèsis* is can only be affirmed by pointing to the tendencies and doings of a *phronimos*; a wise person is inseparable from her or his actions. With this revised understanding of *phronèsis* we can now look to exemplars of wise management practices in the world of business.

Our starting point is the question, What is business for? The idea that the conduct of business takes place solely for the purpose of profit is so deeply rooted as to be almost unquestionable. Yet, there are those in business practice who think and behave otherwise; who maintain that in fact the business of business is fundamentally to provide a service to society and thereby to contribute to the collective good. For these individuals the cultivated disposition to offer a service reflects the old notion of a 'calling'; a vocational opportunity to perfect oneself and at the same time contribute to the common good. Such an orientation, while forgotten by many, nevertheless still underpins the dispositions of experienced 'wise' business people, of whom there remain several significant exemplars. We can profit from examining these as exemplars of *phronimos*.

Take the case of Konusuke Matsushita, the unassuming founder and arguably the greatest Japanese industrialist of the twentieth century. In his book *My Management Philosophy* (1986), and in several subsequent volumes including *Thoughts on Man* (1982) and *The Heart of Management* (2002), he expounds on what we might call an *indirect* and *wise* way of achieving profits and success. For Matsushita, business exists not so much for profit but fundamentally to provide a service to society and to help improve the lives of ordinary people. He insists that 'while profit is essential, it is not the ultimate goal'. Instead, the goal is 'to improve human life' (Matsushita, 1986, p. 10). Thus, 'the true mission of an enterprise is to render the economy and the lives of human beings richer and more plentifully endowed day by day, thereby making society prosperous, peaceful and happy' (Matsushita, 2002, p. 7). Profit, then, is not the be all and end all of business. Rather it must be understood as a form of 'reward' that accrues *on the rebound* to the producer/provider for offering a service that is ultimately valued by society so that the greater the 'contribution to society, the greater in turn is the reward' (ibid., p. 8). Only if their products and services are well received, valued and appreciated will the 'reward' be justified. In other words, profit is not something to be directly sought but rather must come *on the rebound* as a result of the appreciation of the consumer. This deep understanding of the social obligation and hence purpose of business in the context of society enables 'wise' decision-making to take place. It is associated with the deeper paradoxical insight that a company can be highly profitable without being *profit-driven*.

The economist John Kay makes a similar observation, albeit in more populist terms, in a recent book entitled *Obliquity* (2010) where he controversially maintains that paradoxically our goals are best pursued indirectly, and draws (admittedly on selective anecdotes) to support his thesis that *the most profitable businesses are not profit-oriented, the richest people are not really enamoured with money and the happiest people do not seek happiness*. However, Kay does not go on to examine why it is that this paradoxical situation seems to play itself out time and again. What appears missing in Kay's account, and is more seriously considered in Matsushita's philosophical explorations, is a deep intuition that much more goes on beneath the surface of things in the realms of human motivation; that the older tradition of a 'vocation' as a calling to serve the good of humanity exists and persists, albeit in almost unrecognisable form. Matsushita himself offers some important insights on this which will allow us to reconnect with our discovery that *phronèsis* is more about a cultivated resourcefulness of mind than it is a form of knowledge.

Matsushita repeatedly emphasises the importance of managers cultivating what he calls a *sunao* mind. *Sunao* is a Japanese term that denotes meekness, tractability, an open-hearted innocence and genuine sincerity. It is an 'untrapped mind, free to adapt itself effectively to new circumstances'. Such a malleable and tractable mind reflects a trained capacity to 'look at things as they are at that moment' (Matsushita, 1986, p. 63) without bias or preconception. This insistence on the ability to see clearly is reminiscent of the pristine seeing that the English social critic John Ruskin (1927, XV, p. 27) calls the 'innocence of the eye'. It is a freed-up and 'uncluttered' mind that is often associated with Zen training and with the practice of perfecting the oriental arts. The Japanese Zen master D.T. Suzuki maintains that what is most distinctive about the study of eastern arts is that they are 'not intended for utilitarian purposes ... but are meant to train the mind ... to bring it into contact with the ultimate reality' (Suzuki, in Herrigel, 1985, p. 5). Matsushita insists that at Matsushita Electric it is a regular management policy and expectation for managers to assiduously cultivate this *sunao* mind in the 'conviction that it enables us to perceive the real state of all things in society' (Matsushita, 2002, p. 45), thereby enabling wise decision-making in the conduct of human affairs.

Concluding Remarks

Matsushita's *sunao* mind is as close as one can get to the Greek notion of *phronèsis* as practical wisdom. It is a cultivated disposition involving mindfulness and perceptual sensitivity to seemingly complex situations that results in a spontaneous clarity of the situation at hand and thus the appropriate effort and action needed. Such an absorbed non-instrumental doing is also associated with a spontaneous outpouring of effort that results in unparalleled achievements. We call this 'performative extravagance' (Chia and Holt, 2007, pp. 517–21) in which excellence is realised even in the absence of a reward-seeking orientation. In being entirely absorbed and preoccupied with her or his own *phronetic* self-cultivation, the individual's sustained efforts and actions unwittingly produce outcomes that contribute in large measure to the ultimate betterment of society. *Phronèsis*, therefore, corresponds more to a sense of vocation or calling than it does to any kind of career aspiration. Practical wisdom is not a form of technical knowledge transmissible through books but a form of everyday practice that, sustained over time, can produce extraordinary transformations; we are only able to recognise wise acts in hindsight.

Notes

1. '将欲取之, 必固与之', (《道德经》第36章).
2. '指桑骂槐'.
3. '道可道, 非常道。名可名, 非常名。', (《道德经》第1章).

References

Aristotle (1980). *The Nichomachean Ethics*, trans. D. Ross. Oxford University Press.
Bateson, G. (1972). *Steps to an Ecology of Mind: Collected Essays in Anthropology, Psychiatry, Evolution and Epistemology*. Balantine, New York.
Bergson, H. (1992). *The Creative Mind*. Citadel Press, New York (orig. 1946).
Bourdieu, P. (1990). *The Logic of Practice*. Polity Press, Cambridge.
Chan, W.T. (1963). *A Source Book of Chinese Philosophy*. Princeton University Press.

Chang, C.-Y. (1963). *Creativity and Taoism*. Harper & Row, New York.

Chia, R. (2003). 'From Knowledge-creation to the Perfecting of Action: Tao, Basho and Pure Experience as the Ultimate Ground of Knowing'. *Human Relations*, 56(8): 953–81.

Chia, R., and R. Holt (2007). 'Wisdom as Learned Ignorance: Integrating East–West Perspectives'. In E.H. Kessler and J.R. Bailey (eds), *Handbook of Organizational and Managerial Wisdom*. Sage, Thousand Oaks.

Chia, R., and R. Holt (2009). *Strategy without Design: The Silent Efficacy of Indirect Action*. Cambridge University Press.

Dunne, J. (1993). *Back to the Rough Ground: 'Phronèsis' and 'Techne' in Modern Philosophy and in Aristotle*. University of Notre Dame Press.

Dreyfus, H.L. (2001). *On the Internet*. Routledge, London and New York.

Eikeland, O. (2008). *The Ways of Aristotle*. Peter Lang, Oxford.

Eliot, T.S. (2001). *Little Giddings*. Faber and Faber, London (orig. 1942).

Ferguson, N. (2008). *The Ascent of Money*. Allen Lane, London.

Gadamer, H.G. (2004). *Truth and Method*, trans. J. Weinsheimer and D.G. Marshall. Crossroad, New York (orig. 1962).

Heidegger, M. (1959). *Introduction to Metaphysics*. Yale University Press, New Haven.

Heidegger, M. (1971). *On the Way to Language*. Harper and Row, New York.

Herrigel, E. (1985). *Zen in the Art of Archery*. Arkana, London (orig. 1953).

James, W. (1996a). *Some Problems of Philosophy*. University of Nebraska Press, Lincoln (orig. 1911).

James, W. (1996b). *Essays in Radical Empiricism*. University of Nebraska Press, Lincoln (orig. 1912).

Johnson, B. (1989). *A World of Difference*. Johns Hopkins University Press, Baltimore, MD.

Jullien, Francois (2000). *Detour and Access: Strategies of Meaning in China and Greece*. Zone Books, New York.

Jullien, Francois (2004). *A Treatise on Efficacy: Between Western and Chinese Thinking*. University of Hawaii Press, Honolulu.

Kay, J. (2010). *Obliquity*. Profile Books, London.

Liddell-Hart, B. (1967). *Strategy: The Indirect Approach*. Faber and Faber, London.

MacIntyre, A. (1984). *After Virtue: A Study in Moral Theory*, 2nd edn. University of Notre Dame Press.

March, J.G. (1991). 'Exploration and Exploitation in Organizational Learning'. *Organization Science*, 2(1): 71–87.

March, J.G. (2003). 'A Scholar's Quest'. *Journal of Management Inquiry*, 12(3): 205–7.

Matsushita, K. (1982). *Thoughts on Man*. PHP Institute, New York.

Matsushita, K. (1986). *My Management Philosophy*. Japan: PHP Inst. National Productivity Board, Singapore (orig. 1978).

Matsushita, K. (2002). *The Heart of Management*. PHP Institute, New York (orig. 1994).

Merton, R. (1936). 'The Unanticipated Consequences of Purposive Social Action'. *American Sociological Review*, 1: 894–904.

Morin, E. (1992). *Method: Towards a Study of Humankind*, trans. J.L. Roland Bēlanger. Peter Lang, New York (orig. 1977).

Morin, E. (2008). *On Complexity*, trans Robin Postel. Hampton Press, New York.

Nicholas of Cusa (1996). *Idiota de sapienta* (*The Layman on Wisdom and Knowledge*), trans. J. Hopkins. Arthur J. Banning, Minneapolis, MN.

Nishida, K. (1990). *An Inquiry into the Good*, trans. M. Abe and C. Ives. Yale University Press, New Haven (orig. 1921).

Popper, K.R. (1959). *The Logic of Scientific Discovery*. Routledge, London (orig. 1934).

Ruskin, J. (1927). *The Complete Works*. Nicholson and Weidenfeld, London.

Saussure, F. de (1966). *Course in General Linguistics*. McGraw Hill, New York.

Serres, M. (1982). *Hermes: Literature, Science, Philosophy.* Johns Hopkins University Press, Baltimore, MD.

Smith, A. (1894). *Chinese Characteristics*. Fleming H. Revell, New York.

Taleb, N.N. (2007). *The Black Swan*. Allen Lane, London.

Whitehead, A.N. (1929). *Process and Reality.* Macmillan, New York.

Whitehead, A. N. (1933). *Adventures of ideas.* Penguin, Harmondsworth (orig. 1932).

Whitehead, A.N. (1985). *Science and the Modern World*. Free Association Books, London (orig. 1926).

Wittgenstein, L. (1961). *Tractatus Logico-Philosophicus*. Routledge, London.

5
From the Financial Crisis to Wise Management: The Relevance of the 'Return to Aristotle'

Jean-Jacques Rosé and François Lépineux

Introduction

Since 2007 a number of countries have been confronted with a multi-faceted financial crisis whose outcome is still unknown. The unwinding of this early twenty-first century has been marked by an ineluctable gearing: the sub-primes episode has entailed the threat of a collapse of the banking system, the disruption of the commodities market, the risk of a sovereign debt default in several European countries and the stagnation – then the recession – of some developed economies. This ruthless mechanism throws American citizens onto the street, brings governments down in Rome and in Athens, and plunges people in various countries of the South into famine, while the effects of climate change are increasingly visible. In many parts of our planet, it seems that business, financial markets and globalisation engender backward movements and growing conflicts, whereas the Age of Enlightenment had promised progress and perpetual peace.

After the tragedies of the twentieth century, these new dangers and evils – as the financial crisis is but one of the crises that characterise the 'temps des crises' (Serres, 2012) – call for a reflexive meditation on the breakdowns of the economic and financial machine, the present and future disturbances of planetary ecosystems and the failure of modernity's promises. Can the western way of life remain a model for all the peoples of the Earth? Following in the footsteps of MacIntyre and Ricoeur, a 'return to Aristotle' – focusing on the concept of *phronèsis* – opens the way to a transformation of management in a *complex world* shaken by current crises and foreseeable perils, as suggested in 2008 by Richard Nielsen, the president of the Society for Business Ethics.

Any attempt to apply Aristotelian ethics to management presupposes a clarification of the main Aristotelian concepts and of their regained place in contemporary philosophy. That is why this chapter draws on the latest exegeses of the *Nicomachean Ethics* and of the *Politics* to revisit and explain the content of *phronèsis* (practical wisdom) in its application to the economic field and specifically to business. Our objective is to uncover the vigour of the original concept under the accumulated sediments, and to examine to what extent the semantic analysis of *phronèsis* can provide rules for moral judgment or action in order to define forms of wise management adapted to the time of permanent crisis. The time of crises sounds the death knell of quantitative management and calls for wise management so as to safeguard management itself; the reading of the financial crisis through Aristotelian notions allows defining wise management and imposes it.

1. From Crisis to Crisis: Excess, *Hubris* and the Reference to Aristotle

Three years after the beginning of the so-called sub-prime crisis, 2010 was announced as a time for economic recuperation that would have marked the starting point for a new cycle. But this was not the case: a loss of confidence in sovereign debts and the monetary system followed the crisis of private debt. In Europe, the conjunction of threats from the instability of currencies, real economic problems and the perceived failure of democratic systems has begun to evoke the tragic chronology that preceded the advent of totalitarianisms in the 1930s. As we finalise this chapter, problems relating to the European currency and banking system are unresolved, and the EU economy does not show many signs of emerging from recession. The Euro crisis linked to the excessive indebtedness of several countries and the fragility of a number of banks, coupled with the failure of the international community to agree on common goals at the Rio+20 Summit – which leaves major global environmental issues unresolved – gives the impression of a continuing crisis that is going to worsen.

1.1. Stiglitz's and Nielsen's Analyses of the Financial Crisis

In the context of this multifaceted financial crisis, and tired of not being heard, J.E. Stiglitz resigned from his functions before providing in *Freefall* (2010) his testimony, as a witness and as an actor, in taking part in macro decisions at the economic, financial, monetary and political levels, both as chief economist at the World Bank and as an expert for the American Democratic Party. These positions allowed him to trace and interpret the debates that took place, then the choices that were made and the consequences that followed one after another in an inexorable chain reaction toward successive collapses. The diagnosis made by Stiglitz highlights a perversion of agency theory. This disruption occurs when the model elaborated by Berle and Means (1932) is applied to the field of financial investment where it brings about a dilution of responsibilities throughout the whole chain of agents.

The effect of this process is to decouple short-term return from long-term vision, which structurally entails a denaturing of the praxis: agents end up freeing themselves of the rules of the market, forgetting all elementary principles of prudence and playing a game as if it had no limits. 'Thousands of money managers boasted that they could "beat the market"' (Stiglitz, 2010, p. 13). The author's ferocious indictment identifies the factors of a dizzying spiral of excess that has progressively spread to the whole planet: deregulation, financialisation, securitisation, finally leading to a failure of Berle and Means's initial model. How can this reading not conjure up the heroes of Greek tragedy who kept following a path whose fatal outcome was continuously announced by the chorus? Stiglitz endorses this same role of enlightened witness when he recalls, a posteriori, how simply analysing the combined *excesses* of rationality and greed made it impossible not to foresee the fall: 'Capitalism can't work if private rewards are unrelated to social returns. But that is what happened in late-twentieth-century and early-twenty-first century American-style capitalism' (Stiglitz, 2010, p. 110).

There is a striking convergence between the analysis of a major economic actor like Stiglitz and that of a prominent business ethics scholar like Nielsen with respect to the development of the crisis. Nielsen's appraisal of the situation is quite similar: for him, these dysfunctions reveal a kind of *hubris*. In his presidential address to the Society for Business Ethics in 2008 (Nielsen, 2010), he chose to apply a framework of interpretation drawn directly from the *Nicomachean Ethics* (*NE*) to analyse the use of leverage by hedge funds, private equity funds and banks in sub-prime mortgages and high-leverage operations. The catastrophic effects observed on the real economy don't flow from the mechanism itself, but from an *excess* of its use by actors blinded by greed and who have lost all sense of responsibility. In fact, leverage is a determining factor that led to the rise of trade in Phoenician, Greek and Roman societies (Andreau, 1999; Rosé, 2000; Nielsen, 2010). It has accompanied the development of the western economy whose finality had, according to Nielsen, already been theorised by Aristotle:

> In the *Nichomachean Ethics*, Aristotle also considers the idea of praxis within many different spheres of life as action that developmentally changes the actor and the external world. Putting these two ideas of economic/business activity and praxis together, Aristotle can be interpreted as suggesting that the purpose of business activity/praxis is to create wealth in a way that makes the manager a better person and the world a better place. (Nielsen, 2010, p. 299)

1.2. The Convergence between Stiglitz, Nielsen and Aristotle's Contemporary Exegetes

Interestingly enough, a double convergence is appearing: first, between the analysis of Stiglitz and that of Nielsen regarding the financial crisis; and, second, between Stiglitz's and Nielsen's analyses on the one hand, and those of the contemporary exegetes of Aristotle's works on the other – especially the *NE* and the *Politics*. This unexpected coincidence is revealed by the correspondence between the terms chosen by these different authors: whereas an economist like J.E. Stiglitz refers to the contemporary notion of *excess*, a business ethicist like R.P. Nielsen uses both *excess* and *hubris*, and the specialised translators and commentators of the *NE* and the *Politics* remind us of the place of *hubris* in ancient Greek culture. Indeed, the contemporary notion of excess is the modern formulation of the ancient concept of hubris; this equivalence finds echoes in the growing stream of research based on the return to Aristotle in contemporary philosophy in general and in the field of business ethics in particular.

Hubris – commonly understood today as 'excessive or overwhelming pride and arrogance' – can be viewed as a major phenomenon of our age: humanity crosses irreversible thresholds and peaks one after the other (climate, energy, demography, food etc.). But *hubris* is primarily a concept of ancient Greece, where it was born 25 centuries ago. In the Greek world, *hubris* brings misfortune, whereas virtue, justice, the city, success and happiness can only be conceived of within the limit. Such is the condition man must accept as his very nature, according to the principles of the seven sages of Greece: in Delphi, 'know thyself' leads to 'nothing in excess'. In the wake of Socrates, this finiteness was paradoxically elevated by Plato to the status of a standard of perfection: 'limit, moderation, number, form, all names that aim at expressing the same

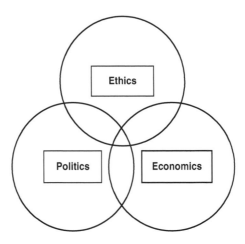

Figure 5.1 'Intersection not subordination' between three fields of action
Source: Ricoeur, 1991: 433.

reality' (Aristotle, 2002, II, p. 144). Confronted with *hubris*, the Greek tradition (from Homer to tragic theatre) has opposed it through *phronèsis*.

Nielsen and Stiglitz share the same diagnosis: the globalised economic system no longer functions in a manner consistent with the original pattern of capitalism, to the extent that it produces more 'harm to others' than goods fairly shared between all. But the reference frame is different: whereas Stiglitz focused on agency theory, Nielsen adopts Aristotelian ethics. This change allows a deeper understanding of the aforementioned phenomena related to the crisis, as the Aristotelian conceptual universe renders possible *both* to explain the reversal of the finalities of business praxis in the globalised world, *and* to elaborate reforms to avoid such a reversal. This dual movement – explaining the reversal *and* being able to remedy it – rests on a dialectical linkage of economics with politics and ethics, according to the diagram proposed by Ricoeur (Fig. 5.1):

> It is because politics raises specific problems and difficulties, irreducible to economic phenomena, that its relationships with ethics are themselves original and even more acute. That is why I propose the following figure which displays three intersecting circles ... : (in Nielsen, 2010, p. 316)

This three-fold linkage (economics/ethics/politics) was first developed by Aristotle in the *Politics*, which provides the first historical formulation of the concepts of western economic thought, presented by Aristotle in a political work that is clearly articulated with his *Ethics*. In particular, the famous distinction drawn by the Stagirite between economics and chrematistics in book I of *Politics* points to two different attitudes towards money: wealth-getting for the needs of one's household, which Aristotle views as an honourable art of acquisition; and accumulation by means of exchanges on the market, where money is hoarded for itself – a dishonourable obsession. This distinction is thus defined, as in the case of ethical notions, by reference to limits and finality:

> But the art of the wealth-getting which consists in household management ... has a limit; the unlimited acquisition of wealth is not its business. And therefore, in one point of view, all riches must have a limit ... The source of the confusion is the near connection between the two kinds of wealth-getting ... accumulation is the end in the one case, but there is a further end in the other. (Aristotle, 2009)

Aristotle's linkage of economics with politics and ethics prefigures the superposition of epistemological fields made in the twentieth century by Ricoeur in *From Text to Action: Essays in Hermeneutics* (1991), as illustrated by Figure 5.1 above. The second part of this chapter will now proceed with the semantic analysis of the *phronèsis* concept.

2. Aristotle's Concept of *Phronèsis*: The Cornerstone of Wise Management Today

2.1. Clarifying Three Aristotelian Notions: Equal, Intermediate, Fair

The system of definitions of the two Greek words *ison* and *meson*, corresponding to the equal–intermediate–fair conceptual complex, is at the core of Aristotelian ethics. In *NE* Aristotle builds the fundamental concepts of any moral thinking (such as wisdom, justice, good, evil, virtues and vices) from the central notion of middle or intermediate. These two terms (middle and intermediate) have been the subject of various definitions and differing interpretations, even of mistranslations. This is notably due to the variety of texts through which these concepts have been progressively determined over time. A number of contemporary commentators have committed themselves to clarifying the content, the meaning, and the links between these notions (Gauthier and Jolif in Aristotle, 2002; Aubenque, 1963, 2011; Chateau, 1997a; Chateau, 1997b; Ricoeur, 1997; Romeyer Dherbey and Aubry, 2002; Rorty, 1980; Wiggins, 1980).[1] They have thus shown how, to a large extent, interpretation problems originate in the way Aristotle links the two words *ison* and *meson* in a system of homogeneous and contrasted definitions.

Ison (equal) is defined by reference to *meson* (intermediate, mean), which differentiates itself according to whether it is applied to things or it is thought in relation to us (Aristotle, 1999, *NE*, II, 5, 1106a, pp. 26–32):

> In everything continuous and divisible it is possible to take more, less and equal, and each of them either in the object itself or relative to us; and the equal is some intermediate (meson)[2] between excess and deficiency. By the intermediate in the object I mean what is equidistant from each extremity, this is one and the same for all. But relative to us the intermediate is what is neither superfluous nor deficient; this is not one, and is not the same for everyone. (Irwin's translation, adapted and cited in Brown, 1997, p. 79)

The same notion (the equal) falls within two opposite definitions, depending on the subject to which it is attributed. If, because of the identity of the substantive, these two definitions are confused with one another, virtue for instance (or other moral notions) shall be considered as a *mean* which becomes tinged with a vague idea of mediocrity.[3] This mix-up, which is quite common, entails a lack of understanding of the main notions of Aristotle's ethics and accounts for the rather usual devaluing of his philosophical thought as a whole. A classic example of this devaluation is the 'centrist' reading of the mean amount (or of the happy medium) which is rigorously in contradiction with the Aristotelian texts, since for Aristotle the mean and the middle, in relation to us, are a summit, a perfection, an *excellence*:

> Whereas to feel these feelings at the right time, on the right occasion, towards the right people, for the right purpose, and in the right manner, is to feel the best amount of them, which is the mean amount – and the best amount is of course the mark of virtue. And similarly there can be excess, deficiency, and the due mean in actions. (Aristotle, 2003, *NE*, II, 1106b, p. 93)

Aristotle has the ambition of achieving universality for the *mean amount*, which remains in his work a transversal notion for all domains of reality – physical, living, spiritual – as underlined by Ricoeur (1992):

> Aristotle thus is the prolongation of a great Greek tradition, more precisely an Athenian tradition marked by Solon and Pericles. But

the stroke of genius ... is to have given a philosophical content to the idea received from the tradition ... Aristotle finds in the equal the character of intermediateness between two extremes, which he carries from virtue to virtue. (p. 201)

This relative middle (for us) between too much and too little allows defining the fundamental notions of ethics insofar as the structure of normative reasoning rests upon it, as Lesley Brown (1997) shows clearly:[4]

To grasp Aristotle's point it is vital to note some double meaning which a translation cannot capture. There is the double use of the Greek comparative whereby it can mean both 'more F' and 'too F', and a matching double use of the Greek *ison*, which can mean both (descriptively) equal and (normatively) fair or right, and of the Greek *meson*. The heart of the distinction between the two kinds of *meson* is the contrast between a non-normative and a normative notion. (p. 79)

The same term, *ison*, denotes different meanings because this notion can proceed from two distinct modes of knowledge, depending on the object to which it applies: descriptively (equal) and normatively (fair or right). Similarly in French 'un partage égal' (an equal sharing) has various significations according to whether it concerns, for instance, the measurement of a physical object or a moral assessment; the substantive 'égalité' (equality) may denote fairness, or even justice as is the case for the French Republican motto. This semantic analysis shows that the fair – or the right – in relation to us is neither necessary nor always identical. Such a result brings up two questions: (1) Is the fair (or right) in relation to us a matter of moral relativism? (2) Otherwise, how should this fair (or right) in relation to us be defined in each individual case? A relevant answer to the second question may be the best way to refute the relativism suggested by the first. This forms the basis for the theoretical importance of this equal – intermediate – fair complex, conceptualised by Aristotle from an ideal that was a constituent part of ancient Greek culture,[5] exalted by Homer and Hesiod before it became the spring of tragedy.

That is how the semantic analysis of the happy medium enables us to provide a rich answer to the problem that has existed throughout the entire history of philosophy, being the object of the most acute and topical controversies and the foundation of the validity of moral judgment.

As shown by Aubenque (1963, 2011), Aristotle's ethics cannot be dissociated from his ontology and his metaphysics. That is why for him, the field of human action cannot be bound by the same necessary laws as those that rule the sphere of abstract truths such as mathematics according to the Pythagorean and Platonic paradigms. Ethical virtue cannot be a matter for the science (*episteme*) of necessary truths, but only for an art (*techné*) such as navigation, strategy, architecture or politics: Pericles is the ideal type of the *phronimos* – a wise leader for the *polis*.

2.2. How the Return to Aristotle Leads to Wise Management: MacIntyre's and Ricoeur's Insights

Ricoeur's and MacIntyre's contributions are essential as they provide a pathway between the 'quantitative/descriptive' on the one hand and the 'normative' on the other. From Hume until Nietzsche, modernity has prohibited the passage from the descriptive to the normative; these two authors proclaimed the impossibility of avoiding moral relativism from the moment that the illusions of beyond-worlds (gods, or the foundation of transcendence and norms) were dispelled. As a result, modernity has condemned the economic sphere to remain in amorality – a thesis notably shared by Milton Friedman: according to 'modern' thinking, the whole economic activity is considered as amoral and can never be moral.

However, the economic realm is not only about the measurable and quantitative. Insofar as economic activities involve human beings, they fall under the sequence of finalities, and consequently the moral rule. That is why in order to reach wise management, it is necessary to break with modernity and to adopt another paradigm. The return to Aristotle represents a relevant means to break away from this 'amorality of the economic sphere' thesis of modernity, and to accomplish the paradigm shift. Hence the interest of actualising the ideas of the Stagirite: the Aristotelian conceptualisation of *phronèsis* is the spring that enables the definition of wise management for the twenty-first century.

In terms of traditional logic, the *phronimos–phronèsis/ison–meson* conceptual complex is not a subject but an attribute which can (or must) characterise *praxis*; the purpose of ethics is to define the content of this attribute by an empirical method which permits to seize it, not in an abstract and theoretical way, but in a concrete and practical manner, that is, taking into account the circumstances. Aristotle carefully insists on the importance of reckoning all the circumstances in order to determine, through deliberation, the right decision and its implementation modes. These circumstances fall into six categories (Aristotle, 2003): (1) the agent;

(2) the act; (3) the thing that is affected by or is the sphere of the act; (4) the instrument, for instance a tool with which the act is done; (5) the effect, for instance saving a man's life; and (6) the manner, for instance gently or violently.

This empirical way to perceive the normative, as well as the construction of the transcendent on the basis of the descriptive and the narrative, bears the seal of Aristotle (Rosé, 2009), according to a Hippocratic paradigm (Nussbaum, 2001b) that rests on two principles: (1) the sense of possible which will always lead Aristotle to subject himself to the real, to the given conditions; and (2) the importance of reaching and preserving a state of equilibrium (*isonomia*) between two extremes or two excesses (Aristotle, 1991).

The question of how to overcome the successive challenges of Hume and Nietzsche, and consequently of the foundation of morality, is one of the obsessions of Ricoeur's work. That is why in *Oneself as Another* Ricoeur indicates that he shares with MacIntyre (2007) and Nussbaum (2001a) a way of thinking, ethics and politics in a perspective that is supported by the contemporary rigour of the sciences while preserving the traditional ambition of the philosopher; the intellectual path taken by Ricoeur in *Oneself as Another* embraces the whole of modern ethical thinking, from the Cartesian cogito onwards, and ends with the *return to Aristotle*. For Ricoeur, this *return to Aristotle* is essential because it enables one to separate the search for a foundation – which, according to him, ought to be abandoned – from the upholding and strengthening of an architectonics of ends, built upon the notions of *phronèsis* and mean amount:

> If we are able to show that the deontological viewpoint is subordinate to the teleological perspective, then the gap between ought and is will appear less unbridgeable than in a direct confrontation between description and prescription or in a related terminology, between judgments of value and judgments of fact. (Ricoeur, 1992, p. 171)

Such an approach is very close to that of MacIntyre who, in *After Virtue*, also attempts to respond to the question, What does philosophy become after the failure of modernity's promises? For MacIntyre, this failure lies in the repudiation of the foundations of the promises of the Enlightenment:

> It was because a moral tradition on which Aristotle's thought was the intellectual core was repudiated during the transition of the

fifteenth to seventeenth centuries that the Enlightenment project of discovering new rational secular foundations for morality had to be undertaken. And it was because that project failed, because the views advanced by its most intellectually powerful protagonists, and more especially by Kant, could not be sustained in the face of rational criticism that Nietzsche and all existentialist and emotivist successors were able to mount their apparently successful critique of all previous morality. (2007, p. 117)

For Ricoeur and MacIntyre, the only way to take on the challenge posed by Hume and Nietzsche is an attitude which accepts the lack of any foundation, in contrast to the position adopted by Rawls or the thinkers of the 'Frankfurt School' (Adorno, Apel, Habermas) who persevere in their quest for an ultimate foundation and who, each in their own way, denounce the contemporary *return to Aristotle*. Now it is precisely this *return to Aristotle* which provides Ricoeur and MacIntyre with the concepts that enable them, at the same time, to accept this lack of a foundation on a theoretical plane and to preserve a robust frontier between *hubris* and *phronèsis* on the practical level. Such is the intellectual path proposed by these two philosophers, if *wise management* is to be anything else than rhetorical smartness to conceal what MacIntyre calls the *manipulating nature of management* and business.

The Aristotelian interpretation of *phronèsis* has made its way across the centuries because it possesses a unique force in philosophy in the face of the polysemous nature of ethical questioning, which has never ceased to manifest itself beyond the moving appearances of successive reflections that have transformed contingent events into the history of societies. The unity of ethical questioning is hidden in the dialectical sequence of ideologies, through the prism of which the different civilisations express these same questions. The *phronimos–phronèsis/ison–meson* conceptual complex provides a framework of interpretation that grasps what is *one* through the historical variation of the forms of action. That is why, even now, the *phronèsis* concept allows us to gather in the same movement three functions which fall under disciplines (respectively: humanities and social sciences, ethics and hermeneutics) that have become heterogeneous according to the *Weltanschauung* of modernity, and to highlight their unity:

• Perceive and evaluate situations, behaviours, deliberations, as well as individual and social choices in their contingent, spatio-temporal and transcultural diversities;

- While submitting them to a moral obligation whose necessity is the result of a transcendence;
- This transcendence being itself founded on an architectonics of finalities which may be seized by a hermeneutics of daily life.

Phronèsis consists of the unity of these three functions assembled by Aristotle in a *hexis*[6] – a term that points out an ability to act, an active tendency of the mind, and that is usually translated by contemporary exegetes as 'disposition' or 'state' (see for instance Rackham's translation of *NE*, Aristotle, 2003). These three functions are assembled so that reason, combined to motivation, holds the clear-sightedness and force to impose individual and collective choices, articulated according to the finalities of the just and the good. The spring of this framework of interpretation is the back-and-forth motion from the descriptive to the normative; this motion appears to be a valuable setting for the different streams of western philosophy (analytical and continental alike) which, since the middle of the twentieth century, has continually been called upon to think situations and events characterised by the chain reactions of the various kinds of *hubris* and all their consequences.

This explains and justifies the power of the *return to Aristotle* for many contemporary authors who have been confronted in the political arena with murderous tragedies and are now faced with a globalisation process that brings massive prosperity to some emerging countries but remains blind in the face of enduring or resurgent poverty and environmental threats. The antagonisms and contradictions of the twentieth century have seemed to make western reason teeter, both with regard to philosophy (Husserl, Heidegger, Arendt) and to humanities and social sciences (Popper, Kuhn). In parallel, the development process of the so-called emerging countries over the past few decades has aroused a plurality of critical views of western reason that are legitimately founded on the historical traditions and the cultures of these countries (Dumont, 1985, 1991; Virmani, 2006; Duplaix and Bousteau, 2011). The *return to Aristotle* has consisted of an array of multiple attempts to come up with, on the theoretical level, an adequate answer to the different forms of the crisis of western reason and civilisation. The same applies on the practical level (Solomon, 1992; Knight, 2007, 2008); the question of the feasibility of wise management takes its place in this overall trend.

Amidst the turmoil caused by the ongoing financial crisis and the forthcoming global systemic crises, a *phronèsis* thought anew on the basis of the conceptual core of Aristotelian ethics permits us to take a future-oriented stance: 'Not back to the Greeks, but forward with the

Greeks' (Taplin, 1989). Revisiting the *phronèsis* concept may seem appropriate for three major reasons:

1. It should be envisioned in the context of globality, not on the scale of the Greek polis.
2. Beyond the traditional philosophical approach, this concept can be enriched by a transdisciplinary approach.
3. It can provide guidance for the desirable 'great transition' towards a green economy and a fair society.

The vocation of this revisited *phronèsis* is to inspire the decisions that enable all of us – and especially managers – to master action

1. According to the assessment of a right balance;
2. Which can only result from the respect of limits;
3. These limits being themselves determined by the ordering of means subordinated to an architecture of finalities.

Conclusion

Based on the observation and analysis of the sequence of contemporary events, Stiglitz (2010) and Nielsen (2010) share the same fertile diagnosis: the combined excess of rationality and greed is the driving force behind the financial crisis – and even the global crises – which both nurture and threaten from within our system/economy/culture/world. The analyses of Stiglitz and Nielsen combined with the reconstruction by contemporary exegesis of the *phronimos–phronèsis/ison–meson* complex allow describing in a pertinent manner the current financial and economic crisis, within which management is a powerful force. It remains to be considered how the key concepts of Aristotelian ethics can enable contemporary managers to attain a degree of wisdom, that is to say an ability to discern this happy medium which preserves from excess, thus allowing them to prevent the foreseeable sequence of systemic crises – beyond the financial crisis that started in 2007.

MacIntyre and Ricoeur show us that in order to get out of the modern illusion, it is necessary to revert to Aristotle and to find again his distinction between the happy medium applied to things and the happy medium in relation to us. Aristotle views the economic realm as consisting of a mix of things and us; therefore it is a matter of coupling the quantitative, measurement-based approach of management with the ethical dimension – practical wisdom, within the meaning of *phronèsis* – which results in 'wise management'. To determine wise management it is necessary to go through the core Aristotelian ethical notions and to have a perfect command of their content; the happy medium, for instance, is not to be considered a mere compromise between two excesses, but as the construction of an excellence towards which one can only asymptotically tend.

Aristotelian ethics is not just about applying rules or not; it is a question of virtue, disposition and character, which are the result of sound education. This naturally leads to a reflection on the nature of educational programmes delivered by business schools: do these institutions really train virtuous leaders and managers as they claim? The simple observation of the uninterrupted succession of corporate scandals and wrongdoings released daily through the media casts some doubts on the credibility of their promises. The question of the reform of business schools is now debated in various circles, academic or not. Can management education evolve from a focus on the quantitative to a focus on the normative? If such a shift can be accomplished, if virtuous leadership behaviour can really be taught, and if business schools' students are trained – beyond management techniques – in values-led management, indeed in *wise* management instead of (financial) value management, then a transformation of the economic system will become possible. However, contrary to common beliefs, the normative can be more constraining and demanding than the quantitative: this might be one of the reasons why reforming business schools is such a difficult task.

Our subsequent work will aim to determine under what conditions *phronèsis* can effectively become the key to a management founding its action on a systemic and future-oriented vision of the world; in other words, the key to a *wise management* capable of bringing under control the global systemic crises of the twenty-first century. In subsequent contributions to research we will strive to demonstrate how *phronèsis* can be the means that renders possible the integration of moderation into governance, so that economic transition and paradigm shift do not remain utopias but actually become the finalities of business praxis. Our approach will rely on the following elements:

- An attempted synthesis of the main routes that are drawn today, including: *excellence* as a business ethics paradigm (Solomon, 1992), the dialectical construction of virtue (MacIntyre, 2007) and the personalist and hermeneutical reading (Melé, 2009);
- Combined with the systemic integration of the empirical contribution of humanities and social science (Rooney, McKenna and

Liesch, 2010; Sternberg and Jordan, 2005; Schwartz and Sharpe, 2010) to management practice and education delivered by business schools;
• According to the three levels of application of practical wisdom (micro–meso–macro) – which call for a framework of analysis based on multilevel governance.

Yet there is no guarantee that such an intellectual endeavour – founding wise management on *phronèsis* revisited – will consist of a quiet theoretical approach, nor that it will be successful: the outcome is never certain. It is a struggle: one of the innumerable battles of the twenty-first century. But there is also hope, as MacIntyre suggests, that we have reached a turning point:

> What matters at this stage is the construction of local forms of community within which civility and the intellectual and moral life can be sustained through the new dark ages which are already upon us ... This time however the barbarians are not waiting beyond the frontiers; they have already been governing us for quite some time. And it is our lack of consciousness of this that constitutes part of our predicament. We are waiting not for a Godot, but for another – doubtless very different – St Benedict. (2007, p. 263)

Notes

1. As well as Brown, 1997, which includes a substantial critical bibliography, see pp. 77–8 n. 2 and pp. 81–2 n. 12.
2. 'Meson in its most basic use means middle or intermediate; in its normative use it means something like intermediate and correct or more simply appropriate. I have retained the traditional translation mean using mean states for mesotes. Irwin renders mesotes by mean and uses intermediate for meson but this cannot capture the normative sense which the word undoubtedly had in some uses' (Brown, 1997, p. 79 n. 6).
3. Girard notes that 'the Latin translators of Aristotle have translated happy medium by mediocritas – this might explain that' (2010, p. 262 n. 1; our translation).
4. The argument relies on the thorough analysis and the discussion conducted by Gauthier and Jolif (in Aristotle, 2002, II, part I, p. 137 seq.).
5. Among other authors, see Dodds, 1959; De Romilly, 1992; Taplin, 1989; Vernant, 1965; Vernant and Vidal-Naquet, 1982.
6. Aristotle's concept of *hexis* is closely related to Bourdieu's concept of habitus – namely, a 'system of dispositions' (Bourdieu, 2003, p. 190) that determines the position of the subject in a social field. Aristotle doesn't neglect the social dimension for the construction of ethical notions.

References

Andreau, J. (1999). *Banking and Business in the Roman World.* Cambridge University Press.

Aristotle (1991). *Politique*, vol. I, trans. and introduction J. Aubonnet. Les Belles Lettres, Paris.

Aristotle (1999). *Nichomachean Ethics*, trans. T. Irwin. Hackett, Indianapolis.

Aristotle (2002). *Ethique à Nicomaque*, 4 vols, trans. and introduction and comments R.A. Gauthier and J.-Y. Jolif. Peeters, Louvain.

Aristotle (2003). *The Nichomachean Ethics*, trans. H. Rackham. Harvard University Press, Cambridge, MA (orig. 1926).

Aristotle (2009). *Politics: A Treatise on Government*, trans. B. Jowett, rev. J. Barnes. Needland Media, Amazon Kindle.

Aubenque, P. (1963). *La prudence chez Aristote.* PUF, Paris.

Aubenque, P. (2011). *Problèmes aristotéliciens, Vol. 2 – Philosophie pratique.* Vrin, Paris.

Berle, A., and G. Means (1932). *The Modern Corporation and Private Property.* Macmillan, New York.

Bourdieu, P. (2003). *Méditations pascaliennes.* Editions du Seuil, Paris.

Brown, L. (1997). 'What Is "the Mean Relative to Us" in Aristotle's "Ethics"?' *Phronèsis*, 42(1): 77–93.

Chateau, J.-Y. (ed.) (1997a). *La vérité pratique, Aristote, Ethique à Nicomaque, Livre VI.* Vrin, Paris.

Chateau, J.-Y. (1997b). 'L'objet de la phronèsis et la vérité pratique. Sur l'unité et la cohérence de l'Ethique à Nicomaque'. In J.-Y. Chateau (ed.), *La vérité pratique, Aristote, Ethique à Nicomaque, Livre VI*, pp. 185–261. Vrin, Paris.

De Romilly, J. (1992). *Pourquoi la Grèce?* Editions de Fallois, Paris.

Dodds, E.R. (1959). *The Greeks and the Irrational.* University of California Press, Berkeley.

Dumont, L. (1985). *Homo aequalis – Genèse et épanouissement de l'idéologie économique.* Gallimard, Paris.

Dumont, L. (1991). *Essais sur l'individualisme – Une perspective anthropologique sur l'idéologie moderne.* Editions du Seuil, Paris.

Duplaix, S., and F. Bousteau (2011). *Paris–Delhi–Bombay, L'exposition.* Catalogue. Centre Pompidou, Paris.

Girard, B. (2010). *Aristote. leçons pour (re)donner du sens à l'entreprise et au travail.* Maxima Laurent du Mesnil éditeur, Paris.

Knight, K. (2007). *Aristotelian Philosophy, Ethics and Politics from Aristotle to Macintyre.* Polity Press, Cambridge.

Knight, K. (2008). 'After Tradition? Heidegger or MacIntyre, Aristotle and Marx'. *Analyse & Kritik*, 30: 33–52.

MacIntyre, A. (2007). *After Virtue: A Study in Moral Theory.* University of Notre Dame Press (orig. 1981).

Melé, D. (2009). 'Integrating Personalism into Virtue Based Business Ethics: The Personalist and the Common Good Principles'. *Journal of Business Ethics*, 88: 227–44.

Nielsen, R.P. (2010). 'High-leverage Finance Capitalism, the Economic Crisis, Structurally Related Ethics Issues, and Potential Reforms – 2008 Society for Business Ethics Presidential Address'. *Business Ethics Quarterly*, 20(2): 299–330.

Nussbaum, M.C. (2001a). *The Fragility of Goodness: Luck and Ethics in Greek Tragedy and Philosophy*. Cambridge University Press.

Nussbaum, M.C. (2001b). 'The Protagoras: A Science of Practical Reasoning'. In E. Millgram (ed.), *Varieties of Practical Reasoning*, pp. 89–100. MIT, Cambridge, MA.

Ricoeur, P. (1991). *From Text to Action: Essays in Hermeneutics*. Northwestern University Press, Evanston, IL. French edition: (1986). *Du texte à l'action*. Editions du Seuil, Paris.

Ricoeur, P. (1992). *Oneself as Another*. University of Chicago Press.

Ricoeur, P. (1997). 'A la gloire de la Phronèsis, Ethique à Nicomaque, Livre VI'. In J.-Y. Château (ed.), *La vérité pratique, Aristote, Ethique à Nicomaque, Livre VI*, pp. 13–22. Vrin, Paris.

Romeyer Dherbey, G., and G. Aubry (eds) (2002). *L'excellence de la vie – Sur l'Ethique à Nicomaque et l'Ethique à Eudème d'Aristote*. Vrin, Paris.

Rooney, D., B. McKenna and P. Liesch (2010). *Wisdom and Management in the Knowledge Economy*. Routledge, New York.

Rorty, A.O. (ed.) (1980). *Essays on Aristotle's Ethics*. University of California Press, Berkeley.

Rosé, J.-J. (2000). *Contribution à la lecture de la nouvelle traduction de 'Economie et société dans l'antiquité' (Max Weber)*. Séminaire 'Le commerce romain, fonctionnement, règles, mentalités', EHESS-SHADYC, Marseille.

Rosé, J.-J. (2009). 'Corporate Responsibility and Global Social Contract: New Constructivist, Personalist and Dialectical Perspectives'. In H.-C. de Bettignies and F. Lépineux (eds), *Business, Globalization and the Common Good*, pp. 369–416. Peter Lang Academic, Oxford.

Schwartz, B., and K. Sharpe (2010). *Practical Wisdom – The Right Way to Do the Right Thing*. Riverhead Books, New York.

Serres, M. (2012). *Temps des crises*. Le Pommier, Paris.

Solomon, R.C. (1992). *Ethics and Excellence – Cooperation and Integrity in Business*. Ruffin Series in Business Ethics. Oxford University Press, New York.

Sternberg, R., and J. Jordan (eds) (2005). *A Handbook of Wisdom: Psychological Perspectives*. Cambridge University Press.

Stiglitz, J. (2010). *Freefall: America, Free Markets, and the Sinking of the World Economy*. W.W. Norton & Co., New York.

Taplin, O. (1989). *Greek Fire*. Jonathan Cape, London.

Vernant, J.-P. (1965). *Mythe et pensée chez les Grecs*. Maspero, Paris.

Vernant, J.-P., and P. Vidal-Naquet (1982). *Mythe et tragédie en Grèce ancienne*. Maspero, Paris.

Virmani, A. (2006). 'Repenser la RSE à partir de la philosophie hindoue'. In J.-J. Rosé (ed.), *Responsabilité sociale de l'entreprise – Pour un nouveau contrat social*, pp. 305–16. De Boeck, Brussels.

Wiggins, D. (1980). 'Deliberation and Practical Reason'. In A.O. Rorty (ed.), *Essays on Aristotle's Ethics*, pp. 221–40. University of California Press, Berkeley.

6
'To Know as We Are Known': Locating an Ancient Alternative to Virtues

Mark Strom

Is Aristotle Enough?

In *After Virtue*, Alasdair MacIntyre argues that a single moral tradition shaped ethical reasoning from Aristotle until the Enlightenment after which it became fragmented in service of individualism and ultimately 'emotivism' (2007, pp. 6–35).[1] Notwithstanding the diversity of the writers and contexts that influenced it, MacIntyre believes this tradition – epitomised and canonised in Aristotle – shared a stable sense of 'a cosmic order which dictates the place of each virtue in a total harmonious scheme of human life' (2007, p. 142). Linking this cosmic order and the Aristotelian system of virtues were 'background concepts of the narrative unity of human life' (228). According to MacIntyre, this narrative gave stable meaning to the virtues for the better part of two millennia.

This consensus began to unravel in the eighteenth century. MacIntyre believes that Nietzsche's radical critique and abandonment of ethical systems was the logical consequence of the fragmentation that began with the Enlightenment. Thus MacIntyre famously framed his thesis in a question: 'Aristotle or Nietzsche?' (2007, p. 113). According to MacIntyre, there is 'no third alternative' (p.118) – we must recover the virtues-based schema of Aristotle's *Nicomachean Ethics*.

Any framework for virtues today requires a narrative and conceptual framework that can speak to the complexities of the modern social context. But the story and beliefs behind the Aristotelian schema are in fact *alien* and *opposed* to the needs of today's organisational contexts. In particular, the Aristotelian schema is irrevocably elitist, not egalitarian; framed for keeping the status quo, not for transformation; and rationalist, not relational.

Locating Aristotle's Schema in Socio-historical Context

MacIntyre believes that the narratives of Homer and Athens adequately underpin the Aristotelian virtues. But those narratives assumed a cosmic order that upheld the stratification of society. MacIntyre acknowledges that this *is* the classical story: *'Phronèsis* like *sophrosune* is originally an aristocratic term of praise. It characterises someone who knows what is due to him, who takes pride in claiming his due' (2007, p. 154). And,

> For Homer the paradigm of human excellence is the warrior; for Aristotle it is the Athenian gentleman. Indeed according to Aristotle certain virtues are only available to those of great riches and of high social status; there are virtues which are unavailable to the poor man, even if he is a free man. And those virtues are on Aristotle's view ones *central to human life*. (2007, p. 182; emphasis mine)

In reading western ethical thought as variations on a single tradition, MacIntyre has oversimplified in two directions. First, he has missed the radically alternative vision of (at least) one of the traditions he has incorporated (2007, p. 147). Second, he has flattened the tensions and contradictions that arguably constitute the dynamic of western thought. New concepts were not simply added to an Aristotelian system. For example, love has come to figure largely in western accounts of ethics and virtues, even of wisdom. Wirzba and Benson (2008, p. 10) go so far as to claim that 'Love is not just an "add-on" to wisdom but a central *feature* of being wise'. That may be claiming too much, but a cluster of other-centred concepts – compassion, humility, kindness – does seem to have become established in contemporary lists of virtues. Each concept is a radical departure from Aristotle. How did this shift come about?

Recovering a Socio-historical Reading of Paul

The ideas of Paul (formerly Saul) of Tarsus, called the apostle, have been obscured by anachronistic 'Christian' readings of his letters – a fault sometimes as ubiquitous in critical readings as in conservative readings. Whenever Christianity has been complicit in patriarchy, intolerance, neuroses and political agendas, the apostle is usually singled out as the source.

The claims about Christianity may be substantial; but blaming Paul is to read him back to front, a point acknowledged by the French neo-Marxist philosopher Badiou (2003, p. 4). For example, understood in historical and social context, rather than as the advocate of patriarchy, Paul turns out to be one of the strongest advocates in classical literature of the equality of women with men; awkward texts notwithstanding (1 Corinthians 11; 14; 1 Timothy 2; see Winter, 2003, *passim*).[2]

Contemporary observers did not know how to characterise the groups known only as followers of 'The Way' (Acts 9:2; 19:9; 24:14). Believing they were *not* religious (many suspected they were atheists), their contemporaries eventually named them *christianoi* (Acts 11:26; 26:28). The *-ianoi* is akin to our '-ism'. It signalled a political group, and the early groups did not want the tag (Judge, 1972). There are ample historical grounds for distancing Paul from the religious and institutional conventions that followed within a generation or two. Some examples will help to introduce Paul's break with classical tradition.[3]

First, Paul avoided Aristotle's core vocabulary of *arête* (virtue). This is noteworthy when elsewhere he freely co-opted and reframed civic and political vocabulary, often controversially (e.g. *kurios* 'lord', *ekklesia* 'gathering', *soma* 'body', *doxa* 'honour', *evangelion* 'good news', *charis* 'grace' etc.). Generally, Paul either used Graeco-Roman vocabulary as per its contemporary usage, or reframed the terms to invert classical ideas and convention. Interestingly, he avoided the vocabulary of leadership.

Second, Paul's *use* of *phronèsis* is a radical departure from Aristotle and Graeco-Roman moral philosophy. In the Book of Philippians, Paul employed *phronèsis* and its cognates (Phil. 1:7; 2:2, 5; 3:15, 19; 4:2, 10) as a way of knowing ('have this mind') patterned after Christ as anti-Caesar (Phil. 2:6–11; Horsley, 1997, 2000). The spectacle of a humiliated–glorified 'lord' here provided Paul a reference point for a new way of being-in-knowing (*phroneo*) expressed in acts that ignore rank and subvert status (vv. 3–4): 'Do nothing out of selfish ambition or vain conceit. Rather, in humility value others above yourselves, not looking to your own interests but each of you to the interests of the others.' Aristotle most certainly 'would have been horrified' (MacIntyre, 2007, p. 184). For Paul, I believe, *phronèsis* no longer signalled a practical conventional mindset, but a radically relational mindset.

Third, several other innovations help locate Paul's innovations. He gave no place to *andreia* (courage), and he reworked the other cardinal virtues (Horsley, 1982, pp. 105–6). He inverted *charis* (grace) from a mark of the gentleman benefactor who accepts the obligations of reciprocity, to the basis of an unprecedented egalitarianism (Harrison, 2003).[4] Paul's positive use of *metamorphoō* (transform) was unprecedented in classical literature. His radical egalitarianism – 'neither Jew nor Gentile, neither slave nor free, nor male or female' (Galatians 3:28) – led him to invert the common 'body' metaphor and to speak of *all* people as gifted (Romans 12; 1 Cor. 12–14). When he wrote that he sought to become 'all things to all people' (1 Cor. 9:21), this was not a chameleon-like lack of what we now call integrity, but an unprecedented sense of commitment to the other.

These innovations and improvisations, common enough to us now, amounted to a dramatic departure from classical and Graeco-Roman views of life and society. MacIntyre does not overstate the case when he says that Aristotle 'would have been horrified by St Paul' (2007, p. 184). Paul's life did not match the classical virtues; indeed, contemporary observers would be likely to regard Paul as unstable, unseemly and lacking in the cardinal virtues.[5] Yet, ironically, his life and thought is closer to the mark of our own idea of integrity, a notion that finds little support in the classical tradition (Judge, 1982, 1983). Paul's story of a Jewish messiah was wrapped in dramatic reversals and inversions of social conventions that in turn inspired further transformations in social practice.

Paul's life and thought offers a (tacit) critique of the elitism and conventionalism of Aristotle and the Hellenistic moral philosophers. He may also offer an alternative mode of being, knowing and relating to the Aristotelian schema of virtues: perhaps even a little more amenable to our own modern purposes.

Moving toward Paul's Innovations

Rank and status defined social experience in the first century. Rank marked a person for life and could only be changed by adoption or decree. A man (almost always a man; Winter, 2003) was deemed a leader by rank (Clarke, 1993). In reading *Nicomachean Ethics*, it may be assumed that virtues make the leader. Indeed, Aristotle's virtues read to us like those attributes whose practice (*habitus*) could transform any manager into a leader of great character and influence. But Aristotle and his peers believed that only a man of rank ('the superior man') was capable of sustaining true virtue. Social superiority *preceded* virtue and made it attainable. The four cardinal virtues – wisdom, justice, temperance and courage (tellingly, *andreia*, 'manliness') – were not agnostic of rank. Taken together they signified the self-contained man who lived up to the privileges and responsibilities of his place in the social hierarchy (Judge, 1982). This was the common meaning of 'know yourself'.

Rank was fossilised status (Judge, 1982). The markers of status were similar to our own: fame, friends, wealth, beauty, education, social standing, success, largesse, popularity and, less regarded today, oratory. The moral maxims shed light on status. A total of 254 maxims are known from extant lists over a thousand years (Judge, 1993). The persistent favourites were: know yourself, pick your time, nothing to excess and the cost of commitment. The context of these four was the virtue *philotimia*, the love of ambition. The maxims illuminated the path by which a man might improve his own position.

So how did *philotimia*, the love of ambition, become the vice of self-service? And how did love as self-giving, *agape*, become a virtue? These are in large part the legacies of Paul (and the New Testament Johannine literature). They begin with the man who called *agape*, love, the greatest of all (1 Cor. 13:12).

The Innovation of Grace

Paul came to view humanity – past, present and future – as headed by two 'Adams' (Rom. 5; 1 Cor. 15). To be 'in' the first Adam meant to participate in an order characterised by death, condemnation and flesh. Its animating principle was *law*. To be 'in' the second Adam meant to participate in an order characterised by resurrection, justification and spirit. Its animating principle was *grace*.

Law and grace were antithetical. According to Paul the law was intended to promote life but could only arouse death (Rom. 7:7–11). Unlike the Graeco-Roman moral philosophers (Malherbe, 1986), Paul rejected keeping law or moral codes as the means to human flourishing. In tune with Paul's insight, Wirzba and Benson (2008, p. 6) write, 'Unconditional love ... is love that literally has no (even legal) "conditions"'. So if law could only feed ego and shame, where did Paul ground the behaviours of human flourishing?

Paul introduced something as offensive as it was unprecedented: identification with an anti-hero and an un-sophisticate; indeed, with a humiliated man. Taking the traditions of the crucifixion and resurrection of Jesus of Nazareth as his starting point (1 Cor. 15:1–8), Paul read the experience of the one he called the Christ, and by extension his own experience, as establishing a paradigm of rising-within-dying. Human flourishing, for Paul, came by imitating the reversal of rank and expectation exemplified in the Christ story. Paul amplified this by three more paired contrasts: rising-within-dying is to be experienced as wisdom-in-foolishness, strength-in-weakness and joy-in-suffering.

Paul seemed to regard his life as a continual 'dying' to the binary expectations of society and to its marks of performance and status

(2 Cor. 4). At the same time, he claimed to experience 'rising' as a sense of identity, calling and relationship free from any law. His freedom, he intimated, needed no moral compass (Rom. 7:6; Gal. 5:1). He seemed to advocate a 'relational' mode of life that did not need recourse to moral theory, schema or law.

Congruent with his own message, Paul modelled humility, compassion and love – no doubt inconsistently (I have no interest here in venerating him). Today we call these virtues; but, to his contemporaries, they were scandalous, not virtuous. They were excessive and unbecoming to a man (always a man) of social and intellectual standing. They clearly break the bounds of Aristotle's 'mean'. In Rome, as in Athens, a noble man worked to augment his fame and opportunities: 'Roman *principes* sought fame, and to get to the top. Self-advertisement and the proclamation of achievement were essential tools in the armoury' (Hillard, 2008, p. 107). This is the background to the scandal of Paul's unseemly boasting in 2 Corinthians 10–12: not *that* he boasted, for that was expected of a great man (Forbes, 1986), but that he boasted of his *weakness*. In place of self-promotion and particularly self-sufficiency, marks of the Aristotelian 'superior man', Paul regarded his dependency as a context for grace and renewal (2 Cor. 12:9).

Today we tend to understand humility and inclusiveness as virtuous.[6] But in Paul's day, virtue confirmed rank and status. Indeed, to read humility, compassion, inclusiveness et al. back into Aristotelian *arête* and *phronèsis* is to miss the latter's social context of rank, status and the love of ambition. We do better to look to the radical who appeared four centuries later.

Grace, Paul believed, had relativised rank, discredited status, dignified all without discrimination and opened the way for personal and social transformation. Yet Paul was not constructing a new moral code or schema of virtues (Lategan, 1990). Rather he was laying the ground for the transformation of relationships.

The Innovation of Transformation

Two 'world stories' dominated the first century: the little-known story of Israel bearing a promise to the world (Gen. 12:1–3), and the pervasive story of Augustus and his *pax Romana*. Paul dissented from both.

Paul viewed the story of Rome as false. Reading his letters as moral or religious homilies we will miss the highly political associations of his thought (Horsley, 1997). The profession 'Jesus is Lord' was an affront to 'Caesar is Lord'. In a hymn (Colossians 1:15–20) Paul's description of Christ appropriates imperial titles. Taubes goes so far as to call Paul's message a 'declaration of war against Rome' (2004, p. 13).

The Jewish story was Paul's own story as a member of its religious and intellectual elite, and as a former campaigner against Rome. But Paul's penchant for reversals extended to his reframing of the story of his own people. Paul consistently constructed his message on the pre-Israelite promise to Abraham for the world (Gen. 12:3), not on Moses, the architect of Israel's social, legal and moral structures (Badiou, 2003, p. 103; Strom, 2011). Paul reframed Israel's story from nationalism to universalism. To Paul, Rome was the wrong world-story; Israel carried the true world-story – but had missed its ending! How did he convey this startling prospect?

In Rom. 12:1–3, Paul gave one of his more succinct summaries of the implications of what was now emerging as a nascent alternative worldview. Here Paul opened a dangerous possibility: that someone living within and under Rome might 'not conform to the patterns of this world, but be transformed by the renewing of your mind' (v. 2). Anachronism disposes us to hear 'not conform' through religious or moral filters as 'don't do bad or impious things'. But the context and vocabulary carried clear *political* overtones.

Paul wrote to small groups of dissenters in Rome to strengthen them in their counter-cultural stance. Economy, politics and the imperial cult were wedded throughout the empire, and *liturgia* ('worship'; Rom. 12:1) indicated responsibilities due to the emperor. Paul urged his groups to redirect their deepest loyalties. The 'patterns of the world' (*suschematisesthe to aioni touto*) are the 'schemas of the age'. What would Paul have regarded as the schemas of his age?

His letters reveal (not always tacitly) critiques of dualism, rank and status, the nationalism of his compatriots and the power of imperialism over every aspect of life. Paul's call to be transformed, *metamorphoō*, is the first use of the word positively in classical literature. Classical philosophy and society overwhelmingly censured change. Paul's vision of personal, social and even cosmic transformation was a striking innovation that gave rise to further social improvisation and innovation (Judge, 1984; Strom, 2001, pp. 73–100). Today we view adaptation and openness to change as a virtue. But to Aristotle and the Graeco-Roman moral philosophers, change was to be censured. The virtues *constrained* innovation.

Paul believed that grace was the new ground of identity. It undercut elitism (Rom. 12:3–5) and established the new social obligation to love (13:8). Notwithstanding his pragmatism about authority (13:1–7),

Paul's message was as subversive to the inner logic of the imperial capital as it was to the conventions of rank and status (vv. 6–21). A new account of being–knowing–relating was unfolding and taking hold.

The Innovation of a Relational Epistemology:
Aka Faith, Hope and Love

Confidence in reason was both the genius and the Achilles heel of Greek philosophy.[7] The tendency of philosophy to become detached from people, 'often locked [it] into an abstract cycle of debate in general terms, driven more by the sheer rationality of the tradition than by reference to any actual social situation' (Judge, 1975, p. 191).

Audiences would have identified Paul as a sophist or philosopher though he never described himself in either way (Winter, 2001). At Corinth, a city that Dio noted for its aggressive sophists (*Oration* 8.9–12), Paul had alienated certain groups by his refusal to assume the role of a professional orator serving under their patronage (1 Cor. 2:1–5; 2 Cor. 10:10).

Paul distanced himself from the Corinthian sophistic tradition. Where oratory was central to success, rhetorical skill was 'power, whether for good or for ill' (Gempf, 1993, 260). Paul's refusal of oratory (1 Cor. 2) went against the codes of sophistic ambition and excellence. His choice to work with his hands was an affront earning him the formal enmity of the aggrieved powerbrokers (Marshall, 1987). Their offer – patronage with the usual expectation of honour returned – was entirely unexceptional. They would have provided Paul with a platform for his Corinthian career in exchange for his professional services and his support of their privileged position (Winter, 2001).

Paul was deeply aware of how reason and oratory aided the status of the educated. He sharply criticised the arrogance and deceit that lurked in the claims and counter-claims of philosophers. He dismissed philosophy as having failed to deliver the certainty and enlightenment it promised (1 Cor. 1:18–21). Nowhere was his struggle clearer than with the intellectual and social conceit of influential members of his Corinthian groups (1:26–31; 4:10–13; 2 Cor. 10:1–6). Paul makes the contrast stark: 'Knowledge (*gnosis*) puffs up, but love (*agape*) builds up' (1 Cor. 8:1). Benson (2008, p. 29) captures the heart of the tension: 'Whatever this *gnosis* may be, the Corinthian church clearly think it empowers them – and that is what disturbs Paul'.

In a crucial Pauline text, 1 Corinthians 13, the theme is clearly love (*agape*) but the context is knowledge. After censuring the factionalism of his readers (1:10–17), Paul argued for a reversal of intellectual expectation and a reorientation of rationality (1:18–2:16; Stowers, 1990). The Corinthians had transposed their new experiences of their new 'graces', gifts (*charismata*), to markers of status (12:12–26). In the midst of advocating a consensual and collaborative reordering of their meetings, Paul pointed to 'a more excellent way ... love' (12:31).

The passage opens with a provocative summary of the goal of classical philosophy – 'to know all things' (1 Cor. 13:2). This is surely one of the most succinct and pointed summaries of the goal of classical philosophy in the extant literature. What follows is perhaps also its most radical extant critique – 'but had not love'. Paul positioned *agape* (love) as profoundly other-centred; in this sense it was the *antithesis* of *arête* (virtue).[8]

In contemporary terms, we read the admonitions of the central section (1 Cor. 13:4–7) as virtuous but this was not so in Paul's day. Indeed, to 'keep a record of wrongs' (v. 6) was what a Corinthian, Athenian or Roman man *should* do as he pursued his own ambition within the bounds of the all-encompassing obligations and reciprocity of the patron–client relationship (Harrison, 2003). We begin to glimpse a radical departure from virtue as a way of structuring relationship: Aristotelian virtues would direct Paul's readers inward; Pauline love directed his readers outward.

Paul ends with knowledge (1 Cor. 13:8–12). He has grown from one who knew as a child to one who knows as an adult. Now he knows in part; one day he will know in full. So, then, 'these three remain: faith hope, and love – and the greatest of these is love' (v. 12).[9] Paul has not switched from the epistemological to the moral: he is still talking about the ways we know. While *knowledge* remains incomplete, Paul says, he *knows* by faith, hope and particularly love. Badiou captures the sense of it: 'love ... alone effectuates the unity of thought and action in the world' (2003, p. 91). Similarly, Wirzba and Benson (2008, p. 3) write, 'when the rigour of love is pursued, the very character of our knowing undergoes transformation'.

As far as we know, faith, hope and love entered western vocabulary as a triad with Paul either from 1 Corinthians 13 or from 1 Thessalonians 1:3 and 5:8 (two of his earliest and non-disputed works). It is, perhaps, a challenge for the contemporary mind to put off centuries of anachronistic readings to glimpse the triad as other than religious, spiritual or moral virtues. But in lived experience, faith, hope and love are ways of knowing available to all peoples of all persuasions of all time. Historically the triad found new prominence in the story and sources that eventually yielded Christianity. But faith, hope and love are *not* specifically religious or spiritual (Bauer, 1979, pp. 600–3). What *is* novel is the way Paul used them to reframe rationality and social relations. Paul challenged classical epistemology with a profoundly 'ordinary' yet innovative account of knowing as human and relational.

It is ironic that Paul's innovations would later be inverted and domesticated in the ethical, religious and political structures of the classical–Christian alliance that dominated western thought and society for over a millennium and a half.

Re-evaluating the Western Story

The story of Rome was its destiny to rule the world: *Romanitas*, Rome eternal and universal, the centre of the universe. Paul's story could not help but clash with this story and with the central tenets of classical philosophy. He had unleashed ideas into the world and no one could foresee the consequences.

Augustine represents a watershed in the convergence of these two great traditions. Following Paul, he read faith, hope and love as subverting autonomy and grounding reason in experience. Yet Augustine remained caught in the historical novelty of framing a new path for the academy and the *polis* based on an idea that had critiqued the foundations of both.

In Paul's account of faith, hope and love, Augustine saw the outline of an alternative epistemology. The classical starting point had been the autonomous knower working his way toward certainty by reason alone (Gottlieb, 2000). But there can be, as Augustine put it, no understanding except faith precedes it. His famous dictums carry the point: 'faith seeks understanding';[10] 'understanding is the reward of faith';[11] 'we believe in order that we might understand';[12] and 'he who loves aright believes and hopes rightly'.[13]

In his study of the unravelling of the classical system, Cochrane wrote that Augustine was 'recommending faith, not as a substitute for, but as a condition of understanding' (2003, p. 44). It had always been so, but classical philosophy seemed to miss the point that *faith in reason* powered rationality. Augustine, however, saw it and this is why Polanyi regarded him as the first 'post-critical' philosopher (1958, p. 266).

The worlds of Plato and Aristotle, and Paul and Augustine, came to be inextricably linked. Augustine crafted a remarkable intellectual break from classicism, yet he remained a Platonist. Christendom baptised the elitism of classicism, confused the idea of the kingdom of God with *Romanitas* and (at last) provided a cosmology that could support unparalleled discovery in science and technology. Augustine's *City of God* rivalled Plato's *Republic* and Aristotle's *Politics* in the breadth of its political and social vision. In his *Letter to Arsacius* (*c*.362), Julian the Apostate pins the Galileans' (i.e. Christians) subversivion to the order of *Romanitas* on their novel conventions of open dialogue, literacy and hospitality. His advice to the priests of the old Roman gods: plagiarise! Though his own agenda soon died with him, he needn't have bothered: the emerging synthesis of Paul's innovations with classical thought was already well under way. In time it would sustain that which it had subverted, *Romanitas*, under the twin (and often opposed) guises of the Church of Rome and the Holy Roman Empire.

Our reading of Paul's innovations, and their subsequent inversion, suggests that the western tradition is not about one (mostly) coherent tradition that became lost or dismissed (contra MacIntyre). It is about *two* competing traditions whose clash of ideas continues to enrich an unstable but highly productive hybrid: status and grace; convention and transformation; abstract rationality and relational ways of knowing.

These tensions shape every context of leadership and organisational complexity. Wisdom, I believe, lies in exploring these tensions, not in obscuring them.

On the Contemporary Significance of the Pauline Innovation of Grace

The ambiguity, contradictions and anomalies that accompany organisational complexity require ways of knowing that do not mask, but embrace, uncertainty. Complexity is more than complication: more than the sum of many puzzles amenable to logic. Complexity is fuzzy, ambiguous and uncertain. Managers grappling with organisations seek to arouse engagement and innovation. What is needed, I believe, is less a system or ethics of virtue that directs managers inward than a relational mode of knowing and being that directs them outward.

Understood in its historical place as the origin of western concepts of equality and egalitarianism, grace continues to bear a radical edge (Warren, 2002).[14] Conventional management approaches to cultural change and engagement have relied on hierarchy and cascaded messages. Meaning is created by the few, certainty is assumed and desired and control is paramount. Interaction is too often limited to communication and people are 'engaged' passively. Unlike Paul's own practice, there is rarely a compelling collective story large enough, and generous enough, to give room for people to write their own stories within it; nor it seems is there often the invitation or means to do so.[15]

Being attentive to grace takes managers in a very different direction. We can view hierarchy as an artifice: pragmatically useful, but no true indicator of capability, brilliance or natural networks of conversation. Instead, we can acknowledge that meaning *is* being created by the many in conversation. We can give up on certainty but seek a proper confidence. Networks of conversation open the possibility of co-design. We can work to honour story and to champion agency and voice.

On the Contemporary Significance of the Pauline Innovation of Transformation

Our concepts of paradigm, change, engagement and innovation arguably derive, via a long and winding path, from Paul's idea of transformation. Few leaders have ever accomplished the scale of change that Paul triggered in anything like the complexity of his context. Julian was incensed at its ubiquitous and profound impact on the foundational ideas and structures of the Roman Empire.

Central to Paul's idea of transformation is a renewal of the mind that enables discernment of the 'schemas of the age'. I have argued above that the schemas for Paul were dualism, rank and status, nationalism, and imperialism. The first two clearly continue to be part of organisational life and contribute to its complexity. The last two are arguably present by analogy at least.

Dualism is not hard to find: theory vs practice; strategy vs operations; analysis vs customer experience. We transpose 'best practice' from the other side of the world and wonder that it fails. The problem is our failure to translate abstract ideas to new contexts and relationships. Paul grounded rationality in context, experience and relationship – modes of knowing now championed in design-thinking as crucial for grappling with the complexity of 'wicked problems' that defy rationalistic problem-solving (Vickers, 1981; Golsby-Smith, 1996; Buchanan 1992).[16]

Paul was pragmatic about rank but savage on status. The effect of this novelty was to shift the obligations of rank from self-advancement to the wellbeing of others. What followed was a radical equalising of people that paved the way for literacy and improvisation. Modern organisational structures provide accountability but tend to circumscribe work and value; in this sense they work against innovation. Cultures do not change until their leaders step down in their worlds. Innovation is always happening, generally at the edges: a leader who holds rank lightly and eschews status is disposed to walking at the edges and being attentive to the brilliance that flourishes there.

The martial metaphors of capturing markets and killing competitors transpose nationalism and imperialism to commerce. The morality or otherwise of these expressions is not my point. What interests me is the dispositions that open up or close deeper possibilities. Martial metaphors lend themselves to mergers and acquisitions (plunder and alliance), not to innovation and organic growth (curiosity and imagination). Likewise, martial or competitive metaphors are fundamentally binary: win–lose. Complexity requires modes of non-binary knowing – renewals of the mind – that can see beyond the schemas of the marketplace.

Paul pinned transformation on a renewal of the mind, an idea he regarded as a mark of community, not simply of individual experience. Given the prevailing emphases upon analysis, it is somewhat ironic that few organisations promote a strong intellectual life. It is a mistake to identify reason with the reductionism, fragmentation and abstraction of managerial practice (Saul, 2001, 2003). These modes of thought are not only lacking in the relational nuances and instincts of faith, hope and love, but, in my experience, are also lacking in genuine intellectual rigour. Reports, presentations and meetings too frequently meander for want of a sharp question to focus the mind. We look to analysis to give us strategy. We do not analyse our way to the future. Conceptualising a vision and a path to achieving it is an act of the imagination: a compelling hypothesis framed as a choice on behalf of a desired story. I have seldom seen strategies that yielded genuine transformation.

On the Contemporary Significance of the Pauline Innovation of Faith, Hope and Love

Decoupled from religion, we may begin to appreciate and embrace faith, hope and love as *sapiential* ways of knowing: dispositions that pave the way for insight, nuance and an apt confidence. Hope and even love, though perhaps still marginal to most discussions, have found their way from social to corporate discourse (Senge, 1992, pp. 384–5; Senge, et al., 2004, p. 107; Kahane, 2010, *passim*). Nonetheless faith may still feel too religious for corporate discourse.

While there are distinctly Christian perspectives on faith, I suggest that faith is not an exclusively or even originally Christian or religious concept, but a phenomenon intrinsic to human experience. There *is*, however, something distinct about Paul's use of *pistis* (faith) and *pisteuo* (to believe).[17] The crux is the link Paul made between faith and his reframing of *charis* (grace). This juxtaposition of faith and grace enabled the idea of relationship as a gift independent of any moral, intellectual or social merit, and not dependent upon the obligations of reciprocity – only the debt to love.

The preamble of the Charter of the United Nations makes clear that our affirmation of equality is an act of faith: 'We the peoples of the United Nations determined ... to reaffirm faith in fundamental human rights, in the dignity and worth of the human person, in the equal rights of men and women and of nations large and small'. We likewise choose to believe that transformation can be positive, and that knowing must take account of matters of the heart and of relationship. We commit ourselves to these beliefs and act upon them. That is to say, we have faith in them.[18] Thus Aristotle had to believe that a life of *eudaimonia* was possible and desirable before he could describe it or argue for it.

Over the last decade the journal of the Institute of Advanced Studies in Culture at the University of Virginia, the *Hedgehog Review*, has chronicled and stimulated intellectual discourse ranging across questions of morality, dignity, justice, equality, emotion, individualism, multiculturalism, citizenship, religion, pluralism, secularism, ontology and more. In places the discourse has embraced faith beyond religious bounds:

> the secular 'should not be thought of as the space in which real human life gradually emancipates itself from the controlling power of "religion" and thus achieves the latter's relocation.' In the historical processes of European secularization, the religious and the secular are inextricably bound together and mutually condition each other. Asad has shown how 'the historical process of secularization effects a remarkable ideological inversion ... For at one time "the secular" was a part of a theological discourse [*saeculum*]', while later 'the religious' is constituted by secular political and scientific discourses, so that 'religion' itself as a historical category and as a universal globalized concept emerges as a construction of Western secular modernity. (Casanova, 2006, p. 10)[19]

In discussions of 'weak ontology' as a mediating position between foundationalism and relativism, the language of faith has been invoked to describe *how* we hold our deepest-level commitments to concepts such as human dignity and morally defensible change.[20] Building on the seminal work of Stephen White (1991), Connolly argues that an 'existential' or 'onto-political' faith infused with 'a distinctive sensibility ... is important to political thinking and theory, to the micropolitics of everyday life, and to the macropolitics of an entire state' (2005, p. 28).

Connolly goes on to argue that faith (and hope and love) are both *ubiquitous* (if tacit) and *necessary* in social, political and corporate discourse. Interestingly, he argues this position as an atheist and an 'immanent naturalist':

> Immanent naturalists seek to tap in ourselves and others a preliminary attachment to the abundance of being over identity ... bestowing importance upon the interinvolvements [*sic*] between language, affect, faith, and sensibility ... We discern that we, too, are inhabited by a faith-infused doctrine that can be supported by argument but that has not been definitively established – the faith/philosophy of immanent naturalism. We seek to pluralize more broadly and deeply than heretofore religious impulses, philosophical orientations, and experiences of faith. (Connolly, 2005, p. 34)

Narrative has experienced a renaissance in social and business literature. Stories are vehicles of human identity and meaning. If explanatory frameworks assume and build upon reason, stories assume and build upon faith: 'Reason's indefatigable attempts to unmask and track down the fallacies of our beliefs will leave us shivering in the cold, for only beautiful stories – not truth – can console us' (Illouz, 2010, p. 19).

In these dialogues faith is clearly finding voice and currency in secular discourse. Here faith (and hope and love) takes on the character of an epistemological *disposition* amenable to ambiguity and uncertainty and, above all, to the humanness of complexity. These are not epistemological *steps*. There is no faith > hope > love process, whether linear or iterative. Nonetheless, following Paul, the neo-Marxist philosopher Badiou sees a conceptual and dispositional priority to love: 'love is precisely what faith is capable of ... [for it] alone effectuates the unity of thought and action in the world' (Badiou, 2003, pp. 90–1).

The language of faith (and hope and love) offers a constructive alternative to the language of autonomy and certainty.[21] It provides a mode of epistemological description amenable to narrative structures of identity and meaning that are not amenable to analysis. It is a mode open to the reappraisal of craft and community as keys to organisational change and managing complexity.

Analysis, plans and strategies remain vitally important. But grappling with complexity requires ways of knowing that are relational, not binary. The abstraction, fragmentation and reductionism of analysis and planning tend to reinforce the illusion that complexity can be reduced to a stream of choices. If complexity is viewed as a suite of problems, then the right method plus the right statistics may seem to solve any problem.[22] This leaves little room for the plain humanness of things too big to grasp, the serendipity of imagination and innovation, and the role of care and engagement in occasioning insight. The language may be archaic and irrecoverable, but faith, hope and love draw attention to the 'indwelling' that invites and enables innovation in the face of complexity.[23]

Conclusion

Paul represents a watershed in the forging of western thought. He provided a unique framing of being-in-knowing as relational. In doing so he countered, and offered, an alternative to the elitism and assumptions of autonomy and certainty so intrinsic to classical life and thought. His innovation of grace reframed *phronèsis* from Aristotelian conventionality to a mindset that opened the way to the modern ideas of equality and fraternity. Transformation became a universal hope. In tackling the nexus of elitism and knowledge, he reframed knowledge as relational: 'to know as I am known', animated by faith, hope and love.

Translated to our milieu and contexts, these innovations can question *and* strengthen our contemporary appeals to virtue, Aristotelian or otherwise, as we seek the wisdom and leadership to grapple with complexity, ambiguity and mystery.

Notes

1. For the most part this chapter will adopt a critical stance toward aspects of the thought of both Aristotle and MacIntyre. I should therefore like to commence with a caveat to this criticism. I am in many respects an admirer of Aristotle's brilliance, particularly in his reworking of Plato. I also appreciate MacIntyre's formidable scholarship, particularly his exposition of Aristotle and his critique of Nietzsche.
2. I use references that relate to Pauline texts in the New Testament and have abbreviated these after their first use.
3. For the background to Paul's thought as innovative in Graeco-Roman context, see Strom (2001, pp. 182–99). There I likened Paul's 'method' to musical improvisation.
4. 'Paul was attracted to *charis* as a leitmotiv for divine beneficence because the Augustan "age of grace" had ensured that nobody would be able to compete

against the munificence of the Caesars' (Harrison, 2003, p. 351; Greek characters in original).

5. See my discussion of Paul and morality (Strom, 2001, pp. 142–56). Paul may appear to us to exhibit the cardinal virtues: wisdom, self-control, justice and courage. What is lacking in Paul is the crucial nexus of virtue and social privilege. In classical and Hellenistic society, wisdom was that which upheld social stratification, justice that which gave a man the reward/punishment due to him (i.e. according to his rank), self-control was the mark of a superior man, and courage was exemplified in a man who upheld his own honour. See the extensive citation and discussion of Graeco-Roman moral texts in Malherbe (1986).

6. I have elsewhere contributed a chapter on humility to a work on leadership and virtue (Strom, 2003). I noted there that several of the virtues included in that work would never have been so regarded by the classical writers. Now also Dickson (2011, pp. 83–96).

7. In the first half of this section I am drawing on Strom (2001, pp. 105–14).

8. This is an admittedly difficult concept for modern readers. We may read virtues such as justice and wisdom as relational. But the classical virtues need to be read in light of the social nexus of rank, status and ambition. From Homer through Aristotle to writers contemporary with Paul, wisdom, justice, temperance and courage were understood to be exemplified in the self-contained man (e.g. Dio Chrysostom, *Oration* 49.8–11; Seneca, 'On the firmness of the wise man', 6.3–8). The classical ideal remained *ataraxia*, detachment (e.g. Plutarch, *Moralia* 83E, 86A, 83BC). In Phil. 2:3 Paul turned *tapeinos* (humbled, abased), a term only used negatively in classical literature (Bauer, 1979, p. 804), into the *virtue* of *tapeinophrosune* (humility, modesty). For the evidence from non-literary sources, see the discussion of three first-century eulogies in Horsley (1982, pp. 33–6, 40–3; and 1987, pp. 10–17). For a full discussion illustrated from the primary sources, see Strom (2001, pp. 58–67).

9. A parallel to 1 Cor. 13:13 comes in a seventh-century BCE poem attributed to Tyrtaeus: 'this is virtue, this is the noblest prize and the fairest' (frag. 12). The virtue is courage. In the *Symposium* Plato lauds love as 'originally of surpassing beauty and goodness' (197c–e). For Maximus of Tyre, love 'is a thing superb … It is everywhere confident, despises all things, and subdues all things' (*Dissertations*, 20.2). In both the term is *eros*, not *agape*. For Plato *eros* is idealised in the intellectual and physical (sexual?) relationship between a man and a youth. For Maximus *eros* is the passion that drives a man to face all obstacles and enemies. Paul's use of *agape* in 1 Cor. 13 commends other-centredness. Elsewhere I have demonstrated the innovation this represents in Graeco-Roman thought (Strom, 2001, pp. 142–56, 189–95). I happily acknowledge my indebtedness to my *Doktorvater*, Edwin Judge. See the representative articles of Judge's nearly six decades of scholarly leadership in Harrison (2003) and Scholer (2008).

10. *On the Trinity*, XV, 2.2.

11. Tractate 29.6.

12. Sermon 126.

13. *Enchiridion* 31.117.

14. On the history and implications of the idea of grace for society, see the essays collectively titled 'Individualism' in the Spring 2002 edition of *The Hedgehog*

Review. Warren writes, 'The life of grace is fundamentally "others-oriented" – social and connectional ... In other words, grace compels one to have an ethic of service, to be others-oriented rather than individualistic and self-protective. As such, it might be a key, or even essential, to the growth of a genuinely multicultural society' (2002, p. 34). See also Bellah (2002).

15. On Paul's practice as reframing leadership in terms of wisdom, improvisation and narrative, see Strom (2003, 2007).

16. From a different perspective, John Ralston Saul makes a similar argument for weighting reason as *only* equal to common sense, ethics, imagination, intuition and memory (2001, pp. 265–315). See also his earlier account of the rise of rationalism in managerial thought (Saul, 1993, pp. 77–107).

17. Not that the terms are unique. The vocabulary of faith (*pistis*) and believing (*pisteuo*) is well attested in the classical and Hellenistic sources with the same semantic field as Paul's use (Bauer, 1979, pp. 660–5). It is also worth noting the common ground of Aristotle and Paul. If Paul's use of faith for human–divine relationship renders its use inappropriate in our contexts, then the classical understanding of virtue as a divine gift (e.g. Hierocles, *On Duties* 1.3.53–4) should equally exclude our appropriation of *virtue*. Aristotle assumes that *eudaimonia* and *arete* are divine – indeed 'anything that men have is a gift of the gods' (*Ethics* 9.1). Like Plato and the Pre-Socratics, Aristotle viewed human life as a microcosm (mini-cosmos) patterned after the gods.

18. In analytical epistemology faith is sometimes viewed as incompatible with knowledge (Creel, 2001, pp. 105–7). Knowledge is limited to things that can be established by syllogistic or inductive methods. Yet reason depends upon faith. Methodologically, if knowledge is 'properly justified true *belief*', reason can only work retrospectively on belief. Substantially, confidence in reason can only be established as an inductive argument based on empiricism: i.e., arguments framed according to Aristotle's three logical maxims (and other modalities of logic) continue to seem to work; fallacies continue to seem to fail. But this is a step removed from establishing the reasonableness *of reason*. One must assume reason works since any syllogistic argument *for* reason must *assume* reason: it is circular. We have faith in reason. Perhaps we would do better to limit the claims for reason (Saul, 2001, pp. 266–315) acknowledging with Aristotle that logic can only address what 'cannot be other than it is' (*Posterior Analytics* 71b, 73a).

19. Casanova is here quoting from Asad (2003, p. 191). See the essays collectively titled 'After Secularization' in the Spring/Summer 2006 edition of *The Hedgehog Review*.

20. See the essays collectively titled 'Commitments in a Post-Foundationalist World: Exploring the Possibilities of "Weak Ontology"' in the Summer 2007 edition of *The Hedgehog Review*. The articles are based on the seminal work of White (1991).

21. Marjorie Grene, a colleague and major interpreter of Michael Polanyi, opened her exposition of Plato's *Meno* with an account of how the assumptions of autonomy and certainty have shaped the history of western philosophy (Grene, 1974), p. 17.

22. Saul (1993) offers a history of reason's journey post-Descartes into instrumental reason. The title of Descartes' 1637 work is instructive: *A Discourse on Method*. I would argue that modern managerialism combines faith in

method with faith in statistics. On the epistemological and social upheavals created through the rise of statistics, see Cohen (2005).
23. By 'indwelling' I am echoing the work of Michael Polanyi. His theory of all knowing as *personal* knowing may help locate faith, hope and love epistemologically. Critiquing 'objectivism', Polanyi asserted that all knowledge is *personal* knowledge made possible by 'indwelling' what we seek to know (1958, p. 300). Polanyi admired Augustine, describing his view of faith as epistemic as the first 'post-critical philosophy' – the name Polanyi gave his own work (p. 266).

References

Agamben, G. (2005). *The Time That Remains: A Commentary on the Letter to the Romans.* Stanford University Press.

Aristotle (1960). *Posterior Analytics. Topica.* Leob Classical Library, 391, trans. H. Tredennick and E. Foster. Harvard University Press, Cambridge, MA.

Aristotle (1966). *Ethics (Nicomachean)*, trans. J. Thomson. Penguin, London.

Asad, T. (2003). *Formations of the Secular: Christianity, Islam, Modernity.* Stanford University Press.

Badiou, A. (2003). *Saint Paul: The Foundation of Universalism.* Stanford University Press.

Bauer, W. (1979). *A Greek–English Lexicon of the New Testament and Other Early Christian Literature*, 2nd edn, ed. W. Arndt and F. Gingrich. University of Chicago Press.

Bellah, R. (2002). 'The Protestant Structure of American Culture: Multiculture or Monoculture?' *The Hedgehog Review*, 4(1): 7–28.

Benson, B. (2008). 'The Economies of Love and Knowledge in Paul'. In N. Wirzba and B. Benson (eds), *Transforming Philosophy and Religion: Love's Wisdom*, pp. 28–41. Indiana University Press, Bloomington.

Buchanan, R. (1992). 'Wicked Problems in Design Thinking'. *Design Issues*, 8(2): 5–16.

Casanova, J. (2006). 'Rethinking Secularization: A Global Comparative Perspective'. *The Hedgehog Review*, 8(1): 7–22.

Clarke, A. (1993). *Secular and Christian Leadership in Corinth: A Socio-historical and Exegetical Study of 1 Corinthians 1–6.* E. J. Brill, Leiden.

Cochrane, C. (2003). *Christianity and Classical Culture: A Study of Thought and Action from Augustus to Augustine.* Amagi, Indianapolis.

Cohen, L. (2005). *The Triumph of Numbers: How Counting Shaped Modern Life.* W.W. Norton & Company, New York.

Connolly, W. (2005). 'White Noise'. *The Hedgehog Review*, 7(2): 26–34.

Creel, R. (2001). *Thinking Philosophically: An Introduction to Critical Reflection and Rational Dialogue.* Blackwell, Boston.

Dickson, J. (2011). *Humilitas: A Lost Key to Life, Love, and Leadership.* Zondervan, Grand Rapids.

Forbes, C. (1986). 'Comparison, Self-praise and Irony: Paul's Boasting and Conventions in Hellenistic Rhetoric'. *New Testament Studies*, 32: 1–30.

Franz, D. (2009). 'Pillar, Ledger, and Mission: Ontologies of the American Corporation'. *The Hedgehog Review*, 11(2): 7–18.

Gempf, C. (1993). 'Public Speaking and Published Accounts'. In B. Winter and A. Clarke (eds), *The Book of Acts in Its First Century Setting: Vol 1. Ancient Literary Setting*, pp. 259–303. Eerdmans, Grand Rapids.

Golsby-Smith, T. (1996). 'Fourth Order Design: A Practical Perspective'. *Design Issues*, 12(1): 5–25.

Gottlieb, A. (2000). *The Dream of Reason: A History of Philosophy from the Greeks to the Renaissance*. Allen Lane, London.

Grene, M. (1974). *The Knower and the Known*. University of California Press, Los Angeles.

Harrison, J. (2003). *Paul's Language of Grace in its Graeco-Roman Context*. Wissenschaftliche Untersuchungen zum Neuen Testament 2, Reihe 172. Mohr Siebeck, Tübingen.

Harrison, J. (ed.) (2008). *E.A. Judge: The First Christians in the Roman World: Augustan and New Testament Essays*. Mohr Siebeck, Tübingen.

Hillard, T. (2008). 'Augustus and the Evolution of Roman Concepts of Leadership'. In J. Beness (ed.), *Studies in Honour of Margaret Parker*, II, pp. 107–52. Macquarie Ancient History Association, Sydney.

Horsley, G. (ed.) (1981–89). *New Documents Illustrating Early Christianity*, vols I–V. Macquarie University Press, Sydney.

Horsley, R. (ed.) (1997). *Paul and Empire: Religion and Power in Roman Imperial Society*. Trinity Press, Harrisburg.

Horsley, R. (ed.) (2000). *Paul and Politics: Ekklesia, Israel, Imperium, Interpretation*. Trinity Press, Harrisburg.

Illouz, E. (2010). 'Love and Its Discontents: Irony, Reason, Romance'. *The Hedgehog Review*, 12(1): 18–32.

Judge, E. (1972). 'St Paul and Classical Society'. *Jahrbuch fur Antiqiuty und Christentum*, 15: 19–36.

Judge, E. (1975). 'St. Paul as a Radical Critic of Society'. *Interchange*, 16: 191–203.

Judge, E. (1982). *Rank and Status in the World of the Caesars and St. Paul*. The Broadhead Memorial Lecture, 1981. University of Canterbury Press, Christchurch.

Judge, E. (1983). 'Christian Innovation and Its Contemporary Observers'. In B. Croke and A. Emmett (eds), *History and Historians in Late Antiquity*, pp. 13–29. Pergamon, Sydney.

Judge, E. (1984). 'Cultural Conformity and Innovation in Paul: Some Clues from Contemporary Documents'. *Tyndale Bulletin* 35: 3–24.

Judge, E. (1993). 'Ancient Beginnings of the Modern World'. *Ancient History*, 23(3): 125–48.

Kahane, A. (2010). *Power and Love: A Theory and Practice of Social Change*. Berrett-Koehler, San Francisco.

Lategan, B. (1990). 'Is Paul Developing a Specifically Christian Ethics in Galatians?' In D. Balch, E. Ferguson and W. Meeks (eds), *Greeks, Romans, and Christians: Essays in Honour of Abraham J. Malherbe*, pp. 318–28. Fortress, Minneapolis.

MacIntyre, A. (2007). *After Virtue: A Study in Moral Theory*. University of Notre Dame Press.

Malherbe, A. (1986). *Moral Exhortation: A Greco-Roman Sourcebook*. Library of Early Christianity, 4. Westminster, Philadelphia.

Marshall, P. (1987). *Enmity in Corinth: Social Conventions in Paul's Relations with the Corinthians*. J.C.B. Mohr, Tübingen.

Plutarch (1928). *Moralia I–II*, trans. F. Babbitt, Loeb Classical Library, 222. Harvard University Press, Cambridge, MA.

Polanyi, M. (1958). *Personal Knowledge: Towards a Post-critical Philosophy*. University of Chicago Press.

Polanyi, M. (1966). *The Tacit Dimension*. Doubleday, New York.

Saul, J.R. (1993). *Voltaire's Bastards: The Dictatorship of Reason in the West*. Penguin, London.

Saul, J.R. (2001). *On Equilibrium*. Penguin, Melbourne.

Scharmer, O. (2009). *Theory U: Leading from the Future as It Emerges*. Berrett-Koehler, San Francisco.

Scholer, D.M. (ed.) (2008). *Social Distinctives of the Christians in the First Century: Pivotal Essays by E.A. Judge*. Hendrickson, Peabody.

Seneca (1928–35). *Epistulae Morales. I–III*, Leob Classical Library. Harvard University Press, Cambridge, MA.

Senge, P. (1992). *The Fifth Discipline: The Art and Practice of the Learning Organization*. Random House, Sydney.

Senge, P., O. Scharmer, J. Jaworski and B. Flowers (2004). *Presence: Exploring Profound Change in People, Organizations and Society*. Nicholas Brealey, London.

Stowers, S. (1990). 'Paul on the Use and Abuse of Reason'. In D. Balch, E. Ferguson and W. Meeks (eds), *Greeks, Romans, and Christians: Essays in Honour of Abraham J. Malherbe*, pp. 253–86. Fortress, Minneapolis.

Strom, M. (2001). *Reframing Paul: Conversations in Grace and Community*. IVP, Chicago.

Strom, M. (2003). 'Humility'. In C. Baker (ed.), *The Seven Heavenly Virtues of Leadership*, pp. 3–15. McGraw-Hill, Brisbane.

Strom, M. (2007). *Arts of the Wise Leader*. Sophos, Auckland.

Strom, M. (2011). 'From Promised Land to Reconciled Cosmos: Paul's Translation of "Worldview," "Worldstory" and "Worldperson."' In P. Church, T. Bulkeley, T. Meadowcroft and P. Walker (eds), *The Gospel and the Land of Promise: Christian Approaches to the Land of the Bible*, pp. 14–27. Pickwick, Eugene, OR.

Taubes, J. (2004). *The Political Theology of Paul*. Stanford University Press.

Vickers, G. (1981). 'The Poverty of Problem Solving'. *Journal of Applied Systems Analysis*, 8: 15–21.

Warren, H. (2002). 'Authority and Grace: A Response to Robert Bellah'. *The Hedgehog Review*, 4(1): 29–34.

White, S. (1991). *Sustaining Affirmation: The Strengths of Weak Ontology in Political Theory*. Princeton University Press.

Winter, B. (2001). *Philo and Paul among the Sophists: Alexandrian and Corinthian Responses to a Julio-Claudian Movement*. Eerdmans, Grand Rapids.

Winter, B. (2003). *Roman Wives, Roman Widows: The Appearance of New Roman Women and the Pauline Communities*. Eerdmans, Grand Rapids.

Wirzba, N., and B. Benson (2008). 'Introduction'. In N. Wirzba and B. Benson (eds), *Transforming Philosophy and Religion: Love's Wisdom*, pp. 1–11. Indiana University Press, Bloomington.

7
Wise and Virtuous Leadership: The Contribution of Confucian Values to Business Leadership

Li Yuan

Introduction and Background

Leadership is deemed as a highly context-based, complex outcome of dynamic interaction between the leader, follower and situation; and it continues to be a highly researched, yet elusive topic. Since the industrial revolution, with the advent of the modern economy and globalisation, the practice of leadership has more often been linked to effectiveness and efficiency in promoting organisational performance and profits (Nahavandi, 2000), and as a result of such emphasis, business researchers and practitioners often tend to focus on business leaders' competences that directly relate to promoting business profits as the most important, or even the only, criterion for good/effective leadership. Unfortunately, the mainstream of leadership theories of the twentieth century, including trait theory, behavioural theory, situational theory, contingency theories and so forth, has not placed sufficient emphasis on the ethical aspects of leadership. Following Enron and other prominent ethical scandals in almost every type of organisation in recent years, people are asking, what is wrong with our business leaders?

Over the last three decades, China has achieved remarkable economic growth and social transformation. The opening-up policy and economic reforms in the late 1970s spurred people to pursue wealth and profit, and the accelerating process of globalisation has exposed Chinese people to an unprecedented access to a multi-valued environment. Consequently, Chinese traditional values, virtues and norms have been greatly undermined due to the concussion of ruthless profit-minded orientation. This has led to the rise of many unethical business practices in recent years (for example the scandal of food safety, the environmental crisis, labour rights and so forth). Like their unethical, overseas counterparts, these Chinese leaders were not perceived to be weak, but they all were deemed to have acted *unwisely* (Jones, 2005), and they are held to be responsible for the (unethical) values and beliefs held in their organisation's culture (Collins, 2001; Krames, 2003).

In China, the recent campaign for corporate social responsibility (CSR) and the development of 'human-based' and 'virtue-based' business models initiated by local business reflect a rising concern about the apparent absence of business ethics (Ip, 2011). Although there has been much research on ethical leadership in the past decade, and on a worldwide scale (see Brown and Trevino, 2006), it has become necessary to build leadership ethics by resorting to indigenous and traditional Chinese wisdoms, especially Confucianism. This may be because, first, in spite of the global homogenising of organisational processes, managerial practices and leadership styles, Chinese cultural values are still the most significant factor in determining and shaping Chinese business organisational, managerial and leadership practices (Liu, 2009; Kerr, 1983; Redding, 1990; Wah, 2010; Warner, 2008). The process of the formation and transformation of Chinese management has been marked by some ingrained factors relating to their deep-rooted traditional culture and value systems as well as historical evolution, and therefore Chinese leadership research cannot be isolated from the Chinese cultural context. Second, a significant quality of any management approach rooted authentically in Chinese cultural values, especially as defined in philosophical Confucianism, is the inseparability of ethics from the practice of leadership (Chen and Lee, 2008). Confucianism was understood as the foundation, or one of the pivotal factors, that supported and promoted the meteoric rise of the East Asian economies in the 1980s and early 1990s (Chan, 2008). Although Confucian ethics may have a lot in common with its western counterpart, and elements such as righteousness, benevolence, trustworthiness, justice and so on, some Chinese traditional virtues possess a uniquely Confucian understanding: such as *li* 礼 (ritual propriety), *junzi* 君子 (exemplary personhood), *zhongyong* 中庸 (moderation) and *zhongshu* 忠恕 (loyalty and altruism). These virtues exemplify the distinctiveness of Confucian-based Chinese leadership. Third, in 1988, 75 Nobel Prize winners made a statement in Paris that if humankind is to survive in the twenty-first century, they must draw wisdom from Confucius (Wah, 2010). Confucian ethical leadership may indeed offer productive insights for managers within other cultural settings.

Towards such an end, in this chapter I propose a concept of Confucian meritocracy by incorporating selected merits (intelligence, knowledge and ability) with Confucian virtue or moral worthiness, and this may be taken as one criterion for evaluating wise and effective leadership. Wise and virtuous business leadership in modern society not only benefits organisation, but also serves the wellbeing and harmony of society as a whole, rather than narrowly and instrumentally chasing business profits at the expense of the common good.

Meritocratic Leadership

The term *meritocracy* is a satirical invention of Young (1958), who wrote the classic satire or fantasy, *The Rise of the Meritocracy*. Young envisioned a future social system in which outcomes such as power, status, jobs and wealth are distributed on the basis of merits (i.e. intelligence and effort). Without the irony Young intended, the term is now applied to the advanced capitalist systems of reward allocation and status attainment (Scully, 1997), and the definition of merit is broader and includes ability, training and experience. Meritocracy is considered by many to be an ideal justice principle (Hing et al., 2011; Scully, 1997) as it promises people equal and adequate opportunities to achieve success, as determined by individual merits – this is the key principle behind the much-publicised American Dream (McNamee and Miller, 2004; Hing et al., 2011; Yuan, 2012).

Following the lead of western economies, meritocracy as such is growing in recognition in much of the business world as one of the main underpinnings of HR management (Yuan, 2012), for example by identifying merit (i.e. effort + IQ) as the basis for appointments and distribution of rewards to individuals. Meritocracy ensures that only those deemed outstanding and able can reap the rewards of modern capitalism. Those less able must necessarily suffer the consequence of their lack of appropriate ability. Meritocracy thus assumes that those who distinguish themselves by special knowledge, skill and other valued abilities can make better decisions and should decide for those less able; it attempts to explain or justify meritocratic leaders and their roles in society. Such business leaders must necessarily possess appropriate knowledge, skill and ability in areas of management, sales, finance and marketing and so forth. This meritocracy entails a leadership of the most talented by ensuring that any advancement within the hierarchy of organisations is restricted to those individuals who demonstrate relative superiority in knowledge and skill – qualities that determine and predict superior organisational performance and profits. It is believed that effective leadership will result in creating a culture of meritocracy and that meritocracy will also create effective leaders within the organisation (Vieira, 2011).

The isolation of merit from considerations of ethical value and a concern for humanity in general is one of the factors that have contributed to a proliferation of crises in financial markets and industries across the world. In fact, it is frequently the most talented individuals in terms of merit who are responsible for ethical failures, resulting in serious negative ramifications (McNamee and Miller, 2004). Consequently many researchers (such as Trevino, Butterfield and Mcabe, 1998; Trevino, Hartman and Brown, 2000; Yang, 2011) have noted that merits (IQ, ability, skill etc.) cannot be fundamental, and hence are the only valid method for understanding and evaluating leadership, as a person may have all the identified leadership competencies but with little moral sense. This will nullify his or her merit and may even lead his or her organisation in the wrong direction. The harmful effects of leaders' lack of virtue often spill outside of organisations and can have severe negative consequences for society as a whole (Bennis, 2007). Meritocracy may be more justifiable than hereditary aristocracy or arbitrary power (Tan, 2009), but it needs to be kept in check by ethical criteria to prevent leaders with merits from abusing their power. Thus, the need for an ethical approach to organisational leadership is becoming increasingly urgent as the social, environmental and economic costs of 'moral hazard' are realised both in China and other countries.

Confucian Meritocracy

As crime, corruption and unethical behaviour in the corporate world continue to expose the gulf between knowledge (including the ability that comes with knowledge) and virtue (Tan, 2009), the value of Confucian philosophy is found in its thoroughgoing integration of knowledge and virtue, resulting in the inseparability of merit and ethics.

For Aristotle, ethics is closely associated with practical wisdom, which mostly refers to some kind of capacity or traits of character and qualities of mind by means of which people can live social life in a correct way. The practical application of wisdom has been highly appreciated in the Confucian tradition as well. Here, it demonstrates a clear tendency towards ethicism. Within the various differences connoted by Aristotelian '*phronèsis*', Confucianism can still be deemed as a kind of practical wisdom (de Bettignies et al., 2011; Chan, 2008; Ip, 2011), and it is manifest in classics such as *Analects* and *Daxue* (Yao, 2006; Yu, 2009) and so forth. Confucian wisdom has had an appeal for thousands of years and is still being applied to solve the paradoxes and perplexities of daily life (Yao, 2006). Confucian wisdom focuses on the fulfilment of a life that comes with the full development of humanity, and it prompts people to act properly and morally according to the constantly changing *Way* or *Dao*, the principle of the universe.

Aristotelian practical wisdom has the problem-solving capacities of cleverness and shrewdness, but differs from the latter in that it is not ethically indifferent, and a practically wise person should be an ethical person at the same time (Yu, 2006). In other words, acting rationally and acting ethically do not seem to be identical, as the former is associated with intelligence or cleverness without ethical sense (Yu, 1998). Also, as Aristotle pointed out, '*knowing* about them [just and good acts] does not make us any more capable of *doing* them' (see the *Nicomachean Ethics*, Aristotle, 1976, p. 221), and he distinguishes the former as one kind of wisdom, namely theoretical wisdom (*sophia*), which is a combination of knowledge of fundamental principles (*nous*) and knowledge of what follows from those principles (*theoria*). Confucians also acknowledge problems arising from the incongruity between knowing and acting. According to Yao (2006), an advantage Confucian ethics has over Aristotelian ethics, in solving these problems, seems to be that Confucians in general do not place intellectual activity above (or away from) practical wisdom.[1] In this holism they do not therefore refer to wisdom either as a state of the mind or a behaviour pattern or an attribute of the soul, but as the whole process of self-cultivation guided by an insightful understanding of universal principles. Confucian masters grasp wisdom with intellectual development, but this intellectual capacity is never considered to be purely cognitive (Yao, 2006). According to Confucius the wise, *zhizhe* (智者) involves both intellectual and ethical achievement. Without virtuous behaviour, even if one is incredibly knowledgeable, one cannot be considered wise.

In this chapter, I therefore propose a 'Confucian meritocracy' as a leadership standard which fully values knowledge/ability/skill and ethics. Confucian meritocracy ensures that merit based upon virtue should be given priority of consideration along with any merit based upon intelligence, skill and ability. Confucian meritocracy requires leadership of the *wise*, those who possess both virtue and ability in the Confucian sense. Moreover, although Confucians respect both the virtuous and the talented, if with limited options, Confucians would prefer to put leadership authority in the hands of those who would exercise leadership virtuously – the moral elite – rather than entrusting power to those are intelligent, skilful and knowledgeable but are lacking in virtue, and thus would be likely to lead to bad decision-making. The practice of enterprise is not merely a commercial exercise, but also a moral praxis. To make an enterprise function, what a leader needs is some knowledge and skills of good management; but the key to any successful moral praxis is ethical excellence or virtue. Confucian values and ethics, including benevolence and compassion, loyalty and morality, righteousness and trustworthiness, moderation and propriety, and so on, are the moral principles that may be seen to underlie human actions, and therefore these should be fully studied and integrated into the construction of 'Confucian meritocratic leadership', which values highly those leaders who have both virtue and ability.

Confucian Virtues Relevant to Leadership[2]

For Confucius, a leader should be not only knowledgeable, but also, and perhaps more importantly, virtuous. Confucians lay much emphasis on the 'rule of virtue' (*de zhi* 德治), which means the best way for rulers to govern is through means of *de* (德 virtue). Within traditional ancient Chinese culture, the word *de* (德) incorporates both meanings of virtuous conduct (*dexing* 德行) and virtuous character behind the behaviour (*dexing* 德性) (Lai, 2010). Confucius says, 'One should govern with virtue. He is like the northern star: it takes its proper place and other stars rotate around it' (*Analects* 2.1).[3] Some specific Confucian virtues relevant to leadership are held in common with western concepts of management ethics, such as benevolence, righteousness and trustworthiness, so this review will identify some virtues which possess a uniquely Confucian understanding, such as *li* 礼 (ritual propriety), *junzi* 君子 (exemplary personhood), *zhongshu* 忠恕 (altruism and loyalty) and *zhongyong* 中庸 (moderation). These latter virtues, which exemplify the distinctiveness of Confucian-based Chinese leadership, are given particular attention in this chapter.

From an ethical point of view, Confucian wisdom is closely related to, or even determined by, virtue, which is often represented by *ren* (benevolence or humanity), the supreme virtue and the sum total of all virtues of Confucian virtues. The character *ren* (仁) is composed of two parts: a standing man on the left and *er* (the number two) on the right. So *ren* is an extensive love of human beings, and through the cultivation of the 'Way', enables a moral person to have concern for both the physical and moral wellbeing of others. However, unlike the love theory of Mozi (墨子), who advocated universal love for all, and Christianity, which advocates love for everyone including one's enemy, Confucian love is graded according to the proximity and distance of each relationship. For Confucians, to deny the graded relationship is to obstruct the path of humanity and righteousness and even destroy the harmony of all things, as the hierarchy of everything that exists in the universe naturally follows the Dao, the basic principle of the universe and of human society. An individual can be human only in relationship to other human beings in a society, and *ren* can only be defined and realised through relationships and interactions with others, and further a harmonious and moral society can only be built and maintained through recognising hierarchy and the central leadership role of the moral person (*junzi*). The fulfilment of humanity (*ren*) occurs by doing moral behaviour according to the principle of *li*.

Li (礼 *Ritual Propriety*)

Li, or rite/ritual propriety, indicates a pattern of behaviour that is the foundation of human virtue. Virtue is realised in concrete human acts, and acts are of a pattern with certain features which are represented by *li*:

> they are all expressive of 'man-to-man-ness', of reciprocal loyalty and respect ... Men are by no means conceived as being mere standardised units mechanically carrying out prescribed routines in the service of some cosmic or social law. Nor are they self-sufficient and individual souls who happened to consent to some social contract. Men become truly human as their raw impulse is shaped by *li*. *li* is the specifically humanising form of the dynamic relationship of man-to-man. (Fingarette, 1998, p. 7)

Li is the inherent requirement of morality, and as a code of conduct, it is manifested by moral behaviour. *Li* supports proper cooperation behaviour in China through the realisation that individuals interact with each other according to the principle of *li*. A virtuous leader must fully understand the code of *li* and behave according to *li*. He must then sow it into the organisational culture, in order to cultivate a moral atmosphere in an organisation in which members will interact in an appropriate way through internalising *li* as their moral code as well. As Confucius says,

> if you govern them [the common people] with decrees and regulate them with punishments, they will evade them, but will have no sense of shame. If you lead with virtue (*de*) and regulate them with

rules of propriety (*li*), people will have a sense of shame and abide by the rules. (*Analects* 2.3)[4]

Confucians view society as a community of interrelated responsibilities in which to achieve a moral, just and harmonious society the principle of *li* also recommends that an individual should do what is proper to fulfil his position (Romar, 2002). So it requires a leader of an organisation to understand well his role, tasks and position in the process of management and rectify his mind and heart to apply the proper attitudes and knowledge to fulfil his role. That is, except behaving according to *li* as common people, leaders must set themselves higher moral standards and measure their moral behaviour with regard both to their role as superiors and to how their actions will impact those around them.

Junzi (君子 *Exemplary Personhood*)

The goal of government in Confucianism is to build a harmonious society in which people live in peace and prosperity. This goal requires the government to foster a climate of virtue by providing a role model. Confucianism holds that *junzi* (君子), or gentlemen/exemplary persons, and *Xiaoren* (小人), or petty persons, would not make equally good decisions, and that they will choose different means or ends, corresponding to the inequality of moral merits. When virtuous leaders lead the way, the followers tend to be virtuous. Confucius says, 'if the leader strives for goodness, the people will follow him in being good. The virtue of *junzi* is like wind; the common people's virtue is like grass. Grass always bends in the direction of the wind' (*Analects* 12.19).[5] A good leader must be a *junzi* in the first place. As a role model, *junzi* should be virtuous himself and then lead others by virtue, and therefore develop a positive moral climate in a virtuous circle. Just as Confucius says, 'government means correctness. If you set an example by being correct, who would dare to remain incorrect?' (*Analects* 12.17).[6]

Confucius has an apparent, negative attitude towards profit-making in business activities. Confucians constantly associate 'profit' with the 'inferior man'. The Master says, 'The *junzi* is conversant with righteousness; the inferior man is conversant with profit' (*Analects* 4.16).[7] Benevolence and righteousness were regarded as the primacy over profit (see *Mencius* 1.1). The *Daxue* (*Great Learning*) also stated that 'financial profit is not considered as real profit whereas righteousness is considered the real profit' (Chan, 1963, p. 94). However, it should be noted that Confucians did not disparage profit, especially business profit as a whole, or at least emphasised that it was not the main goal of Confucians. As long as profit-making activities are not for selfish and instrumental purpose, and for the good of the whole community, profit itself is not the target of condemnation for Confucius. Contrarily, these statements above mean to exhort one to strive to attain human virtues such as humanity, righteousness, trustworthiness and so forth, and profit should not be set as their primary or exclusive goal of life; profit should merely be the involuntarily consequence of the moral behaviour of *junzi*. So a Confucian leadership of an enterprise, as a *junzi*, will regard moral attainment as more important than seeking material wellbeing (Cheung and King, 2004, p. 248).

Zhonghu (忠恕 *Altruism and Loyalty*)

Master Zeng (曾子) once pointed out that the *Dao* of Confucius consists in *zhong* (loyalty) and *shu* (altruism, like-hearted consideration) (*Analects* 4.15).[8] The Confucian Golden Rule says, 'Do not do to others what you do not want them to do to you' (*Analects* 15.24).[9] This is the Confucian altruism, or *shu* (恕), which encapsulates the reciprocal principle of interrelationship among individuals (Wang, 1999). In the context of leaders' and followers' relationship, the Confucian reciprocity is reinforced in *The Great Learning*: 'If a leader treats you in a way you dislike, do not treat those whom you lead in the same way; if those whom you lead treat you in way you dislike, do not treat your leaders in the same way'.[10] *Shu* is intimately related to *ren*, as if one can think about and treat others as one would oneself, one has undoubtedly attained humanity. Confucius says,

> For a man of *ren* is one who, wishing to establish himself, helps others to establish themselves; wishing himself to be prominent, helps others to be prominent. He is able offer himself as an example. This may be called the approach to *ren*. (*Analects* 6.30)[11]

In contrast with the foundations of reciprocity in western concepts, such as will/reason/duty (Kant), the disinterested and benevolent spectator (Mill), and fairness (Rawls), the Confucian *shu* is based on interpersonal connection (relationship with different distances) and human virtues (Chan, 2008, pp. 352–3).

As an important moral conception, the *zhong* (loyalty 忠) appears 17 times in the *Analects*. Due to the principles of *Five Cardinal Relationships* (五伦) and the *Three Bonds* (三纲), consequently *zhong* on the part of the inferior implies faithful support for the superior, which may be illustrated by complete dedication to the superior and a willingness to sacrifice one's self-interest (Chen, 2002, p. 341). In other words, people who are lower in the hierarchy must respect and obey the one who is in higher status (Hackley and Dong, 2001). However, Confucius does not advocate the kind of blind loyalty that prevailed in many later dynasties in China (Huang, 1997, p. 22). *Zhong* ought to be understood and realised through mutual obligations between the superior and the subordinate, instead of through a purely unilateral commitment from below. In the *Analects*, when Duke Ding asks about how a ruler should treat his ministers, and how ministers should serve their ruler, Confucius replies, 'a ruler should employ his ministers in accordance with *li*; the ministers should serve their lord with loyalty (*zhong*)' (*Analects* 3.19).[12] A leader will win his followers' loyalty as long as he treats them with *li*; what a leader can expect from his employees depends on what the employees expect and have got from the leader.

Zhongyong (中庸 *the Doctrine of Mean*)

The goal of social harmony and ultimately the harmony of the whole nature is consistent with the Confucian concept of *zhongyong* and the way of the Dao (Nuyen, 1999). *Zhongyong* is a situation in which every proposition and viewpoint can coexist without any bias and prejudice. It is the original status of thinking before philosophy differentiates from it.

When there are no stirrings of pleasure, anger, sorrow or joy, the mind is in the state of equilibrium; when those feelings have been stirred, when they are in the neutral degree, they are in the state of harmony. The equilibrium is the great root from which grow all the creatures in the universe, and the harmony is the fulfilment of the Dao of society. If the states of equilibrium and harmony are both attained, heaven and earth will be in perfect order, and all things will be nourished and flourish (*Li Ji*, Zhong Yong).[13]

This is the ideal of grand harmony in Confucianism: the absence of extremes is the foundation of the world, and if human beings follow through the cultivation of *zhongyong*, they will become exemplary persons and the world will be harmonised so that the Dao of humanity will be prevalent (Li, 2004, p. 177).

For Aristotle, the notion of human virtues is intimately connected with the ethical mean, and for each virtue, there is an appropriate mean. Aristotle defines virtue as a 'purposive disposition, lying in a mean that is relative to us and determined by a rational principle' (see Aristotle, 1976, p. 101). The Aristotelian 'mean' seeks for the equity of human beings so as to obtain the real morality, whereas the Confucian ideal has broader meaning. The Confucian 'mean' is based on the perception of the fundamental neutrality of all nature. The Confucian ideal tries to reach harmony of the whole world, which means heaven, earth and humans all in their proper place, everything never going to an extreme and remaining in a harmonious balance. An ideal Confucian leader is one who possesses the idea of balance, moderation and appropriateness:

> He [the leader] is similar to heaven and earth, and therefore never violates the natural order of things. His knowledge covers all things in the world and his way of wisdom would help all things, and therefore he does not exceed the mean. He moves in all directions and yet does not lose central direction. He enjoys life and nature given by heaven and knows the mandate of heaven. Hence he is free from worries. He is able to settle people in their land and devote himself to works of benevolence, and thus he is capable of loving. (*I Ching*, Xici)[14]

The secular understanding of *zhongyong* in later dynasties often deviated from what Confucians intended, and became a synonym for compromise, conservatism and sophisticated slickness. These words are far from the Confucian *zhongyong* which is not about going along with the flow without contention; it is not about unprincipled compromise; it stresses timely and appropriate actions; the true harmony is in his heart. As Confucius says, 'the *junzi* is harmonious but not conformable; the petty man is conformable but not harmonious' (*Analects* 13.23).[15] *Zhongyong* strongly opposes radically extreme and reckless destruction of social relations and natural laws. It requires a leader to reach equilibrium in conflicting and complicated situations, without amoral compromise; he should always be flexible in his behaviour according to timing and situation but firm in his basic moral principles.

In summary, for Confucians the contrast between the wise and the unwise is not that the former have knowledge and competence while the latter do not, but that the former is virtuous while the latter is wicked (Yao, 2006). Although wisdom needs to be substantialised through intellectual development, this intellectual capacity needs to be moralised. By moralising the intellectual capacity, the true 'wise' can therefore be distinguished from the superficial 'clever'. Confucius says, 'the man of wisdom is free from delusion; the man of humanity is free from anxiety; the man of courage is free from fear' (*Analects* 9.29).[16] A man who has the real wisdom to discern right from wrong, the real *ren* to know the Dao of humanity and the real courage[17] to do what is righteous fear-lessly can be considered as *junzi*, the exemplary person who perfectly integrates merit with virtue.

Discussion and Conclusion

In short, modern society tends to isolate merit from considerations of ethical value as the basis for appraising leadership. Talented but unethi-cal leaders are often considered as effective leaders by their pandering to the short-term interests of their shareholders. The Confucian meritoc-racy that I propose in this chapter aims to couple merits (intelligence, knowledge and ability) with virtue or moral worthiness (and the latter is given priority), and these two aspects together should be taken as a criterion for evaluating effective leadership.

To leaders, the central managerial challenge is, on the one hand, to organise human resources, develop harmonious interrelationships and establish the rules of interaction in order to achieve collective objec-tives; yet, on the other hand, it is to make wise strategic decisions for the organisation's development, which should be based on fully under-standing related policies and law, consumers' needs, its competitors, the outside environment and so forth. All these factors, either inside or outside of an organisation, are better considered in 'relationships'. The crux to grasp Confucian thinking in depth is to put it in the con-text of 'relationship': Confucian virtues, including *ren*, righteousness, trustworthiness, *li*, *zhongshu*, *zhongyong*, *junzi* and so forth, only exist, and must be fulfilled, in the interdependency and interrelationships of human beings and the outside world, as Confucians view society as a community of interrelated responsibilities, and individuals cannot exist independently. To achieve the constant harmony of society, people must behave properly according to their roles and in accordance with *li*: treat others the way one would like others to be treated; keep a moderate mind and behave flexibly according to timing and the situation, and do not violate radically and extremely the Dao of humanity.

So, wise and virtuous leaders would not take for granted that they are distinguished, talented and own the absolute authority of leadership, and thus isolate themselves from their employees. Rather, such leaders will involve a dynamic network of relationships, will view themselves as a centre of relationships in the organisation, which means they know that their behaviour – morally or immorally – will set an example and strongly affect their followers. Moreover, they will try to create a good balance between the interests of the organisation and the larger interests of society, as harmonious social relationships are of utmost importance to them. Although some forms of immorality in business may lead to quick profits, and therefore produce a resplendent illusion of effective management and leadership, ethical leadership in the Confucian sense of possessing both virtue and merit will benefit the business and the whole of society in the long run.

To offer an ethical approach to organisational leadership, from the perspective of Confucian meritocracy, there is an effective standard. This standard would have three levels to judge whether a leadership is effective: first, does she or he reach inner peace and harmony by the constant self-cultivation of virtue? Second, does his or her organisation build or maintain a harmonious environment for its employees? Finally, does his or her organisation make some contribution to the harmony and wellbeing of the whole of society? These three levels concern oneself, the internal context and the external context respectively. To achieve harmony among these three levels requires wise leadership possessing both virtue and merit in the Confucian sense.

Specifically, in addition to the business profit that his or her organisation has gained, Confucian virtues,[18] including benevolence, trustworthiness, *li*, *zhongyong* and so on, combine with the three levels of harmony and should be integrated in the evaluation criteria of effective leadership. Furthermore, as evaluation criteria, each virtue must be mutually integrating, constraining and supporting, as each single virtue by itself will not be enough to assess leadership in practice. In the spirit of Confucian concern for individual moral cultivation and communal harmony, the public would evaluate an organisation's leadership through a more holistic, critical and dynamic way by taking Confucian merits (talent and virtue) as the criteria. Consequently, the general population can be influenced and educated by exemplary leadership. Yet, the specific criteria and processes of evaluating leadership which are based on Confucian meritocracy are not the focus of this chapter and will be delimited here. It may well provide a topic for our continuing and future research.

Notes

1. For Aristotle, the best life should be that which most fully exercise one's rational activity – the life of contemplation (Yu, 1998).
2. Different from Aristotle's virtue, which hinges on practical wisdom, Confucian virtue is contingent on humanity in interrelated social relationship. The former emphasises how a person as a self-determining being can live well in society, and the latter emphasises how a person as a relationship-determining being can live morally and properly in society (see Yu, 1998).

3. '为政以德。譬如北辰。居其所，而众星共之。' All Confucian texts are translated from the original by the author except where otherwise attributed.
4. '子曰: 道之以政, 齐之以刑, 民免而无耻; 道之以德, 齐之以礼, 有耻且格。'
5. '… 子欲善而民善矣。君子之德风, 小人之德草, 草上之风, 必偃。'
6. '政者, 正也, 子帅以正, 孰敢不正?'
7. '子曰: 君子喻于义, 小人喻于利。'
8. '子曰: "参乎！吾道一以贯之。" 曾子曰: "唯。" 子出。门人问曰: "何谓也?" 曾子曰: "夫子之道, 忠恕而已矣!"'
9. '子贡问曰: "有一言而可以终生行之者乎?" 子曰: "其恕乎。己所不欲, 勿施于人。"'
10. 《大学》。'所恶于上毋以使下; 所恶于下毋以事上'.
11. '夫仁者, 己欲立而立人, 己欲达而达人。能近取譬, 可谓仁之方也已。'
12. '定公问: "君使臣, 臣事君, 如之何?" 孔子对曰: "君使臣以礼, 臣事君以忠"'.
13. (礼记. 中庸). '喜怒哀乐之未发谓之中, 发而皆中节谓之和。中也者, 天下之大本也; 和也者, 天下之达道也。致中和, 天地位焉, 万物育焉'.
14. (易经.系词上) '易与天地准, 故能弥纶天地之道。… 与天地相似, 故不违。知周乎万物, 而道济天下, 故不过。旁行而不流, 乐天知命, 故不忧。安土敦乎仁, 故能爱。' Translated by Chung-ying Cheng (2011).
15. '君子和而不同, 小人同而不和'.
16. '子曰: 智者不惑, 仁者不忧, 勇者不惧'.
17. For Confucius, wisdom and courage, like humanity, are characterised by a moral colour, to be distinguished from worldly intelligence and daring (Huang, 1997, p. 20). *Yong* refers to the courage to do what is righteous.
18. Here, it is vital to note that Confucian virtues must be inherited and transformed in the context of modern society. For example, the *Three Bonds* (三纲) is obviously now outdated, and it merely shows the idea of relationship bounded by certain moral standards or virtues.

References

Aristotle (1976). *The Nicomachean Ethics*, trans. J.A.K. Thomson. Penguin, Harmondsworth.

Bennis, W. (2007). 'The Challenges of Leadership in the Modern World: Introduction to the Special Issue'. *American Psychologist*, 62(1): 2–5.

de Bettignies, H.-C., P.-K. Ip, X.-Z. Bai, A. Habisch and G. Lenssen (2011). 'Practical Wisdom for Management from the Chinese Classical Traditions'. *Journal of Management Development*, 30(7/8): 623–8.

Brown, M.E., and L.K. Trevino (2006). 'Ethical Leadership: A Review and Future Directions'. *Leadership Quarterly*, 17: 595–616.

Burns, J.M. (1978). *Leadership*. Harper and Row, New York.

Chan, G.K. (2008). 'The Relevance and Value of Confucianism in Contemporary Business Ethics'. *Journal of Business Ethics*, 77: 347–60.

Chan, W.-T. (1963). *A Sourcebook of Chinese Philosophy*. Princeton University Press.

Chen, G.M. (2002). 'The Impact of Harmony on Chinese Conflict Management'. In G.M. Chen and R. Ma (eds), *Chinese Conflict Management and Resolution*, pp. 3–18. Ablex Publishing, Westport, CT.

Chen, C.C., and Y.T. Lee (eds) (2008). *Leadership and Management in China: Philosophies, Theories and Practices*. Cambridge University Press.

Cheng, C.-y. (2011). 'Confucian Global Leadership in Chinese Tradition: Classical and Contemporary'. *Journal of Management Development*, 30(7/8): 647–62.

Cheung, T.S., and A.Y. King (2004). 'Righteousness and Profitableness: The Moral Choices of Contemporary Confucian Entrepreneurs'. *Journal of Business Ethics*, 54: 245–60.

Collins, J. (2001). *Good to Great*. HarperCollins, New York.

Fingarette, H. (1998). *Confucius: The Secular as Sacred*. Waveland Press, Prospect Heights, IL.

Hackley, C.A., and Q.W. Dong (2001). 'American Public Relations Networking Encounters China's Guanxi'. *Public Relations Quarterly*, 46(2): 16–19.

Hing, L.S., D.R. Bobocel, M.P. Zanna, D.D. Garcia, S.S. Gee and K. Orazetti (2011). 'The Merit of Meritocracy'. *Journal of Personality and Social Psychology*, 101(3): 433–50.

Huang, C.-C. (1997). *The Analects of Confucius: A Literal Translation with an Introduction and Notes*. Oxford University Press.

Ip, P.-K. (2011). 'Practical Wisdom of Confucian Ethical Leadership: A Critical Inquiry'. *Journal of Management Development*, 30(7/8): 685–96.

Jones, C.A. (2005). 'Wisdom Paradigm for the Enhancement of Ethical and Profitable Business Practices'. *Journal of Business Ethics*, 57: 363–75.

Kerr, C. (1983). *The Future of Industrial Societies*. Harvard University Press, Cambridge, MA.

Krames, J.A. (2003). *What the Best CEOs Know: Seven Exceptional Leaders and Their Lessons for Transforming any Business*. McGraw-Hill, New York.

Lai, C. (2010). 'Virtue Ethics and Confucian Ethics'. *Dao*, 9: 275–87.

Li, C.Y. (2004). 'Zhongyong as Grand Harmony – An Alternative Reading to Ames and Hall's Focusing the Familiar'. *Dao: Journal of Comparative Philosophy*, 3(2): 173–88.

Liu, H. (2009). *Chinese Business: Landscapes and Strategies*. Routledge, Abingdon.

McNamee, S.J., and R.K. Miller (2004). *The Meritocracy Myth*. Roman and Littlefield, Lanham, MD.

Nahavandi, A. (2000). *The Art and Science of Leadership*. Prentice Hall, Upper Saddle River, NJ.

Nuyen, A.T. (1999). 'Chinese Philosophy and Western Capitalism'. *Asian Philosophy*, 9(1): 71–9.

Redding, S.G. (1990). *The Spirit of Chinese Capitalism*. De Gruyter, New York.

Romar, E.J. (2002). 'Virtue Is Good Business: Confucianism as a Practical Business Ethics'. *Journal of Business Ethics*, 38(1/2): 119–31.

Scully, M.A. (1997). 'Meritocracy'. In R.J. Ely, E.G. Foddy and M.A. Scully (eds) (2003), *A Reader in Gender, Work and Organization*, pp. 284–6. Blackwell, Oxford.

Tan, S.-H. (2009). 'Beyond Elitism: A Community Ideal for a Modern East Asia'. *Philosophy East and West*, 59(4): 537–53.

Trevino, L.K., K.D. Butterfield and D.M. Mcabe (1998). 'The Ethical Context in Organizations: Influences on Employee Attitudes and Behaviours'. *Business Ethics Quarterly*, 8: 447–76.

Trevino, L.K., L.P. Hartman and M. Brown (2000). 'Moral Person and Moral Manager: How Executives Develop a Reputation for Ethical Leadership'. *California Management Review*, 42: 128–42.

Vieira, W. (2011). 'Leadership and Meritocracy'. Available at http://waltervieira.com/leadership-and-meritocracy (accessed March 2012).

Wah, S.S. (2010). 'Confucianism and Chinese Leadership'. *Chinese Management Studies*, 4(3): 280–5.

Wang, Q.J. (1999). 'The Golden Rule and Interpersonal Care – From a Confucian Perspective'. *Philosophy East and West*, 49(4): 415–38.

Warner, M. (2008). 'Reassessing Human Resource Management "with Chinese Characteristics": An Overview'. *International Journal of Human Resource Management*, 19(5): 771–801.

Yang, S.-Y. (2011). 'Wisdom Displayed through Leadership: Exploring Leadership-related Wisdom'. *Leadership Quarterly*, 22: 616–32.

Yao, X.-Z. (2006). *Wisdom in Early Confucian and Israelite Traditions: A Comparative Study*. Ashgate, Farnham.

Young, M. (1958). *The Rise of the Meritocracy*. Penguin, New York.

Yu, J.-Y. (1998). 'Virtue: Confucius and Aristotle'. *Philosophy East and West*, 48(2): 323–47.

Yu, J.-Y. (2006). 'Yi: Practical Wisdom in Confucius's *Analects*'. *Journal of Chinese Philosophy*, 33(3): 335–48.

Yu, J.-Y. (2009). *The Ethics of Confucius and Aristotle: Mirrors of Virtue*. Renmin University Press, Beijing.

Yuan, L. (2012). 'Exploring the Philosophical Underpinnings of Western HRM'. *Frontiers of Philosophy in China*, 7(2): 317–46.

8
Wang Dao Management as Wise Management

Po-Keung Ip

Introduction

The spectacular rise of China as a world economic power has prompted management scholars to probe the management aspect of China's business. One major question asked is whether there is a uniquely Chinese management approach and practice that has emerged in the process (Leung, 2012; Chen and Miller, 2010). This chapter primarily responds to this question by critically examining one traditional Chinese concept that may have relevance to today's management. The chapter reconstructs a concept of *Wang Dao* (王道, Kingly Way of Governance, or Kingly Way), originally proposed in the Confucian classics, and articulates its modern meanings in the context of business. The idea of *Wang Dao* (or *Wangdao*) was first advocated by Mencius as the supreme moral principle of political governance. The idea of *Wang Dao* stood as a minority view of governance amid a dominant ethos of governance during the Warring States period (476–221 BCE) in China. The dominant way of governance in that period was by force and conquest, which resembles the way a hegemon would rule a country. This way of governance was fittingly named *Ba Dao* (霸道, the Hegemonly Way) at that time. *Wang Dao*, in contrast, is governance by benevolence and moral rightness or appropriateness. Its corporate version is articulated as *Wang Dao* management. Whether *Wang Dao* is wise management is contingent on the meanings of wise management and wisdom. The meanings of wisdom, which are often regarded as elusive and difficult to define, are discussed by utilising the results of recent conceptualisations of wisdom in the literature and the sense in which *Wang Dao* is wise is examined. A case that approximates the ideal of *Wang Dao* here is introduced as an illustrative example of how *Wang Dao* may manifest in the real world of business.

Wang Dao as Conceived by Mencius

The idea of *Wang Dao* occupied a pivotal position in the thought of Mencius (or Mengzi, 372–289 BCE), the second Confucian sage. Another leading follower of Confucius, Xunzi (313–238 BCE), contributed substantially to this idea. The idea was articulated alongside another salient idea – *ren zheng* (benevolent governance). Both *Wang Dao* and *ren zheng* were conceived as the right way of ruling a country and stand at the core of the Confucian political ideal and vision which exhorts that politics should be practised in accordance with virtues (*de*) (為政以德, *wei zheng yi de*). These political concepts and ideals have ramifications and applications that go far beyond the domain of politics. They can properly be adapted to the familial, corporate, societal as well as international domains. A corporate version of *Wang Dao* is articulated in the next section.

For Mencius, deploying *Wang Dao* to rule a country is the supremely moral way of governance. It is worth noting that *Wang Dao* governance closely approximates *ren zheng*. Indeed, the two words '*ren zheng*' (benevolent governance) were first coined by Mencius and the idea that they represented has since exerted a lasting impact on Chinese political thinking and culture. In his many dialogues with the princes, dukes and kings about the way of government, Mencius frequently invoked the ideas of *ren zheng*. This idea emerged in one important discourse of Mencius with King Hui of Liang when the latter asked about the way of good government. In response, Mencius cited Qin and Chu, two powerful states at that time that ran the government in ways which were against *ren zheng*. Mencius explained how these states did things that were anti-*ren zheng*:[1]

> The rulers of those States rob their people of their time, so that they cannot plough and weed their fields, in order to support their parents. Their parents suffer from cold and hunger. Brothers, wives, and children are separated and scattered abroad. Those rulers, as it were, drive their people into pit-falls, or drown them. Your Majesty will go on to punish them. In such a case, who will oppose your Majesty? In accordance with this is the saying, 'The benevolent has no enemy.' (*Liang Hui Wang I*)

In another discourse, Mencius positively explained the features of *ren zheng* as follows:

> The way of the people is this: If they have a certain livelihood, they will have a fixed heart; if they have not a certain livelihood, they

have not a fixed heart. If they have not a fixed heart, there is nothing which they will not do in the way of self-abandonment, of moral deflection, of depravity, and of wild license. When they have thus been involved in crime, to follow them up and punish them – this is to entrap the people. How can such a thing as entrapping the people be done under the rule of a benevolent man? Therefore, a ruler who is endowed with talents and virtue will be gravely complaisant and economical, showing a respectful politeness to his ministers, and taking from the people only in accordance with regulated limits. (*Teng Wen Gong I*)

It is clear from the above passage that *ren zheng* means government by *ren* concerns and *ren* acts. *Ren* is the capacity to practise benevolent or kind deeds buttressed by the emotion of benevolence. For Mencius, this capacity to be kind to others, apart from being a cardinal virtue of humanity, is also an inborn human attribute. In addition to *ren*, Confucians also sees *yi* as the virtue or ability to undertake morally appropriate or right acts, as another vital element which often works in tandem with *ren*, for *ren zheng*. In another famous passage (*Liang Wai Wang I*) Mencius explicitly advocated that *ren* and *yi* were the right ways to run a state, in contrast to one based on interests and gain, the dominant ethos of the Warring States Period.

Thus, *ren zheng* and *Wang Dao* in essence refer to governance principally guided by *ren* and *yi*, supported by other moral correlatives. Among these correlatives, there are three additional cardinal virtues: *li* (the ability to follow rituals and norms, or to comply with norms of propriety); *zhi* (the ability to conduct wise acts) and *xin* (the capacity to be trustworthy). These attributes, combined with *ren* and *yi*, form the core that defines the essence of Confucian morality. It was this virtue-based morality that enabled rulers, officials, educated people and commoners to achieve and sustain a moral way of governance and compliance.

Wang Dao is quintessentially ethical governance which requires its institutions, policies, values, leadership and so forth to be guided and constrained by the core moral dictates of benevolence, moral rightness and their correlates. Leaving details of the governance structure and process aside, *Wang Dao* governance and politics are admittedly very high political ideals to achieve. But the difficulty in achieving *Wang Dao* itself is not a definitive proof of its unworthiness or irrelevance, as there are many unanticipated and intervening factors that may hinder its realisation. Its worthiness has to be assessed on its own merits and its relevance has to be gauged by how well it is connected to the real world. For the present purposes, we ask whether *Wang Dao* is a wise way of management.

Is *Wang Dao* Wisdom?

Philosophers have been thinking and debating about wisdom for millennia. Major religions and cultures have produced diverse traditions of wisdom thinking. Recently, the concept has received animated attention from psychologists and social scientists, as well as neuroscientists and evolutionary biologists. This section gives a brief account of ideas of wisdom in western literature coupled with concepts of wisdom in the Chinese tradition to reap some comparative insights.

One influential view in the psychological literature (Sternberg, 2003, p. 152) viewed wisdom as the application of successful intelligence and creativity mediated by values towards the achievement of a common good through a balance among intrapersonal, interpersonal and extra-personal interests, over short and long terms, in order to achieve a balance among adaptation to existing environments, shaping of existing environments and the selection of new environments. This is a highly complicated concept which contains diverse complex elements, and has multiple dimensions, as well as time horizons. Also, intelligence and creativity are taken as the bases for wisdom. They are necessary but not sufficient conditions for wisdom. In a recent formulation, Jordan and Sternberg (2007, pp. 3–4) redefined wisdom as the ability to balance and meet the interests and wellbeing of multiple constituencies over the long and short terms, using information that is based on truth and logic to help balance multiple interests. For Sternberg, wisdom essentially contains values, balanced interests of diverse stakeholders, multiple time horizons, knowledge and logic, and the common good. Management and organisation scholars have tried to articulate management wisdom in different dimensions (Kessler and Bailey, 2007). Nonaka and Takeuchi (2011) see practical wisdom as tacit knowledge acquired from experience that enables people to make prudent judgments and take actions based on actual situations, guided by values and morals. Although less complicated than Sternberg's model, this concept has some broad overlaps with it: practical knowledge, experience and values, among other things. There is a variety of conceptualisations of wisdom in the psychological literature; the bulk of these concepts, by virtue of their having strongly practical connotations, have meanings that approximate that of *phronèsis*.

Philosophical concepts of wisdom can be found in both the western and Chinese traditions. Aristotle's notion of wisdom is a leading representative in the West (Trowbridge, 2011). For Aristotle (2000), there are two kinds of wisdom: *phronèsis*, practical wisdom, and *sophia*, metaphysical wisdom. The former helps people to deal with practical problems in the world. Matters in politics and ethics in social and personal lives are objects of *phronèsis*. The latter kind enables one to master the ultimate nature of the universe. The result of *sophia* is the achievement of knowledge of the supernatural, transcendent and metaphysical realms. The object of *sophia* is metaphysical knowledge. Aristotle identifies a man who possesses practical wisdom to be one who is 'able to deliberate well about what is good and expedient for himself, not in some particular respect, e.g. about what sorts of thing conduce to health or to strength, but about what sorts of thing conduce to the good life in general'. Practical wisdom is 'a reasoned and true state of capacity to act with regard to human goods'. And it is a virtue as well (*Nicomachean Ethics*, VI, 5).

In the Chinese tradition, particularly Confucianism, *zhi*, wisdom, is primarily viewed as a cardinal virtue which helps an individual to achieve the practical and moral ends of a worthy life. It includes the ability to make moral decisions, to lead a moral life, to care for one's family, to rule a country ethically and to be a superior and virtuous person. *Zhi* is seldom conceived in isolation, but is seen as intimately interconnected with *ren* and *yi*, the two other cardinal virtues. For Confucius, the major functions of *zhi* are to work in unison with *ren* and *yi*, as well as other cardinal virtues to aid a person to do the good and right things, to frame intelligent choices, to exercise discretion, to select and follow legitimate rituals or norms and to guide, conduct and bind relationships, both in personal and sociopolitical relations. In so doing, *zhi*, together with *ren*, *yi*, *li* (propriety or ritual-following) and *xin* (trustworthiness), forms the moral core of a virtuous person to do what is considered to be right and good and ultimately to define and sustain the ideal social and moral order of society.

The words 'zhi' (智, wisdom) and 'zhi' (知, knowledge) in Chinese, though having different forms, are used interchangeably in many contexts. They have many semantic overlaps. To be wise sometimes means to have knowledge, but to be wise often means more than having knowledge. Virtues are the critical ingredient in the Confucian sense of *zhi*. The following citation from *Lunyu* (the *Analects*) demonstrates this crucial point: 'Fan Chi asked what constituted wisdom. The Master said, "To give one's self earnestly to the duties due to men, and, while respecting spiritual beings, to keep aloof from them, may be called wisdom"' (*Yong Ye* 22). This passage seems to invoke the respect of spiritual beings as one constituent of wisdom. However, Confucius also advised people to keep a respectful detachment from them. This is consistent with Confucius' predominantly this-worldly concern, which focuses primarily on the imminent issues and concerns of human society, and seldom on matters in the supernatural realm. Imminence, rather than transcendence, is the realm in which wisdom ought to apply and operate. This priority for imminence is particularly pronounced in Confucianism in the classical period, that is, from the Spring and Autumn period (771–475 BCE) to the Warring States period. The following passage in *Lunyu* testifies to this concern:

> Ji Lu asked about serving the spirits of the dead. The Master said, 'While you are not able to serve men, how can you serve their spirits?' Ji Lu added, 'I venture to ask about death?' He was answered, 'While you do not know life, how can you know about death?' (*Xian Jin* 12)

In Confucius' description of 'the three ways' of *Junzi*, the superior moral man, wisdom is viewed as one of them: 'The Master said, "The wise are free from perplexities; the virtuous from anxiety; and the bold from fear"' (*Zi Han* 29). Other attributes of the wise include, 'The wise find pleasure in water; the virtuous find pleasure in hills. The wise are active; the virtuous are tranquil. The wise are joyful; the virtuous are long-lived' (*Yong Ye* 23).

Mencius extended the meaning of *zhi* by conceiving it as one of the four *germs* or *buds* (四端, *sze duan*) of human natural goodness. As an advocate of the innate goodness of human beings, Mencius believed that all human beings are endowed with four basic human moral feelings or sentiments which he saw as the buds of human goodness. They include the feelings of commiseration, shame and dislike, respect and reverence, and right and wrong. Importantly, the feeling of commiseration is the bud of *ren* (benevolence), the feeling of shame and dislike is the bud of *yi* (rightness), the feeling of respect and reverence is the bud of *li* (propriety or norm-complying) and the feeling of right and wrong is the bud of *zhi* (wisdom) (*Gong Sun Chou I*). Indeed, Mencius wrote,

> Everyone has the feeling of commiseration, everyone has a feeling of shame and dislike; everyone has the feeling of reverence and respect;

and everyone has the feeling of right and wrong. The feeling of commiseration nurtures *ren*, the feeling of shame and dislike establishes
yi; the feeling of reverence and respect forms *li*; and the feeling of
right and wrong develops *zhi*. (*Gaozi I*)

Furthermore, Mencius asserted that *ren*, *yi*, *li* and *zhi* are inborn
human attributes, not something imposed on us from outside. How
the four sentiments as seeds of human goodness are interrelated or
functioned together is not entirely clear; what is clear is that they are
bundled together as potential for being and doing good. Mencius also
thought that given the right environment and the proper effort of nurturing, these seeds could flourish into vital virtues that guide and drive
a moral life.

Wisdom for Mencius not only can aid us to distinguish right from
wrong, it is also the result and manifestation of a developing or developed human potential for goodness. The senses of right and wrong here
presumably include both the *cognitive* sense of true and false, and the
moral sense of right and wrong. More importantly, to the extent that
wisdom is seen as the bud of goodness, it is intimately linked to the
realisation of human goodness and destined for a moral purpose. In this
sense, *zhi* is essentially *practical* in nature.

For Confucians, *phronèsis* wisdom is inherently practical and functions for a moral purpose. To conduct one's life successfully in society
requires knowing oneself as well as perceiving the abilities, desires, intentions, characters and behaviours of other people, all of which require
practical wisdom. In other words, it is imperative for people to understand
humanity and society, and the *Dao*² that undergirds and sustains them,
and this level of understanding requires wisdom. In sum, Confucian
wisdom is this-worldly as it is practical and moral. Metaphysical truth
is not the major concern. Confucian wisdom approximates Aristotle's
sense of *phronèsis*.

It is interesting to see whether, and to what extent, this notion of
wisdom shares some commonalities with modern notions of wisdom.
Recent conceptualisations of wisdom from diverse disciplinary sources
identify several of its major characteristics (Meeks, 2009): pro-social attitudes and behaviours, pragmatic knowledge of life, emotional homeostasis, self-understanding, tolerance of diversity, effective handling
of uncertainty and ambiguity, among others. Pro-social attitudes and
behaviours include those that are motivated by the ideal of the common
good with wisdom as a necessity in achieving the common good. To say
that a person has a pragmatic knowledge of life is to say that person

possesses a body of substantive and procedural knowledge of people and society, as well as the capacity to lead a good and meaningful life. Emotional homeostasis refers to emotional stability in the face of uncertainty, and having positive attitudes in the face of adversity, as well as the absence of negative emotions towards others. Self-understanding is the capacity of knowing one's values, goals, desires, strengths and weaknesses as well as a capacity for being self-reflective. Tolerance is the ability to tolerate differences in values and views. The ability to deal with uncertainty and ambiguity is the possession of a mind that recognises the normality of uncertainty and ambiguity in real life, and the ability to deal with them. Rooney, McKenna and Liesch (2010) identify five core elements of wisdom: values tolerance, self-insight, balance of intelligences, emotional understanding and regulation and tolerance of ambiguity and uncertainty. Although using different terms to denote the various core elements of wisdom, these works are focusing on areas which have many overlaps. McKenna (2012) in a recent address reasons that moral commitment (Sternberg, 2004) and conation (Hannah, Avolio and May, 2011) should be added to the core of wisdom. Against this set of attributes, one can see that Confucian wisdom broadly shares several dimensions of the core of wisdom: pro-social, pragmatic, practical, moral and for the human good, among others. To give a full account of these connections requires more detailed analysis that goes beyond this discussion. However, to the extent that *Wang Dao* is quintessentially *ethical* governance with a *practical* mission, it possesses the salient attributes of wisdom – it is wisdom.

Wang Dao in the Corporate World

What would *Wang Dao* mean in the business context? We briefly articulate what *Wang Dao* would mean with respect to corporate values and mission, organisational structure and management, as well as leadership of a *Wang Dao*-inspired firm.

Using a caricature of an ideal-type *Wang Dao* firm, we would be able to identify characteristics of these major aspects. The firm would adopt *ren* and *yi* as its core values to define its missions and goals, structure and process, as well as leadership. *Li* as norms and rules, being the third component of the core, has to be guided and constrained by *ren* and *yi* to have moral legitimacy. Thus, the *Wang Dao* firm could alternatively be named as a *ren-yi* firm (Ip, 2009b). *Ren, yi* and the legitimised *li* would also serve as cardinal principles to shape its strategies, policies and processes. The organisational structure and management practices are guided and regulated by *ren*, *yi* and *li*. People in the organisation – that is, internal stakeholders from the board directors, CEO, managers down to line workers on the factory floor and at the sales counter at the bottom of the organisational hierarchy – would embrace and learn to embrace *ren*, *yi* and *li*, and act in ways that are consistent with them. Leadership would be ethics-driven (Ip, 2011) and a workforce that is ethics-sensitive and competent should be key ingredients of the human capital of the firm. External stakeholders, in particular suppliers and customers, would be treated in ways consistent with *Wang Dao*. To use managing a supplier as an example of Wang Dao management, the firm would use *ren*, *yi* and *li* as the bases to manage ethically a supplier company. This would include ethically guiding, regulating and training how a supplier would handle the labour rights of its workers relating to working hours, overtime, fair compensation, promotion, health and safety, the right to collective bargaining and the right to form independent unions, as well as the dignity and wellbeing of the workers. To further illustrate how *Wang Dao* management is manifested in the real world, a real case is introduced in the next section.

A Case – *Wangdaoism* of Stan Shih

Stan Shih of the Acer Group is the most ardent advocate of *Wang Dao* management among prominent Chinese business leaders in Taiwan in recent years. After founding Acer, Shih had been the company's Chairman and CEO until his retirement from the firm in December 2004. Over more than three decades at the helm of the company, Shih has developed a vision of management that he named '*Wangdao* management' or '*Wangdaoism*'. For Shih, *Wangdaoism* underlies the core of Acer's major management principles and practices.

The Acer Group is a global personal computer company headquartered in Taiwan. It was founded (as Multitech) in 1976 and is now the second largest computer maker in the world. Acer's core business includes producing computer notebooks, tablet computers, servers, storage devices, displays, smartphones and peripherals, and also offers e-business services to businesses, governments and consumers. In the early 2000s, Acer transformed itself into a designer, marketer and distributor of computer and electronic products and services from a manufacturer, while outsourcing manufacturing to contractors. As a global company, Acer has subsidiaries in North America, Australia, India and Europe. As of 2010, it had a revenue of USD 19,978.7 million, profits of USD 480 million, and had a staff of 7757 worldwide (2011).[3]

As the idea of *Wangdaoism* is deeply intertwined with the practices that gave rise to it, it is difficult to separate these practices from the idea. According to Shih, the core elements of *Wangdaoism* include 'Acer 123', 'not hoarding one's knowledge and skill', profit-sharing and joint ownership, empowerment of employees and meritocracy, among other things. In fact, many of these elements were developed in Acer's formative years. The idea of Acer 123 refers to a practice that treats customers as the most important stakeholders, while treating employees as the second and shareholders as the third. The practice of 'not hoarding one single skill' from employees refers to Acer's practice of offering ample training to employees to help them develop their potential abilities. Shih also allowed employees to own shares in the company, who were thus able to share profits together, which was an extraordinary policy for companies at that time. Supporting this management practice are some core beliefs and values which Shih personally dearly holds (Lin and Hou, 2010; Shih and Lin, 1996; Shih, 2011). Shih subscribes to a belief of enlightened self-interest to the effect that a company should aim to create value for others – for example, customers, suppliers, society – while the company would also reap benefits in the process. Executives should use this principle to guide and restrain their self-interests in their corporate thinking and actions. An enlightened self-interest would bring and sustain values and benefits both for the company and other stakeholders, making business sustainable. More importantly, Shih believes that businesses should have a large role to play in society in addition to creating wealth for shareholders. Another core belief that undergirds *Wangdaoism* is Shih's belief in the natural goodness of human nature. This belief is basically Confucian, though Shih does not explicitly admit it. Meritocracy is another major value that underlies Shih's *Wangdaoism*. This relates particularly to the issue of company leadership succession. This value is best reflected in Shih's personal decision not to allow his children to inherit the company, but to allow non-family employees who have the ability to apply for the job. Broadly interpreted, it is easy to see that Shih's *Wangdaoism* shares some of the features of *Wang Dao* articulated earlier in this chapter. Notwithstanding its boldness and outlier innovations, Shih's *Wangdaoism* is still under development and its final version has yet to emerge.

Conclusion

It is clear that *Wang Dao* management is a form of wise management. It is wise because it is ethics-based, strongly social, practical, self-reflective, diversity tolerant, knowledge regarding, and may be long-term oriented, among other things. These are major attributes of a *Wang Dao* firm and its leadership. This chapter has set out a concept of *Wang Dao* and laid out mainly its positive elements, and has fleshed out some preliminary features of its supply-chain management. The full meanings and implications of *Wang Dao* management in all salient aspects of a firm have not been explored. As indicated earlier, a *Wang Dao* firm is, in effect, a *ren-yi* firm that has downsides and challenges (Ip 2000, 2009a, 2009b), which requires further probing. Shih's version of *Wangdaoism*, in its maturity, may not be fully in line with the ideas expounded in this chapter, which is conceptual in nature. The Acer experience suffices as an illustrative, albeit brief, example of the fact that some form of *Wangdaoism* is a realisable management practice. If the features of one single coherent concept of *Wang Dao* management are to be fully worked out, it will probably have a range of varied management styles practised under its name in the real world of business. Finally, notwithstanding Acer's case, how valuable would *Wang Dao* management be to the business world has to be further stress-tested.[4]

Notes

1. The translations below are adopted from those of Legge (2012) and Chan (1963), with my own amendments. The chapters of the cited work are in brackets.
2. Dao means the true principles or ways that regulate humanity and society.
3. In the *2011 Fortune Global 500*, 'Acer' is no. 487 (http://money.cnn.com/magazines/fortune/global500/20110, accessed July, 2012).
4. I thank the editors, especially Mike Thompson, for offering helpful comments that improved the chapter.

References

Aristotle (2000). *Nicomachean Ethics*, trans. W.D. Ross. NetLibrary, Boulder, CO.

Chan, W.T. (1963). *Source Book in Chinese Philosophy*. Princeton University Press.

Chen, M.-J., and D. Miller (2010). 'West Meets East: Toward an Ambicultural Approach to Management'. *Academy of Management Perspectives*, 24(4): 6–16.

Hannah, S.T., B.J. Avolio and D.R. May (2011). 'Moral Maturation and Moral Conation: A Capacity Approach to Explaining Moral Thought and Action'. *Academy of Management Review*, 36(4): 663–85.

Ip, P.-K. (2000). 'Developing Virtuous Corporation with Chinese Characteristics for the Twenty-first Century'. In F.-J. Richter (ed.), *The Dragon Millennium: Chinese Business in the Coming World Economy*, pp. 183–206. Quorum Books, Westport, CT.

Ip, P.-K. (2009a). 'The Challenge of Developing a Business Ethics in China'. *Journal of Business Ethics*, 88(2): 211–24.

Ip, P.-K. (2009b). 'Is Confucianism Good for Business Ethics in China?' *Journal of Business Ethics*, 88(3): 463–76.

Ip, P.-K. (2011). 'Practical Wisdom of Confucian Ethical Leadership – A Critical Inquiry'. *Journal of Management Development*, 30(7/8): 685–96.

Jordan, J., and R.J. Sternberg (2007). 'Wisdom in Organizations: A Balanced Theory Analysis'. In E.H. Kessler and J.R. Bailey (eds), *Handbook of Organizational and Managerial Wisdom*, pp. 3–19. Sage Publications, Thousand Oaks.

Kessler, E.H., and J.R. Bailey (2007) (eds). *Handbook of Organisational and Managerial Wisdom*. Sage Publications, Thousand Oaks, CA.

Legge, J. (2012). *The Works of Mencius*. Electronic Library of Chinese Classics, available at http://ctext.org/mengzi.

Leung, K. (2012). 'Indigenous Chinese Management Research: Like It or Not, We Need It'. *Management and Organization Review*, 8(1): 1–5.

Li, J.T., A.S. Tsui and E. Weldon (2000) (ed.), *Management and Organizations in the Chinese Context*. Macmillan, London.

Lin, H.-C., and S.-T. Hou (2010). 'Management Lessons from the East: An Interview with Acer's Stan Shih'. *Academy of Management Perspectives*, 24(4): 17–24.

McKenna, B. (2012). 'Keynote Address. International Conference on Wise Management in Organisational Complexity, May 23–24'. China Europe International Business School, Shanghai.

Meeks, T.W. (2009). 'Neurobiology of Wisdom – A Literature Review'. *Archives of General Psychiatry*, 66(4): 355–65.

Nonaka, I., and H. Takeuchi (2011). 'The Wise Leader – How CEOs Can Learn Practical Wisdom to Help Them Do What's Right for Their Companies – and Society'. *Harvard Business Review*, May: 59–67.

Rooney, D., B. McKenna and P. Liesch (2010). *Wisdom and Management in the Knowledge Economy*. Routledge, New York.

Shih, S. (2011). 'The Spirit of Wangdao, a speech in Chinese delivered on 23 August'. Available online at http://bschool.hexun.com/2011–08–23/132721452.html (accessed May 2012).

Shih, S., and W. Lin (1996). *Reengineering Acer*. Commonwealth Publishing, Taipei (in Chinese).

Sternberg, R.J. (2003) *Wisdom, Intelligence, and Creativity Synthesized*. Cambridge University Press, New York.

Sternberg, R.J. (2004). 'What Is Wisdom and How Can We Develop It?' *Annal of The American Academy of Political and Social Science*, 591(1): 164–74.

Sternberg, R.J., and J. Jordan (2005). *A Handbook of Wisdom*. Cambridge University Press, New York.

Trowbridge, H.T. (2011). 'Waiting for Sophia: 30 Years of Conceptualizing Wisdom in Empirical Psychology'. *Research in Human Development*, 8(2): 149–64.

9
Wicked Problem: Educating for Complexity and Wisdom

Jay Hays

Introduction

The challenges confronting humanity today are many, stubborn, competing and tangled (Küpers, 2007; Walker, Daniels and Emborg, 2008). They may be more complex and far-reaching than challenges posed at any time in the past (Hinterhuber, 1996; Keating, Kauffmann and Dryer, 2001). The modern age is turbulent and fraught with uncertainty and unpredictability (Crossan, Vera and Nanjad, 2008; Scharmer et al., 2001). To make matters worse, the pace of change is relentless and accelerating. Many of the problems vexing us as we venture further into the twenty-first century are outcomes of past innovations or solutions that seemed fitting at the time, but have come back to haunt us.

There is some expectation that we will persist in making disastrous decisions with far-reaching consequences (Kunsch, Theys and Brans, 2007). This prediction is based on the enduring tendency of human beings to act with preference to narrow self-interest and immediate gain, in addition to showing a decided inability or unwillingness to think of the bigger picture and long-term consequences. Nicolaides and Yorks (2008) write on one of the paradoxes of modern times: 'we are accumulating new knowledge at an ever increasing rate, while at the same time we are confronted with the potential disasters of the unanticipated, non-linear consequences of this accumulating body of knowledge' (p. 50).

This chapter is devoted to overcoming these tendencies and equipping future leaders to safely contend with Pandora's enticing box, with educating for complexity and wisdom as the core solution. It adopts an ecological, living-system approach to exploring the way we currently and might more effectively educate those who will inherit stewardship of the planet. Such an ecological approach is not without precedent. For example, Hays (2010a, 2010b) uses an ecological model to describe collective intelligence and organisational wisdom, while Hearn and Pace (2006) develop the notion of value ecologies in understanding emerging business systems.

The ecological approach advocated intends to equip our leaders, scientists and business people with the toolsets and thinking to solve the biggest challenges of our time, as well as capitalise on opportunities over the horizon (Scharmer, 2009; Scharmer et al., 2001). Environmental concerns and dealing with them is just one example of the kind of thorny problem at issue here, where fundamentally new thinking and significant change in the way we approach problems are needed. The list, unfortunately, is long, with poverty, illiteracy, crime, health issues and, indeed, educational reform, additional examples. Such an ecological approach to education is heretical and radical, assuming that we must discard past practices and the beliefs on which they hinge – that is, change the way we educate – if we are to attain the fresh perspective and novel approaches to problem-solving necessary for sustainable solutions.

Orientation and Key Themes

Several key concepts are entertained in this chapter, namely wicked problems, education, complexity and wisdom. Each of these terms will be briefly defined and their nature and relevance to the central thesis explained. The main argument is: (P1) Conventional higher education does not sufficiently equip young professionals for the complex demands of modern business or to play active, contributing roles in their communities.

In fact, conventional education may actually be counterproductive (Rosch, 2008). Kremer and McGuinness (1998) note that traditional methods of teaching perpetuate dependency and passivity when independent thought and action are needed. Conventional education can be a complex vicious cycle – a dynamic problem system posing a wicked problem as explained below. This wicked vicious cycle may be overcome by implementing modest reforms in learning objectives and strategies, and the structure of the learning environment, including relationships between teachers and students. This represents a second proposition: (P2) Educating for complexity and wisdom in the university classroom is possible.

The reforms suggested in the section below (Educating for Complexity and Wisdom), while perhaps radical to some, are simple, sensible and realistic. It is putting them into practice that is the challenge; or, rather, overcoming the tendency of conventional education to perpetuate itself and inhibit significant change. This is part of the reason why conventional higher education is framed as a wicked problem, or at least educating for complexity and wisdom is. As will be seen, wicked problems require wicked solutions; that is, solutions whose complexity and elegance surpass that of their opponents (Beers et al., 2006; Fleckenstein et al., 2008; Keating, Kauffmann and Dryer, 2001). Thus, a third pivotal proposition: (P3) Educating for complexity and wisdom, while both possible and critical, poses a wicked problem.

Wicked Problems

Complex problems exhibit certain characteristics (Bronner, 1993; Snell, 2001). There is seldom one right answer, though there might be many partial solutions from which to choose (Bekken and Marie, 2007). The problem may have hitherto been unyielding to attempts to solve it. It may appear to have been solved only to later resurface. Solution attempts may also produce unintended, unexpected consequences (Binbasioglu and Winston, 2004; Keating, Kauffmann and Dryer, 2001; Stacey, 1995) or permit the arising of other latent problems (Husted, 1993). Problems of this nature have been called wicked, or messy (APSC, 2007; Calton and Payne, 2003; Gold, 2001; Vennix, 1999). Fleckenstein et al. (2008) have proposed use of an ecological metaphor 'as a way of knowing that is congruent with the complexity and messiness of twenty-first-century meaning making' (p. 389). Walker, Daniels and Emborg (2008) describe wicked or messy problems as 'a tangle of complexity, controversy, and uncertainty' (p. 17), while Beers et al. (2006) write that they 'can be seen as a web of problems' (p. 531).

Being able to work effectively within and upon complex systems requires more than intelligence, knowledge, and experience (Kitchener and Brenner, 1990; Snell, 2001). These attributes are sufficient when encountering typical problems and conventional situations, but not in confronting the new and unexpected (Keating, Kauffmann and Dryer, 2001; Yielder, 2004). Known solutions to unknown problems are as likely to fail or exacerbate the problem as they are to succeed (see Gharajedaghi, 2007, or Stead and Stead, 1994). Gharajedaghi and Ackhoff (1984) wrote, 'Commonly prescribed remedies are increasingly ineffective and often make things worse. The growing number of social crises and dilemmas that we face should be clear evidence that something is fundamentally wrong with the way we think about social systems' (p. 290). Wicked problems require 'a different sort of mind' (Rosch, 2008, p. 154), a new kind of thinking, creative, innovative solutions not before attempted or borrowed from other disciplines thought quite different. According to Reznitskaya and Sternberg (2004), messy problems require a type of thinking that transcends solitary frames of reference. The thinking requisite to solve wicked problems, they assert, is characterised dialogically and dialectically; the former involving fair consideration of multiple perspectives, and the latter integrating or synthesising multiple and opposing views. Bassett (2005) also included dialectic thinking as an attribute of wisdom. Underscoring the contribution of systems-thinking to seeing the whole, Gharajedaghi (2007) observes that 'the ability to synthesize separate findings into a coherent whole seems far more critical than the ability to generate information from different perspectives' (p. 476). Educating for wisdom and complexity would entail 'develop[ing] the habits of mind and action necessary to weigh evidence in the light of multiple truths and act[ing] responsibly as members of a greater global community' (Bekken and Marie, 2007, p. 56).

Intimately knowing the system allows the problem-solver to intervene at the point of greatest leverage and enables better prediction as to the effect that the intervention will have (Hays, 2010a, 2010b).

Wisdom

There are many extraordinary expositions on wisdom, and wisdom is increasingly entering mainstream disciplines (Baltes and Staudinger, 2000; and see, as examples, Grint, 2007; Hays, 2007; Roca, 2008). This section synthesises key points from the literature on wisdom, and stresses its symbiotic relationship to complexity and, together, their gathering importance to educating for the twenty-first century. One instructive definition of wisdom was put forward by Hays (2007):

> Wisdom is essentially doing the right thing. The wise act judiciously and prudently in the appreciation of the fullness of context, respond to complex problems in contentious circumstances in a far-sighted and appropriate manner, and care about and prepare for a future that matters. To neglect the fullness of context and limit our horizons is unwise. (p. 84)

Important facets of this definition include that there is a moral and ethical component in doing the right thing (see Sternberg, 1998). There is, at the same time, an action component: wisdom 'is rooted in action rather than simply reflection' (Grint, 2007, p. 236). A wise act is a deliberate one that concerns the common good; it serves interests greater than the self. Wisdom is less what you know than what you do – how you use your knowledge, experience and skill. One may be potentially wise, but it is only through action that wisdom is manifest (Bierly, Kessler and Christensen, 2000).

While values and definitions of what is right may differ across peoples, situations and even times, the wise will reflect on what is right and best, all things considered, before taking action (Hays, 2007). They will possess a strong moral compass and act in accordance with it. They will not privilege self-interest above concern for the greater good (Baltes and Staudinger, 2000; Bassett, 2005). This suggests that they also know themselves very well and are able to detect their own biases, values and motives and balance them with those of others (Eriksen, 2009; Reznitskaya and Sternberg, 2004). This also reflects that wisdom is not (merely) about intelligence or cleverness: clever individuals might do the smart thing, but remain unwise.

Wisdom as conceptualised here stresses caring and stewardship. There is a concern for the bigger picture and long-term consequences. This means that choices and actions will favour the greater good and posterity over immediate gain; even when additional work or investment is necessary. While implicit, courage and persistence may be required to do the right thing in the face of opposition (Bierly, Kessler and Christensen, 2000). There is an emphasis on understanding as much as possible regarding situations before acting, and taking the perspectives of all concerned into consideration. This implies inquiring, empathising and deliberating before acting, and probably entails a good deal of listening as well (Hinterhuber, 1996). This is one area where the linkage between wisdom and complexity is clearest. Knowing the system, the wise would be more likely to anticipate correctly the outcomes of an intervention (Hays, 2007). Wisdom is complexity understood and enacted (Küpers, 2007).

Finally, the wise will likely promote innovative and sustainable solutions, setting aside what is already known or believed to be the case in favour of knowledge that emerges through inquiry and openness (Purser and Petranker, 2005). Such openness is thought to be an aspect of humility, a virtue which many scholars agree characterises the wise (Grint, 2007; Hinterhuber, 1996; Snell, 2001; Sternberg, 1998). It is humility that allows the wise to accept that they do not know everything or have to be seen as knowing it all; to accept that there is much to be learned. While humility may characterise the wise, it is a crucial aspect of the learner (those learning), as depicted by Brown (2004). What this means for education is that inquiry, curiosity and learning are the most important skills and habits that might be fostered, and should be emphasised over accumulation of knowledge (Nicolaides and Yorks, 2008).

Complexity and Complex Adaptive Systems

Complexity refers to the plurality of components comprising a system and their interrelationships and intermingling of influences (Bonn, 2005; Hays, 2007). The more complex the system, the greater and some-times less obvious the relationships amongst elements (Gharajedaghi, 2007). A system is essentially a set of elements that work together and that are in some measure distinct from other systems and the environment. Living systems work together in concert to achieve some end. The human body is a system. It is complete in and of itself, but it is dependent on the greater environment for sustenance and on other human beings for reproduction. It is an integral part of a vital living ecology, and can really only begin to be understood within its ecological context. The human organism may be a distinct individual within its environment, but it is in no way independent of it. Furthermore, a disaggregation of the body's parts may help define its function but provides little insight into what animates its life. As Bettis and Prahalad (1995) have said, 'reductionism is not a viable approach to studying complex systems. Knowledge of the constituent parts is not knowledge of the whole' (p. 11).

Recalling the sustainability issues introduced earlier, attempts to mas-ter our environment may have irreparable consequences. It remains to be seen whether our intelligence is sufficient to save ourselves and the environment; we need a new kind of intelligence, a new conscious-ness (Brodbeck, 2002; see also, Gidley, 2009). Such intelligence will be characterised as organic and ecological, accepting that we are part of a delicate living system. Such thinking overcomes, or at least comple-ments, mechanical thinking, which conceives of the world as a great machine and we its engineers. We simply must come to see the world through different eyes and think of it more holistically, appreciatively and compassionately. The science of complexity and systemic thinking may provide the way for us to do that (Brodbeck, 2002). This is why they should be requisite parts of educating for the twenty-first century.

Systems-thinking conceives of systems as whole and tries to understand them as such (Keating, Kauffmann and Dryer, 2001; McDonald, 2003).

Systems-thinking is less an analytical skill or process than a synthesising one (Gharajedaghi, 2007). Synthesis is basically the capacity and process of putting multiple and sometimes apparently discrepant or incompatible ideas or elements together (Reznitskaya and Sternberg, 2004). It may include the ability to see or make connections between things that others do not (Bonn, 2005). Thus, it is a creative process, and germane to the innovative thinking needed to solve complex, wicked problems.

Organisations and institutions are complex adaptive systems (Bettis and Prahalad, 1995; Schneider and Somers, 2006). Such systems have definable (though permeable and mutable) boundaries, within which multiple individuals and other elements interact with one another in mutually dependent ways according to the system's structure and function (Schneider and Somers, 2006). Importantly, complex adaptive systems influence the environment as they interact with and act upon it.

A key facet of complexity theory is the concept of emergence: that order, adaptation and evolution may arise from disorderly or seemingly chaotic systems (Stacey, 1995). Scholars are increasingly suggesting that it is from systems, including organisations, at the edge of chaos – in tenuous balance between stability and instability – that new forms emerge. This is particularly important when we consider that human beings strive for stability. At the organisational level, functioning has historically been a drive to solidify the structure and define the relationships amongst parts to maximise efficiency and predictability. In short, we like to control things.

Despite our predilection for control and stability, it is resilience and adaptability that allow us to survive. The energies, unpredictabilities and possibilities at the edge of chaos generate conditions for creative and innovative responses to challenges and the ability to take advantage of opportunities (Lichtenstein, 2000; Lichtenstein et al., 2006; Stacey, 1995). This same concept can be applied to learning and educating for complexity and wisdom.

Organisational systems essentially work how they are designed, whether or not we like the way they operate (Husted, 1993). If we explore the elements of an organisation and their internal and external relationships, we can come to understand the system's functioning – how it works and why it works that way, sometimes counter-intuitively (Stacey, 1995). While they may not work as intended, systems do work as designed. This design may be organic, that is, not entirely planned and methodically imposed (see Dron, 2007); but there is a logic or order to the way systems come into being and, in fact, are ever in a process of becoming, that is not yet finished (Bettis and Prahalad, 1995).

Davidson (2010) notes, 'The future is under perpetual construction and is changed by our movement toward [it] ... our movement toward the future is movement toward an unfinished whole rather than a finished state' (p. 112). 'The world, for Freire, is necessarily unfinished and ever-evolving', observes Yielder (2004, p. 65), and, connecting it to learning, she writes, 'knowing is always becoming and is a permanent stage of discovery' (ibid.). It is also the case that no matter how intentionally well designed, a complex adaptive system's behaviour can never really be known or assured in advance (Keating, Kauffmann and Dryer, 2001). This is due to its emergent, self-organising properties.

Human beings possess the capability to fathom complex systems. Sadly, we are driven to seek simple answers and 'quick fixes', conclude Calton and Payne (2003), Nelson and Harper (2006), Schwandt (2005) and others. Van Woerkom (2004) comments that 'Because most people avoid the problems and uncertainty of conflicts that innovative processes entail ... learning processes tend to be conservative and confirm existing frames of reference' (p. 183). It is much easier to defend a relationship between two variables than to explain multiple elements in systems within systems. We feel more confident when we think we understand a problem and its causality. While comforting, striving for control and certainty is actually counterproductive: 'we limit the potential for novelty and innovation' (Davidson, 2010, p. 115).

Simple solutions for complex problems are fated to fail, as so many unsuccessful projects and initiatives bear out (Hays, 2010a; Rowland and Higgs, 2008). Solutions that first come to mind or seem obvious are probably ill conceived and have not considered the fullness of complex systems (Sice and French, 2006). This insidious process is itself an expression of problem-dynamics embedded in a complex system. Embeddedness is an important systems principle: problems cannot be isolated from the systems in which they are located, or *embedded*. Embeddedness is 'the view that a particular phenomenon can only be fully understood in relation to and as a reflection of other phenomena' (Hutchison and Bosacki, 2000, p. 180).

The system itself is nested within a larger context that must also be understood for viable problem resolution (Devine, 2005; Keating, Kauffmann and Dryer, 2001). This explains why holistic approaches to problem analysis and intervention are more likely to succeed than formulaic ones in complex environments (Clayton and Gregory, 2000; Fraser and Greenhalgh, 2001; Sice and French, 2006).

Causal Loop Diagrams are useful tools for capturing organisational dynamics. Unfortunately, maps of complex systems are messy – tangled webs of components hanging together, the spaces surrounding them uncertain and the mutual influences, or interdependence, amongst elements many, diverse and obscure (Hays, 2007, 2010a, 2010b). Gharajedaghi (2007) explains: 'A set of interdependent variables forms a circular relationship. Each variable co-produces the others and in turn is co-produced by the others. Which one comes first is irrelevant because none can exist without the others' (p. 477). Causal Loop Diagrams and their development can be powerful, helping to comprehend important phenomena related to complex systems and wicked problems. Understanding the genesis of the dampening and unintended consequences of conventional higher education, for example, and determining how best to intervene to educate more effectively for complexity and wisdom provide perfect targets for Causal Loop Diagramming. Moreover, the use of such tools in the university classroom can build sophisticated diagnostic skills and the systems-thinking mind so needed of our graduates today; and should comprise at least part of the solution to one of higher education's most significant wicked problems – educating for complexity and wisdom.

Conventional Higher Education as a Vicious Cycle

Conventional higher education is often criticised for its inability to produce graduates who are work-ready and equipped for the challenges of the twenty-first century. Business and management education has been a particular target of such criticism. Skills, abilities and orientations found lacking include initiative, leadership, communications, problem-solving, judgment, creativity, global awareness and intercultural competence, and a general inability to transfer or apply what graduates have learned in unique contexts (see Hays and Clements, 2012). While there appears to be consensus that shortcomings exist and reform is needed, there is very little written about why or how education fails and what specifically might be done to improve the situation.

These acknowledged deficiencies in university graduates come about, in part, through complex vicious cycles operating insidiously and unintentionally in the classroom, and serve to minimise learner capabilities and undermine future performance. These dynamics persist despite continuing efforts to improve. The higher education system and process have a dampening effect on the level of learning needed in the twenty-first century, while achieving perfectly well what many institutions are designed and often pushed to do: maximise throughput, ensure control and standardisation, and minimise conflict and complexity.

Educational institutions and modern organisations need to do much more to prepare people for dealing effectively with rapid change and complex problems. Increasingly, real life does not mirror the simplistic and formulaic problems presented in classrooms and training centres (Grint, 2007), and believing they do can be counterproductive (Lynch, 1999; Nicolaides and Yorks, 2008). The real world is fraught with paradox and contradiction, confusion and ambiguity, competing demands, wicked problems and disagreement amongst problem-solvers about solutions, and a perceived lack of time to consider situations sufficiently.

If, as Grint (2007) maintains (citing Wilkinson), 'the ability to live with paradox and uncertainty is a prerequisite for leadership' (p. 240), then the way we educate and develop the leaders of tomorrow must incorporate aspects of ambiguity, uncertainty and contradiction; adopting strategies that are themselves wicked.

Wicked teaching and learning strategies would be, amongst other things, provocative, contentious, equivocal, ambivalent, paradoxical, vexing, puzzling and so on – very unlike the way we educate at present: programmed and discrete, as if there is only one correct answer and all problems have one. As Sice and French (2006) have observed, students are trained for prescribed solutions to defined problems; they are not taught to question. Of course it is one thing to advocate delivering education wickedly; it is another thing entirely to do so. Messy education is likely to be resisted and criticised by faculty and students. It is hard to design and schedule. How can you structure for unpredictability? How do you master the game when there are no rules?

Educating for Complexity and Wisdom

Educating for complexity and wisdom is both possible and necessary. To the first point, university-age students and young adults can develop the capacities to

- Think systemically, see the bigger picture and take responsibility for acting in interests greater than their own,
- Deal with ambiguity and paradox,
- Accommodate plurality and diversity of perspective, and
- Become more self-reflective and attuned to insight and intuition.

In short, they can and do become wise. Wisdom cannot be taught directly, but it can be learned (Lynch, 1999), and educators can indirectly teach it (Küpers, 2007; Staudinger and Glück, 2010; Sternberg, 2001), attending to both content and process.

Educating for complexity and wisdom, however, is not possible unless we first change the way we educate (Marsick, 1998; Roca, 2008). Cunningham (1999) asserts, 'we will need to radically rethink our approach in the classroom, moving sharply from the deductive end of the spectrum to a more inductive approach' (p. 685).

The typical didactic approach does not work and a different path to discovery is needed, claims Lynch (1999). Ottewill (2003) agrees, noting that an over-reliance on didactic teaching fosters surface, instrumental learning and passivity rather than deep learning, understanding and independence. Educating must become as messy and unpredictable as the real world (Nelson and Harper, 2006; Pina e Cunha, Cuhna and Cabral-Cardoso, 2004; Schwandt, 2005): complicated, contentious and contextualised; often without clear guidance and where options may be many, but none of them necessarily or obviously best (Hays, 2008). Conceiving of educating for complexity and wisdom as a wicked problem offers guidance into how we might best frame such education, philosophically and practically.

To the second point, educating for complexity and wisdom is absolutely essential. Kunsch, Theys and Brans (2007) and Vennix (1999) have advocated for education in systems-thinking and complex problem-solving. Kunsch, Theys and Brans (2007), in particular, relate these skills and orientations to better decisions and ethical and sustainable behaviour, 'granting long-term survival to human systems and associations' (p. 260). The consequences of persisting to think and act myopically and out of narrow self-interest are intolerable and unsustainable. Something must be done.

Educating for complexity and wisdom, however possible and necessary, does not lend itself to simple prescriptions. We would expect to see wisdom manifest in a curriculum designed to promote it. The curriculum must be far-reaching. Such a curriculum will incorporate, integrate and leverage many aspects, and may create tensions among its many variables – it will be inherently complex and inevitably appear to have attributes of a wicked problem. Fortunately, we have much collective wisdom on which to draw for design and delivery of an educational system for complexity and wisdom. Knowing the nature of complex adaptive systems and wicked problems, we may be less inclined to throw out the curriculum at the first indication of challenge – when things inevitably do not turn out as expected.

Concluding Remarks

This chapter sheds light on how we unintentionally undermine the development of wisdom and complexity competence in our youth. At the same time, it offers hope. There is no reason why the typical university teacher cannot make the most of the possibilities inherent in the complex adaptive system that is the higher education classroom. Progress might feel precarious, circuitous and disorienting – thus must be the wicked path.

While readers may have their own understandings of wisdom and many scholarly definitions will be more precise, the one put forward, here – wisdom is doing the right thing for the greater good, all things considered – is both encompassing and instructive. The definition accommodates complexity and systems-thinking. It advises individuals to (1) consciously and conscientiously decide and act in accord with moral and ethical values and principles; (2) consider the bigger picture and long-term consequences of decisions and actions; (3) take into account multiple stakeholders and their interests and concerns; and (4) do their utmost to understand fully the system in question – what it contains, how it operates and the implications of change.

What is required is a new way of contending with existing wicked problems and those still to arise; and, to this end, a new way of educating. Changing the way we educate, though, is a wicked problem. We currently teach too simplistically, as if answers to the most pressing contemporary questions can be found under textbook headings, as bullet points on PowerPoint slides or on student exam papers. But, there are many factors inhibiting change and, if we think of them at all, we assume or act as if they are out of our hands. Systems-thinking and tools such as Causal Loop Diagrams show us that these factors are within our reach and, often, that we ourselves are integral and instrumental elements of problem systems. The use of such tools and thinking methods in classrooms and laboratories must be expanded as one necessary and practical means to 'complicate the educational process'.

In keeping with escalating complexity, uncertainty and dynamic change, university education must become increasingly and intentionally problematic. It must exhibit characteristics of complex adaptive systems, including tendencies of chaos, emergence and spontaneous transformation. An implication of this is that instructional content cannot be reduced to discrete, tidy chunks that are easy to teach, learn and assess, but are, in the final analysis, pointless – at least apart from the whole system to which they belong and the context only within which they can be understood.

While contrary to conventional instructional wisdom, the tendency to reduce, simplify and disaggregate has insidious impacts on the way learners think, approach problems and value learning. The obvious solution to counteract this tendency is to teach holistically (Bassett, 2005; Hutchison and Bosacki, 2000; McDonald, 2003), which brings us back to complexity and systems-thinking – and the wicked nature of educating for complexity and wisdom. If it were easy, everyone would be doing it.

As a wicked problem, educating for complexity and wisdom might be resisted or discounted – it is, after all, different, unpredictable, quite possibly more work and reliant on a repertoire of skills and behaviours that teachers may not esteem or possess (Marsick, 1998; Hays, 2008). It will take time to reorient teachers and shift curricula, but there is not a more pressing moment than now to begin.

References

APSC (2007). *Tackling Wicked Problems: A Public Policy Perspective*. Commonwealth of Australia, Canberra.

Baltes, P., and U. Staudinger (2000). 'Wisdom: A Metaheuristic (Pragmatic) to Orchestrate Mind and Virtue toward Excellence'. *American Psychologist*, 55(1): 122–36.

Bassett, C. (2005). 'Wisdom in Three Acts: Using Transformative Learning to Teach for Wisdom'. Paper presented at the Sixth International Transformative Learning Conference, Michigan State University, 6–9 October 2005.

Beers, P., H. Boshuizen, P. Kirschner and W. Gijselaers (2006). 'Common Ground, Complex Problems and Decision Making'. *Group Decision and Negotiation*, 15: 529–56.

Bekken, B., and J. Marie (2007). 'Making Self-authorship a Goal of Core Curricula: The Earth Sustainability Pilot Project'. *New Directions for Teaching and Learning*, 109: 53–67.

Bettis, R., and C. Prahalad (1995). 'The Dominant Logic: Retrospective and Extension'. *Strategic Management Journal*, 16(1): 5–14.

Bierly, P., E. Kessler and E. Christensen (2000). 'Organization Learning, Knowledge and Wisdom'. *Journal of Organizational Change Management*, 13(6): 595–618.

Binbasioglu, M., and E. Winston (2004). 'Systems Thinking for Identifying Unintended Consequences of IT: Packaged Software Implementation in Small Business'. *Journal of Computer Information Systems*, 45: 86–93.

Bonn, I. (2005). 'Improving Strategic Thinking: A Multilevel Approach'. *Leadership & Organization Development Journal*, 26(5): 336–54.

Brodbeck, P. (2002). 'Implications for Organization Design: Teams as Pockets of Excellence'. *Team Performance Management*, 8(1/2): 21–38.

Bronner, R. (1993). 'Decision-making in Complex Situations: Results of German Empirical Studies'. *Management International Review*, 33(1): 7–25.

Brown, S. (2004). 'Learning across the Campus: How College Facilitates the Development of Wisdom'. *Journal of College Student Development*, 45(2): 134–48.

Calton, J., and S. Payne (2003). 'Coping with Paradox: Multistakeholder Learning Dialogue as a Pluralist Sensemaking Process for Addressing Messy Problems'. *Business and Society*, 42(1): 7–42.

Clayton, J., and W. Gregory (2000). 'Reflections on Critical Systems Thinking and the Management of Change in Rule-bound Systems'. *Journal of Organizational Change Management*, 13(2): 140–61.

Crossan, M., D. Vera and L. Nanjad (2008). 'Transcendent Leadership: Strategic Leadership in Dynamic Environments'. *Leadership Quarterly*, 19: 569–81.

Cunningham, A. (1999). 'Commentary Confessions of a Reflective Practitioner: Meeting the Challenges of Marketing's Destruction'. *European Journal of Marketing*, 33(7/8): 685.

Davidson, S. (2010). 'Complex Responsive Processes: A New Lens for Leadership in Twenty-first Century Health Care'. *Nursing Forum*, 45(2): 108–17.

Devine, S. (2005). 'The Viable Systems Model Applied to a National System of Innovation to Inform Policy Development'. *Systemic Practice and Action Research*, 18(5): 491–517.

Dron, J. (2007). 'The Teacher, the Learner and the Collective Mind'. *Artificial Intelligence & Society*, 21: 200–16.

Eriksen, M. (2009). 'Authentic Leadership: Practical Reflexivity, Self-awareness and Self-authorship'. *Journal of Management Education*, 33(5): 747–71.

Fleckenstein, K., C. Spinuzzi, R. Rickly and C. Papper (2008). 'The Importance of Harmony: An Ecological Metaphor for Writing Research'. *College Composition and Communication*, 60(2): 388–419.

Fraser, S., and T. Greenhalgh (2001). 'Coping with Complexity: Educating for Capability'. *British Medical Journal*, 323 (October): 799–803.

Gharajedaghi, J. (2007). 'Systems Thinking: A Case for Second-order Learning'. *The Learning Organization*, 14(6): 473–79.

Gharajedaghi, J., and R. Ackoff (1984). 'Mechanisms, Organisms and Social Systems'. *Strategic Management Journal*, 5: 289–300.

Gidley, J. (2009). 'Educating for Evolving Consciousness: Voicing the Emergency for Love Life and Wisdom'. *International Handbook of Education for Spirituality*, pp. 553–61. Springer, Dordrecht.

Gold, J. (2001). 'Storying Systems: Managing Everyday Flux Using Mode 2 Soft Systems Methodology'. *Systemic Practice and Action Research*, 14(5): 557–73.

Grint, K. (2007). 'Learning to Lead: Can Aristotle Help Us Find the Road to Wisdom?' *Leadership*, 3(2): 231–46.

Hall, W. (2005). 'Biological Nature of Knowledge in the Learning Organisation'. *The Learning Organization*, 12(2): 169–88.

Hays, J. (2007). 'Dynamics of Organisational Wisdom'. *Business Renaissance Quarterly*, 2(4): 77–122.

Hays, J. (2008). 'Threshold and Transformation'. *European Journal of Management*, 8(3): 24–46.

Hays, J. (2010a). 'The Ecology of Wisdom'. *Management & Marketing*, 5(1): 71–92.

Hays, J. (2010b). 'Mapping Wisdom as a Complex Adaptive System'. *Management & Marketing*, 5,(2): 19–66.

Hays, J., and M. Clements (2012). 'Transition: Bridging the Gap between Study and Work'. Paper presented at the 9th International Conference on Cooperative Education and Work-Integrated Learning, Where East meets West and Theory Meets Practice, Istanbul, Turkey, 20–22 June 2012.

Hearn, G., and C. Pace (2006). 'Value-creating Ecologies: Understanding Next Generation Business Systems'. *Foresight: The Journal of Futures Studies, Strategic Thinking and Policy*, 8(1): 55–65.

Hinterhuber, H. (1996). 'Oriental Wisdom and Western Leadership'. *The International Executive*, 38(3): 287–302.

Holling, C. (2001). 'Understanding the Complexity of Economic, Ecological, and Social Systems'. *Ecosystems*, 4: 390–405.

Husted, B. (1993). 'Reliability and the Design of Ethical Organizations: A Rational Systems Approach'. *Journal of Business Ethics*, 12(10): 761–9.

Hutchison, D., and S. Bosacki (2000). 'Over the Edge: Can Holistic Education Contribute to Experiential Education?' *Journal of Experiential Education*, 23(3): 177–82.

Keating, C., P. Kauffmann and D. Dryer (2001). 'A Framework for Systemic Analysis of Complex Issues'. *Journal of Management Development*, 20(9): 772–84.

Kitchener, K., and H. Brenner (1990). 'Wisdom and Reflective Judgment: Knowing in the Face of Uncertainty'. In Sternberg, R. (ed.), *Wisdom: Its Nature, Origins, and Development*, pp. 212–29. Cambridge University Press.

Kremer, J., and C. McGuinness (1998). 'Cutting the Cord: Student-led Discussion Groups in Higher Education'. *Education & Training*, 40(2): 44–9.

Kunsch, P., M. Theys and J. Brans (2007). 'The Importance of Systems Thinking in Ethical and Sustainable Decision-making'. *Central European Journal of Operations Research*, 15: 253–69.

Küpers, W. (2007). 'Phenomenology and Integral Pheno-practice of Wisdom in Leadership and Organization'. *Social Epistemology*, 21(2): 169–93.

Lichtenstein, B. (2000). 'Generative Knowledge and Self-organized Learning: Reflecting on Don Schön's Research'. *Journal of Management Inquiry*, 9(1): 47–54.

Lichtenstein, B., M. Uhl-Bien, R. Marion, J. Orton and C. Schreiber (2006). 'Complexity Leadership Theory: An Interactive Perspective on Leading in Complex Adaptive Systems'. *Emergence: Complexity and Organization*, 8(4): 2–12.

Lynch, R. (1999). 'Seeking Practical Wisdom'. *Business and Economic History*, 28(2): 133–5.

Marsick, V. (1998). 'Transformative Learning from Experience in the Knowledge Era'. *Daedalus*, 127(4): 119–36.

McDonald, J. (2003). 'Connecting the Mind, Body and Spirit in Learning'. Adult Higher Learning Alliance at Capital University, Columbus, Ohio. Available at http://ahea.org/files/pro2003mcdonald.pdf.

Nelson, C., and V. Harper (2006). 'A Pedagogy of Difficulty: Preparing Teachers to Understand and Integrate Complexity in Teaching and Learning'. *Teacher Education Quarterly*, 33(2): 7–21.

Nicolaides, A., and L. Yorks (2008). 'An Epistemology of Learning through Life'. *Emergence: Complexity and Organization*, 10(1): 50–61.

Ottewill, R. (2003). 'What's Wrong with Instrumental Learning? The Case of Business and Management'. *Education & Training*, 45(4): 189–206.

Pina e Cunha, M., J. Cuhna and C. Cabral-Cardoso (2004). 'Looking for Complication: Four Approaches to Management Education'. *Journal of Management Education*, 28(1): 88–103.

Purser, R., and J. Petranker (2005). 'Unfreezing the Future: Exploring the Dynamic of Time in Organizational Change'. *Journal of Applied Behavioral Science*, 41(2): 182–203.

Reznitskaya, A., and R. Sternberg (2004). 'Teaching Students to Make Wise Judgments: The Teaching for Wisdom Program'. In *Positive Psychology in Practice* (ch. 11). Downloaded at www.shkodraonline.com (no longer available).

Roca, E. (2008). 'Introducing Practical Wisdom in Business Schools'. *Journal of Business Ethics*, 82: 607–20.

Rosch, E. (2008). 'Beginner's Mind: Paths to the Wisdom That Is Not Learned'. In M. Ferrari and G. Potworoski (eds), *Teaching for Wisdom: Cross-Cultural Perspectives on Fostering Wisdom*, pp. 135–62. Springer, Dordrecht.

Rowland, D., and M. Higgs (2008). *Sustaining Change*. John Wiley, Chichester.

Scharmer, C.O. (2001). 'Self-transcending Knowledge: Sensing and Organizing around Emerging Opportunities'. *Journal of Knowledge Management*, 5(2): 137–50.

Scharmer, C.O. (2009). *Theory U: Learning from the Future as It Emerges*. Berrett-Koehler, San Francisco.

Scharmer, C.O., W. Arthur, J. Day, J. Jaworski, M. Jung, I. Nonaka and P. Senge (2001). 'Illuminating the Blind Spot: Leadership in the Context of Emerging Worlds'. Available at www.dialogueonleadership.org.

Schneider, M., and M. Somers (2006). 'Organizations as Complex Adaptive Systems: Implications of Complexity Theory for Leadership Research'. *The Leadership Quarterly*, 17: 351–65.

Schwandt, D. (2005). 'When Managers Become Philosophers: Integrating Learning with Sensemaking'. *Academy of Management Learning & Education*, 4(2): 176–92.

Sice, P., and I. French (2006). 'A Holistic Frame-of-reference for Modelling Social Systems'. *Kybernetes*, 35(6): 851–64.

Snell, R. (2001). 'Moral Foundations of the Learning Organization'. *Human Relations*, 54(3): 319–42.

Stacey, R. (1995). 'The Science of Complexity: An Alternative Perspective for Strategic Change Processes'. *Strategic Management Journal*, 16: 477–95.

Staudinger, U., and J. Glück (2010). 'Psychological Wisdom Research: Commonalities and Differences in a Growing Field'. *Annual Review of Psychology*, 62: 215–41.

Stead, W., and J. Stead (1994). 'Can Humankind Change the Economic Myth? Paradigm Shifts Necessary for Ecologically Sustainable Business'. *Journal of Organizational Change Management*, 7(4): 15–31.

Sternberg, R. (1998). 'A Balance Theory of Wisdom'. *Review of General Psychology*, 2(4): 347–65.

Sternberg, R. (2001). 'Why Schools Should Teach for Wisdom: The Balance Theory of Wisdom in Educational Settings'. *Educational Psychologist*, 36(4): 227–45.

van Woerkom, M. (2004). 'The Concept of Critical Reflection and Its Implications for Human Resource Development'. *Advances in Developing Human Resources*, 6(2): 178–92.

Vennix, J. (1999). 'Group Model-building: Tackling Messy Problems'. *System Dynamics Review*, 15(4): 379–401.

Walker, G., S. Daniels and J. Emborg (2008). 'Tackling the Tangle of Environmental Conflict: Complexity, Controversy, and Collaborative Learning'. *Emergence: Complexity and Organization*, 10(4): 17–27.

Yielder, J. (2004). 'An Integrated Model of Professional Expertise and Its Implications for Higher Education'. *International Journal of Lifelong Education*, 23(1): 60–80.

10
In Search of Wisdom

John Little

Introduction

In the wake of Enron's collapse, Ghoshal argued that there could be no real consideration of ethics or morality in business schools if they continued to neglect considerations of human intentionality. Intentionality is not only relevant to ethics and morality – but, more deeply, to personal integrity and authenticity in relationships and, thence, to wisdom itself. This chapter takes up the challenge of linking the notion of intentionality to matters of practical wisdom, such as in situations of managerial complexity.

The Canadian philosopher Bernard Lonergan, in his study of the activity of knowing in science, mathematics and common sense, and building upon Greek and medieval philosophy, has shown knowing to be a dynamic, heuristic structure of intentionality. The competencies associated with this structure provide a new way to conceive foundational virtues and their linkage to wisdom. Of special interest regarding this structure is that one can find the data needed to affirm its validity, in oneself, in the distinct operations of intentional consciousness.

Leaders and managers, as stewards of corporate values, add value in their creative insights, judgments and decisions, particularly when drawing on their own life experience, acquired knowledge, personal values, practical know-how and wisdom. Discovery of the structure of intentionality enhances the discernment process of decision-making, specifically the control exercised within it.

This chapter presents Lonergan's intentionality analysis through – and going behind – language and concepts familiar to managers, such as data, opportunity, risk, conflict, values, vision, strategy, plans and performance. It shows, in particular, how questions drive change and facilitate movement through the various levels of the structure. But above all, and most critically important for managers, is the disclosure of the dynamic nature and structure of control – and of self-control in particular. Within management situations of complexity and ambiguity, clear self-control is essential, whether it be to heighten one's vigilance, to innovate, to assess probabilities and risk, to discern positions of conflict, to maintain clarity of purpose or, with courage, to uphold commitments when opposition mounts. The definitive textbook required to analyse intentionality is oneself. Guides can assist one's reading of this 'text' and one's coming to self-knowledge and, thence, to the possibility of wisdom.

This chapter lays out a model of intentionality analysis (*iAM*) as a four-level structure of consciousness and thinking. It can become a map or template for one's journey to self-knowledge as well as for the illumi-nation of the dynamic patterns within practical management situations and daily life. The template also reveals the core competencies required in managerial learning, decision-making and acting. With *iAM*, one has a key to the fuller possession of oneself – the doorway to mindfulness, wisdom and living well with others.

Being a holistic model, *iAM* provides a common frame for notions of the heart, the mind and collaboration with others. It enables one to inte-grate what previously seemed disparate, and provides a clear approach to epistemology, to an enhanced understanding of business and organisa-tion theory, and to an inquiry-based pedagogy of critical realism within business schools.

A director of a large mining company, reflecting some years after the event, told me of the disquiet he felt when agreeing with the Board to proceed with a venture that later proved to be environmentally disastrous. Would he have changed things were he to give voice to his disquiet, I wondered. A government inquiry into the collapse of a state bank reported of one director who had not asked a question that could have alerted the Board to an impending disaster, lest he upstage and embar-rass a more senior board member who should have asked the question, but did not. Why was he so disposed to suppress his own questions? A rogue energy trader with Enron admitted after its collapse that he had not asked himself at the time why he was doing what he was doing because he knew he did not want to know the answer (Gibney, 2005). After the event, this trader had the courage to admit of the self-interest that had prevented him asking the hard question.

Wisdom – the authority of one – was arguably absent in each situation. This chapter takes up the way one can come to managerial wisdom through questions, and offers a base upon which wisdom stands, namely the very self that asks the questions and makes the decisions.

Noting the difficulties reported by Cheng (2005), for example, in treating of wisdom, I take up the topic with caution. My approach, through *intentionality analysis*, offers both the concept and experiential method for disposing oneself to its call.

My chapter has three parts. First, I discuss the relevance of intentionality to both management and wisdom. Second, I present a holistic model of *intentionality analysis* (*iAM*) based on the nature of thinking, and show its relevance to management and wisdom. Third, from the perspective of *iAM*, I consider the personal competencies and conditions conducive to wisdom, and I conclude with a brief reflection for educators.

1   Intentionality and Wisdom in Management

In his provocative analysis of corporate failure, Ghoshal (2005) wrote of the serious effects of the neglect of intentionality. He argued that bad business theories taught in business schools contributed to bad business practices, such as those seen at Enron. Probing behind such theories, he identified significant issues related to knowledge itself.[1] He stressed that the neglect of *intentionality* in theories of decision-making led to a pronounced deficit of moral and ethical formation of students, with a catastrophic effect later on business when these students came to make decisions in practice.

Ghoshal called for urgent and systemic intellectual reform. Although he knew not how to achieve it, nevertheless he invoked the *collective wisdom* of the Academy to initiate it. His concerns about knowledge and intentionality bear directly upon the treatment of managerial wisdom that I put forward in this chapter.[2]

In view of this (prevailing, according to Ghoshal) neglect of intentionality, I offer something new to management thinking, namely in the *intentionality analysis* and method of Canadian philosopher theologian, Bernard Lonergan. I draw, in particular, from his two classic texts, *Insight* (1992) and *Method in Theology* (1972), and also from considerable experience in applying this method to executive education and corporate facilitation.

Lonergan's discovery of intentionality *analysis* – and of its integrating power – resulted from his interest in cognitional theory and his questioning of what *he was doing* when he was knowing and what *others were doing* in their respective knowing in science, mathematics and common sense (such as in business and politics).[3] His generalised empirical method (GEM), goes beyond, yet also lends fresh rigor to, scientific empirical method by its primary reference to data *as* the data of consciousness. Lonergan thus developed fresh *ground* by which to approach questions of epistemology, metaphysics, ethics and the self – each directly relevant to this study of managerial wisdom.

As a new paradigm, intentionality analysis challenges business 'thinking', unduly influenced, as Ghoshal maintained, by the scientific method. Briefly put, science's empiricism regards 'data' as *outside* the human person who, accordingly, is 'put *aside*'. In contrast, GEM effects a turn back to the person by treating 'data' as that of consciousness. This data, termed 'experience' in GEM, includes: all that one gathers into consciousness through one's senses of seeing, hearing, sensing, smelling, touching, tasting; all that one might do with such data through imagining and perceiving; feelings that arise; awareness of self's presence; and all that is within memory including what one has learned in one's life's journey, however difficult or accurate that may be to gather or enunciate. In essence, 'experience' refers to what is given in consciousness and disposed for one to inquire upon, including the *experience* of one's own *thinking*, of oneself as a *thinker* and the contents of one's *thought*. Dreams, also, are constituents of 'experience', and provide a helpful frame to distinguish the data they represent from the later interpretations one may offer when fully awake. Through intentionality analysis, one begins to differentiate within the data of consciousness what may have previously appeared to be implicit, compact and integral; one discovers through this method that one can give the same structure to consciousness, to thinking (as a set of cognitional operations) and, furthermore, to the *subject* (or person) and to the *object* being studied and acted upon.[4]

The Intentionality Analysis Model, *iAM*, developed in this chapter, highlights the 'core' operations and competencies involved in thinking. It provides a fresh way to conceive of knowledge and wisdom and their relevance to the person, to management decision-making and to change. I prefigure *iAM* in Figure 10.1. The circular

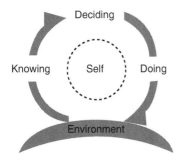

Figure 10.1   Knowing and doing

arrows indicate movement and interdependence of knowing and doing; 'self' signifies the *integrating* agency behind knowing, doing and deciding; 'environment' represents the 'object' of the knowing and doing; and 'decision' links knowing and doing to effect change. Wisdom, as I shall discuss below, lies close to the centre of my model.

2 *iAM*, a Model of Knowing and Doing – and of Thinking

One analyses intentionality by analysing 'thinking', not its thoughts, but its processes. For this one relies on one's own thinking as the definitive textbook and reference.[5] 'Thinking' is a conscious 'mental' *activity* laced with 'self-presence and control'. By *activity*, I mean the *various operations* that one directs, such as, in my case now, in my *searching* for the right word in a sentence, or *wondering* how to dispose my argument, or *deciding* whether to persist with this line of thinking. 'Doing' implies personal intent, namely to achieve some end in view. Hence an inquiry into *what am I **doing*** when I am thinking *intends* an answer – the structure of intentionality – the set of distinct activities (over four 'levels' of consciousness) in knowing and doing. Thus, with a personal question directed towards what one is doing when one is thinking, one begins with *inquiry* to unpack the structure of intentionality.

Inquiry

Lawyers, journalists and teachers know the power of inquiry and of the questions it gives rise to. Governments conduct inquiries to get to the truth of the matter, yet will often predetermine what areas cannot be questioned. Inquiry searches with questions that persist until answers are found. Questions may wander without resolution but, suddenly and unexpectedly, they may break through into new 'ground'. They have found an insight! The detective grasps who did it; the scientist discovers the double helix; the entrepreneur sees a new opportunity.

To find the right question is an achievement, as it is to discover that one's question leads nowhere, and one needs to find another line of inquiry. To dismiss a question may be foolish or betray a reluctance to go where it might lead, such as the energy trader at Enron demonstrated. To arrive at insight is to progress and to 'add value'. To honour questions is to be open; to stop questions is to be closed. To stop, ridicule or divert others' questions is to control.

Inquiry's heuristic force and drive give rise to questions that lie under personal control. But of what is this capacity of control constituted? It too is part of thinking – and furthermore, of *oneself*. It may take courage to stay with one's questions when obstacles, resistance or threatening opposition mount to stop or divert them.

Inquiry signifies an unlimited capacity within us, for there is no limit to the number of questions one can ask, nor in the answers one might find. Inquiry, however, rests when satisfactory answers are found. To inquire, as I have indicated, is already to be 'doing' or performing a distinct intentional act, and to formulate an answer is another kind of 'doing'. What 'lies' between questions asked and answers given are four distinct acts – experiencing, understanding, judging and deciding – that, with their specific kinds of questions and answers, define four specific levels of *iAM*. I now turn to briefly discuss each level in turn.

Experience

As I have indicated, Experience refers to the *data* of consciousness. One can direct one's attention to selections of such data by questions such as *who, when, which* and *what*. The mining company director was fully aware of his feelings of disquiet over the board's decision, yet he suppressed attending to their significance. He ignored their appeal to understand what they signified, but it was of interest to me that he had recalled their presence some years later.

Intentionality analysis is essentially a 'scientific' investigation of experience. One needs to be doing something, however, for one to *experience* the various powers and competencies of thinking. A 'double-take' is needed, a 'meta' look at oneself. For example, in *solving* a puzzle, one can also *be attentive to* what one is doing, such as playing with the data, getting an insight, testing it and moving on. Through this 'meta' look at (and *experience of*) oneself in a range of exercises, one can discover and verify the essential features of *iAM*. This experiential exercise of examining experience reveals the *structure of attention*. It is possibly the first and most difficult skill of *iAM* to practice.

Insight as Understanding

Bethany McLean, a journalist at *Fortune*, driven by a strong hunch that something was amiss at Enron, asked the CEO, Jeffrey Skilling, how the company made its money (Gibney, 2005). Skilling claimed he could not explain; nor was Chief Financial Officer Andrew Fastow helpful. So McLean wrote her article around her unanswered question. The financial community followed with more pointed questions. Thus began Enron's collapse, for there was no insight that held the company together. Bethany had the courage to persist with her question against considerable intimidation from Skilling to divert her.

For one puzzled, searching and seeking to understand, insight is break-through. In *iAM*, insight signifies the 'second level' of consciousness – a 'value-adding' step in management terms. Insight grasps in an instant what was previously hidden and making 'no sense'. It confers unity, identity and wholeness on what was spread out, lacking coherence and unrelated. Through it, one holds things together. Intuitions are insights, though the data that inform them may not be evident. Insights are exclusively private, but unite one with the object of inquiry. Shared insights hold organisations together.

Insights cannot be 'commanded' to occur, but come, often unexpectedly, as relief from the tension of inquiry (with questions such as *how*, *why*, *what is it*). Insights are needed continually in the small matters of practical living – with this author now, in his search for clear expression; with the reader, in seeking to understanding what the author is getting at. It confronts orators as they speak as to which direction to take should they discern they are losing their audience, to journalists to find and ask the penetrating question, the manager to resolve a presenting everyday problem, to the wise person seeking a fitting response to a difficult situation, to a scientist to offer a hypothesis that will explain the data.

Insight must be 'caught' by words and language – and art – to be preserved or shared as concept. Its *formulation* is a further power and skill of intentionality, and presents challenges of its own: language may not be sufficiently refined to 'hold' the insight; one may lack the skill to find the right words; one may make a mistake in the words one chooses; one may be able to express an insight only through metaphor, analogy, story, example or gesture; or be obliged to use a specialist language, such as in science and mathematics. In any event, as insights accumulate and build higher viewpoints, one's concepts may become more abstract, detached from 'experience' and illusory.

Insight lies behind concept, idea, proposition, possibility or hypothesis. Insight and its formulation – the second level of consciousness – together with inquiry and experience constitute the *structure of creativity*, the antechamber through which one must pass on the way to knowledge. Insights are the key to knowing and to wisdom.

Judgment

Insights themselves are not necessarily 'correct'. One may have overlooked some data or 'projected' an interpretation on the basis of similar experiences. For example, one may believe a body of water lies ahead when one sees its glittering appeal on the desert horizon. Only by further walking or by changing position does one come to realise it is a mirage. Insights require testing against all the data and with all relevant questions (generically typified by *is it so*) to determine whether such and such is correct and is so; is fact, not fiction; is real, not illusory; and is true, not false. Then a judgment is made and assent given – or withheld – as to an insight's (and intuition's) truth, reality, coherence and substance.

Reason, absent in insight, is pre-eminent in judgment. Brainstorming, a technique for creative thinking, withholds judgment (and reasons) as it pursues ideas. Judgment grasps that all conditions necessary to validate an insight have been met. In *right* judgment one has knowledge of what *is*. To judge correctly may require strong resolve to resist a tendency to rush to judgment, for example, by not asking all relevant questions.

But it may not be possible to investigate each and every condition with complete thoroughness. Thus one will readily qualify a *yes* or *no* answer with a *maybe*, or *the odds are*, or *probably so*. 'Proven' scientific law, for example is always qualified, open for revision should new data emerge. Management judgment is highly qualified, dependent on accumulated experience and capacity to grasp higher viewpoints and the implications of longer-term horizons.

Furthermore, through attending to one's own conscious experience of the various data of intentionality, one can grasp that there is a recurring pattern within this data, and that one can then affirm that knowing is a compound of inquiring, experiencing, understanding and judging, and, in the degree of competence one has in these powers, one can affirm (know) that one's very self is a *knower* – a compound of being an inquirer, experiencer, understander and judger. Thus the *structure of knowledge* is established as a compound of the three levels of consciousness.[6]

Having arrived at 'knowledge', one may then ask, *so what*, since knowledge provides a secure base from which to act. Knowing that a mirage is an illusion can save one a lot of false hope and expenditure of vital energy were one intent on marching one's way across a desert to quench one's thirst. A *so what* question leads to the fourth level, of decision.

Decision

In decision, one makes a personal stand that continues through time. There is much to attend to in decision-making, particularly since the 'self' and the values one holds (or does not hold) come clearly to the fore. Decision unfolds in three clear stages, each immeasurably rich in context and content and, as I have noted with my opening examples, laced with personal issues. First, there is *deliberation* and discernment. Second, there is *choosing*. Third, there is *action*. Aristotle, in the opening lines of his *Nicomachean Ethics*, indicates that every deliberate action (decision) intends the 'good': 'It is thought that every activity, artistic or scientific, in fact every deliberate action or pursuit, has for its object the attainment of some good. We may therefore assent to the view that has been expressed that "the good" is "that at which all things aim"' (Aristotle, 1958: 4). Deliberation, therefore, is a process of evaluation and a discernment of the 'good' intended by the decision. Inquiry, again, drives the process to resolve the question, will I? Choosing terminates deliberation and initiates action. It is free, full and personal identity with and commitment to the good, as discerned, judged and chosen.

From the perspective of intentionality, deliberation 'sublates' or draws from the products of attention, creativity and knowledge. Through attention, the decision-maker is fully appraised of the situation on which the decision will bear; through creativity, the decision-maker has considered a range of creative options and possibilities for the directions in which the decision might go; through reasoning and experience, the decision-maker has judged the risks and consequences of the various possibilities. But the essence of deliberation must address the question, *is it good?*

In addressing the question of *good*, Finnis has proposed that by asking *why* of any particular benefit sought in a decision, say going to a movie, one would eventually arrive at any one or several of seven *basic goods* (Finnis, 2011). These are goods-in-themselves, needing no further reason. He lists these as: (1) *knowledge* (including aesthetic appreciation) of reality; (2) *skilful performance* in work and play; (3) *bodily life* and the component aspects of its fullness: health, vigour and safety; (4) *friendship* or harmony and association between persons in its various forms and strengths; (5) the sexual association of a man and a woman for mutual support and procreation, as in *marriage*; (6) *harmony within oneself* – between one's feelings and one's judgments (inner integrity) and between one's judgments and one's behaviour (authenticity); and (7) *harmony* with the widest reaches of *ultimate source* of all reality, including meaning and value. These basic goods, he argues, constitute the (universal) human good, implicit therefore within any particular good or benefit one might seek. Although it may be undifferentiated and unrecognised, it nevertheless lies hidden and influential, like 'dark matter', within the heart and depth of us all.

The Structure of Control

Figure 10.2 shows decision and its 'doing' (in *action*) enclosing *iAM*. Decision provides intentional control over the object on which it acts, not only objects in the material world, such as a glass of water, but also over one's very self, one's thoughts and all one's discrete intentional acts, such as those I have discussed above. Figure 10.2 also represents 'I', the self, as controller. For example, in writing this sentence, a control loop is evident, comprising my *experience* of what I type; my *understanding* of what I am typing; my *judging* it appropriate and my *deciding* to continue. Elsewhere, I have treated of this 'I' as the *minder* of the mind or the *heart* of mind – the active, directing presence that oversees and ensures quality performance of each intentional act of enquiry, experiencing, understanding, judging and deciding (Little, 2006).

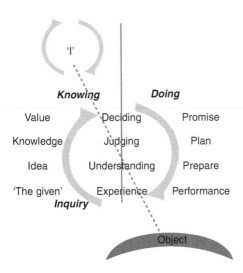

Figure 10.2   *iAM* – the intentional subject

In Figure 10.2 one can attach various 'tags' that designate the 'product' at each stage of knowing and doing. As discussed above, inquiry leads up to 'deciding' through experience, understanding and judging, and then descends to performance through the same levels in reverse. There are thus eight 'products' that 'add value' one to the next: from *that which is 'given'*, as data, to idea, knowledge and value; and then, from deciding, to promise, plan, preparation to performance *that changes the object* as given in experience.

I have discussed how each product adds value to that which precedes it and, in particular, how deliberation about the human good informs decision and the *action* that follows. In considering decision, I have proposed that the value added is the good chosen. It follows that the source of value in each stage is the person, the 'I' – the self, the minder or the heart of mind. From this perspective, the structure of intentionality can represent the conscious, thinking human person, who then becomes the source of value and the agent responsible for implementing countless expressions of the human good in the world. In this sense, *I am* takes on new meaning, as: the receiver, conceiver, knower, valuer, promiser, planner, arranger and performer. The 'object' also has the same structure, namely as: received, conceived, known, valued, promised, planned, arranged for and changed. Within this

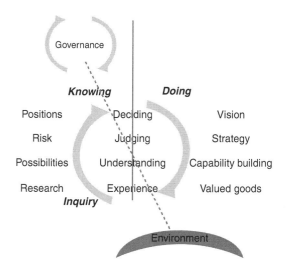

Figure 10.3   iAMO – the intentional organisation

scheme, wisdom (and the wise person) reside, as I shall draw out below, in section 3.

But before I turn to consider wisdom from the perspective of intentionality, let me turn briefly to the *intentional* model of organisation, such as represented in Figure 10.3, and which I call *iAMO*, using terminology that respects *iAM*'s holistic properties.

iAMO preserves the same general structure of four levels – experience, understanding, judging and deciding – that add value through the heuristic drive and direction of inquiry. Thus organisational knowing comprises the following:

1. undertake *research* to gather data from inside and outside;
2. identify opportunities and *possibilities* for future development;
3. undertake feasibility and establish *risk* profiles of possible activities;
4. deliberate on and resolve conflicting stakeholder *positions*,

and organisational doing seeks to effect desired change through a series of subsidiary decisions and actions that:

5. commit to a chosen direction and *vision*;
6. establish *strategy* and policy and secure resources;
7. build *capability*, and;
8. *perform* to deliver valued goods and/or services.

Organisational minding, or self-control, is its governance, which delegates its authority and power to roles spread throughout the organisation to direct and integrate all the above tasks. The corporate good, as a comprehensive set of stakeholder values, is thus the source and power of *intentional* drive of governance and collaboration. This notion of corporate good is located at the centre of governance, and hence of my model. One can also extend this notion beyond the organisation to consider inter-organisational relations and society in general.

In summary, *iAM* is an integral, holistic, heuristic structure of control. It is *integral* in that all parts are necessary for knowing and doing. It is *holistic*, in that it illuminates the dynamics and basis of self-control whether that be of 'me', a group, a team, an organisation or society. It is *heuristic*, in that it discloses itself as a system on the move, that searches and seeks, under the self's direction of inquiry, to bring about some aspect of the human good.

3   Wisdom Disclosed

I now turn to examine wisdom, firstly by taking the model for organisational process, *iAMO*, and then its correlate for the thinking person, *iAM*. *iAMO* can be represented, in summary, as the interaction of three major processes – learn, collaborate and manage – as illustrated on the triangular overlay in Figure 10.4.

To learn, corporate 'thinking' becomes appraised of the realities with which the organisation is engaged and must deal. To collaborate is to secure the active involvement of stakeholders in some form of consultation that leads to a set of clear commitments, contracts or trusts concerning the benefits each seeks. This may involve ongoing processes of conflict resolution and complex deliberations to discern what is equitable and fair. Ultimately, without free and full commitment by stakeholders, the organisation could not function, let alone exist. To manage, then, is to do what is needed to deliver results. It passes down across the four levels in ever-increasing detail of delegation and decision-making.

The three arms can be conceived as held in creative tension by three polarities: discern, lead and make. 'Discern' is the organisation's collective equivalent of the notion of wisdom put forward in this chapter, in that it is deeply attentive to learning yet also mindful of the range and play of stakeholder values and the need to shape equitable and sustainable agreements. Discerning implies deep, collective familiarity with the field, skill in dialectic reasoning and being able to nail the essence of an argument. Leading, in turn, has skills in negotiation, persuasion, rhetoric;

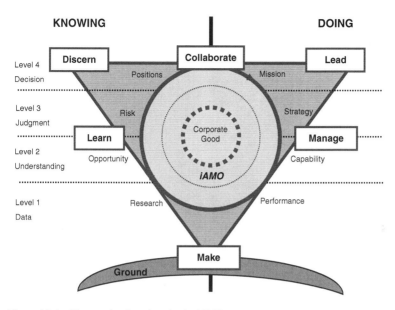

Figure 10.4   Discern, lead and make in *iAMO*

it is able to bring others along by its confidence and personal commitment to a future vision that clearly articulates the corporate good.[7] Making, then, is what is done: under the drive of leading, and through the various levels of management, it delivers 'value' in the goods, services and various exchanges with stakeholders that honour their trust. Each of these polarities is held, in turn, by the 'gravitational' pull of the corporate good that lies at the dark, dense stable centre of our model.

In turning to the model of the thinking person, *iAM*, as in Figure 10.5, the same triangular overlay of learning, collaborating and making applies. Learning directs attention to one's personal development; collaborating refers to those judgments and decisions of trust of intimacy, friendship, collegiality and solidarity with others. Managing refers to the deployment of personal skills and competencies needed to 'change the world', including oneself.

Three polarities pertinent to the person – wisdom, integrity and virtue – hold these three arms in creative tension. Wisdom represents a peak of *self-discernment*, mindful of one's learning and with an eye on one's acting; integrity reflects the notion of *self-leadership*, in which one brings one's deciding and acting into harmony and alignment with one's knowing; and virtue is a high form of *self-making* – as ongoing achievement or habitual

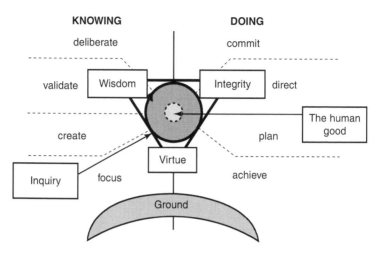

Figure 10.5 Wisdom, integrity and virtue in *iAM*

orientation in attending, understanding, judging and deciding. At the 'dark' stable centre of self, conferring cohesion on wisdom, integrity and virtue resides the notion of the human good.

Figure 10.6 reveals the holistic nature of *iAM* by placing the person within the organisation and as the source of wisdom, integrity and virtue informed ultimately by the human good. These three 'polarities' – wisdom, integrity and virtue – align with the organisation's collective equivalents – discern, lead and make – informed, in turn, by the corporate good. It follows that any development of the person brings these personal qualities to bear upon the organisation, in whole or in part. Any neglect of the person leads to the organisation's corresponding diminishment in whole or in part.

Thus, drawing together these considerations: wisdom as knowledge is grounded in experience, illuminated with insight, in contact with 'being' (what is) and intending what is 'good'. It draws off the rich deposits of memory to reflect afresh on their embedded truth and value. It eschews forgetfulness, but not suffering. It stands with integrity and virtue and is, in turn, sustained by them. It is, in a sense, integral to them. It is perennially open and disposed to abundance and to the unlimited 'other' of being. It beholds the future as a dialectic process of open, critical, collaborative intentionality. It has the ease of authority, not the force of power. It invites, challenges and engages. It is open and attentive, it seizes opportunity, yet it draws on humanity's deepest roots to 'ground' human hope, creativity and enterprise.

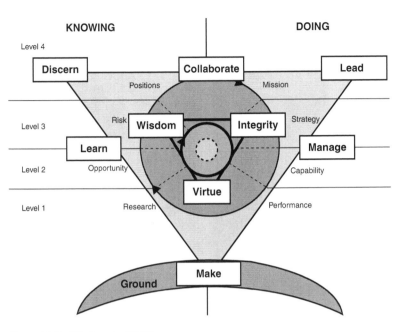

Figure 10.6   Wisdom in *iAMO*

Since the template of wisdom–integrity–virtue 'rests' on the foundational platform of *iAM*, one can define *integrity* as speaking the truth and acting according to the implicit precepts and norms of intentionality, and *virtue* as their cultivated, habitual practice. The precepts and norms of intentionality can be specified as particular skills and competencies in the following way:

- for *inquiry*: be open and persistent; and avoid drifting and brushing questions aside;
- for *experience, be attentive*: be exploratory, discriminating, observant and empathetic; be present; be hopeful for insight; be active with the data; take care not to project false explanation onto the data, nor to 'filter' data; pay attention to and be willing to examine 'uncomfortable' data; recognise feelings as data to be understood;
- for *understanding, be intelligent*: be willing to admit that one does not understand; recognise and foster clarity; in formulating, be accurate and complete, avoid exaggeration or understatement; craft explanation according to the capacities of one's audience;

- for *judgment, be reasonable*: be familiar with the field; ask all relevant questions; do not rely on a single glance. Avoid giving assent without full justification and, mindful of the limits of one's knowing, be humble; avoid arrogance;
- for *decision, be responsible*: be fair, patient, team-spirited, committed, courageous, self-controlled and open to each of the basic human goods; avoid partiality, revenge, grandstanding, laziness, cowardice, impetuosity, superficiality and suppression of a human good.[8]

Within the terms of *iAM*, by carefully attending to and appropriating the skills and competencies associated with each level of thinking – of being open, attentive, intelligent, reasonable and responsible – one develops and takes possession of oneself as open, attentive, intelligent, reasonable and responsible. In the process of this self-knowledge and self-appropriation, it is likely that radical shifts of personal horizon will occur, such as grasping that knowing is more than 'taking a look'; that one's self and others are one in being, united at a hidden depth in search of the universal human good; and that one's own person is an ever-increasing abundance of gift, a product of trust and solidarity with others – a 'being in development'.

Wisdom is therefore a 'product' integral to the process of self-knowledge, self-appropriation and self-making.[9] Wisdom is genuine objectivity which, as Lonergan points out, is the fruit of authentic subjectivity (Lonergan, 1972). Authenticity, in this sense, is the cultivation of these foundational virtues of openness, intelligence, rationality and responsibility. Inauthenticity is understood, therefore, in terms of their neglect, in any number of ways. For example, one can: brush questions aside, filter data, ignore or suppress feelings, be careless with one's insights, be inaccurate in one's formulation, rush to judgment, refuse to consider the legitimate claims of others, and refuse to align one's deciding with one's knowing and to speak what one knows as true.

A Reflection for Executive Education

I have approached the consideration of wisdom through an analysis of intentionality that has, in turn, disclosed the rich, coherent set of norms, competencies and skills of thinking. I have presented my model of intentionality, *iAM*, as integral and holistic, and wisdom, also being integral and holistic, as having its roots in each and every competency and norm. Thus, educators can promote the development of wisdom by giving due attention to these roots. The most effective tool, consistent with *iAM*, is to tap into the power of inquiry.

Thus, in leading a dialogue with the skilful use of questions and with careful, critical listening, in whatever curriculum, exercise, project or method, educators can help their students to question, reflect and recognise experientially, within themselves, the skills and competencies of the four levels of intentionality. Thus, students can be helped to reflect on the consequences that follow from their neglect of these competencies and of the benefits that flow from their careful development and appropriation. But, perhaps more importantly, by their own modelling and instantiation of these skills, educators are more likely to cultivate a similar disposition in their students, managers and clients. Change, after all, must begin with those who lead.

In summary, I have presented an integral, holistic concept for wisdom. With it, I have identified a set of competencies and conditions that accompany its acquisition. I have drawn attention to the central role of inquiry as the key that unlocks the powers of experience, insight, judgment in the development of wisdom, and of the 'self' as its only mediator in words and deeds. I recall the concern expressed at the outset of this chapter, that the experiential method of *iAM* requires self-examination, a process likely to be more effective when facilitated by a trusted, capable guide.

In conclusion, as Ghoshal drew attention to the consequences of neglecting intentionality in business studies, my proposition is that its recovery in business education would not only contribute to the nurturing of managerial wisdom, but also initiate the very intellectual reform for which he called.

Notes

1. He treated, for example, of different epistemologies, a 'pretence of knowledge', inappropriate use of scientific method in research, inadequate accounts of the human person and the negative influence of certain philosophies in management theories.
2. I have dealt elsewhere, at length, using intentionality analysis as *an integrating tool* to address the issues Ghoshal raised about knowledge and business school pedagogy (Little, 2009).
3. Lonergan's careful re-examination of what knowing is came out of difficulties he experienced with the Greek and medieval philosophy of his own formation in handling contemporary developments in knowledge (Lonergan, 1993). As Ghoshal felt drawn by the possibility of a 'grand unification' that would overcome the increasingly specialised, diverse and contending theories and paradigms in management, Lonergan grasped that an integration of

knowledge lay within the study of consciousness, namely within the ambit of intentionality analysis.

4. Flanagan, defining consciousness as 'an awareness immanent in certain acts and in the subject of those acts ... [which] is preliminary to attending and sets the conditions for attending', explores the emergent awareness, understanding and self-affirmation that follows by attending to the different acts of conscious experience, and provides a helpful understanding of what empiricism entails (Flanagan, 1997: 132).

5. Lonergan engages the readers of *Insight* to discover from their own thinking as they read *Insight* that his examination of knowing in science, mathematics and common sense has universal validity.

6. In this structure of knowledge, one thus has what can be defined as epistemology, or a method by which one comes to know. What one has as a result of knowing is *being*. This, in turn, discloses metaphysics as an account of *being*.

7. The corporate good is the set of short- and long-term sustainable benefits sought by all stakeholders. Wise governance establishes what is fair and equitable from their respective and often competing demands.

8. Daly and the author developed a two-day workshop for executives – a range of practical 'thinking' exercises and management problems to explore *iAM* and the requisite skills. This list of Daly's is from one of the exercises that identify the skills used in various stages of the workshop.

9. Self-making is also self-authoring, or writing one's own 'text'. Personal *authority* is thus its product, as is evident in wisdom.

References

Aristotle (1958). *The Nichomachean Ethics*, trans. J.A.K. Thomson. Penguin, Harmondsworth.

Cheng, C.-Y. (2005). 'Preface: What Is Wisdom?' *Journal of Chinese Philosophy*, 32(3): 317–18.

Finnis, J. (2011). *Collected Essays*, vol. III. Oxford University Press, New York.

Flanagan, J. (1997). *Quest for Self-Knowledge*. University of Toronto Press.

Ghoshal, S. (2005). 'Bad Management Theories Are Destroying Good Management Practices'. *Academy of Management Learning and Education*, 4(1): 75–91.

Gibney, A. (screenwriter) (2005). *Enron: The Smartest Guys in the Room*, A. Gibney (producer). Magnolia Pictures, USA.

Little, J. (2006). 'Trust in the Mind and Heart of Corporate Governance'. In G.J. Rossouw and A.G.J. Sison (eds), *Global Perspectives on Ethics of Corporate Governance*, pp. 49–65. Palgrave Macmillan, London.

Little, J. (2009). 'Lonergan's Intentionality Analysis and the Foundations of Organization and Governance: A Response to Ghoshal'. PhD thesis, Australian Catholic University, Melbourne. Available at www.lonerganresource.com/dissertations.php.

Lonergan, B. (1972). *Method in Theology*. University of Toronto Press.

Lonergan, B. (1992). *Insight – A Study of Human Understanding*, vol. III, *Collected Works*. University of Toronto Press.

Lonergan, B. (1993). *Topics in Education*. University of Toronto Press.

11
Giving Voice to Values: An Innovative Pedagogy for Values-driven Leadership Education

Mary C. Gentile

Is there a place for education for wisdom in management education? And if there is, how could it be achieved? In their book, *Wisdom and Management in the Knowledge Economy*, Rooney, McKenna and Liesch (2010) discuss the unique responsibilities and challenges of management education and they pose several difficult questions. They wonder how business education can educate the *whole person*, preparing the individual to reflect upon, question and actively *choose* the objectives they are pursuing in their professional lives, as opposed to merely imparting tools and analytics that students might employ unquestioningly to the tasks set before them. They lament the lack of critical commentary by business schools on the role and purpose of business in our lives and wider society, even while they point out the difficulty in pursuing such a critique when the schools are so closely tied, economically, to the businesses they might call into question. At heart, Rooney, McKenna and Liesch are questioning whether business schools are primarily institutions for higher learning and education, or whether they are something more akin to vocational training? This is a genuine question, not mere rhetoric.

Professional schools all face this dilemma to some degree. To what degree do western schools of medicine critique western medicine, for example? Is the inclusion of a course or two on alternate healing modalities sufficient to constitute a genuine questioning of assumptions about the definition of health and sickness, or the politics of health-care costs and access? And consider the furore raised in recent years by legal scholars in the arena of critical legal studies. To what extent has this intellectual controversy penetrated and impacted the typical law student's training? The answers to these questions vary by school and by professor and by student, of course. But the tension between intellectual critique and practical training does exist, to varying degrees, in each of these professions. Some might argue that it is especially prevalent for business schools, precisely because unlike the law and medicine, business broadly defined (as opposed to particular fields like accounting) has not necessarily yet met the criteria for being a profession (Khurana and Nohria, 2008).

The questioning of whether business schools do, should and/or can provide a kind of vocational training on the one hand, or some higher form of education on the other, will likely continue; but I would like to shift the terms of this debate somewhat. I would like to suggest that regardless of which side one comes down on in this particular conversation, there is still room for – and even a necessity for – *education for wisdom* in management education. I define this as an education that provides both the knowledge and tools and analytics required to be a skilful business practitioner, and also the opportunity and guidance and practice in the kind of critical reflection about the purpose to which one will apply those same knowledge and tools.

Although few would quibble with the need to convey the facts and tools mentioned above, there are lots of barriers around providing guidance and practice in *critical reflection about the purpose of business*. The first of these barriers, alluded to above, is more of a political barrier: the very consumers of business school graduates – companies that hire them – are looking for skilful practitioners, even insightful strategists, but not necessarily for managers who are questioning the role of the company in wider society. Beyond this barrier, however, business school faculty members are not always interested or comfortable with this sort of critical reflection either. For one thing, many of them are not trained in these types of questions; their doctorates and especially their research are often more narrowly focused upon the applications and impacts of particular business practices in their functional domain – that is, the optimal conditions for new product launch; the factors that impact success or failure of cross-border joint ventures or acquisitions; the impacts of different executive compensation schemes on firm performance; the variety of models available for project finance initiatives and so on – rather than upon a wider questioning of the long-term and broader implications of business practice and trends. This broader sort of question is often left to the historians and the sociologists, for many reasons (some of them quite reasonable).

Another barrier is faculty discomfort with so-called *normative*[1] discussions and lessons in the classroom. Faculty members are often hesitant, for legitimate reasons, about discussions rooted in explicit moral or values-based assumptions and foundations. Faculty do not want to suggest that they have 'the answer' when it comes to such questions, nor do they want to venture into territory that may trigger accusations of cultural or ethical narrowness. Rooney, McKenna and Liesch (2010, p. 203) suggest that discussions around 'wisdom' in management contexts are challenging because they are subjective, untestable, unpredictable and normative. After all, a scholar's credibility and self-confidence is largely rooted in the degree to which their work can be supported empirically and 'objectively'.

With regard to the first barrier mentioned above (company demand), although I understand the economic need as well as professional responsibility for business schools to provide training that is, in fact, useful to the companies who recruit and hire their graduates, I do not believe that this sort of training precludes the inclusion of the kind of critical reflection I am talking about here. In fact, arguably it is this sort of deep thoughtfulness about the role and purpose of business, as well as the state-of-the-company/industry that enables the business school graduate to ensure a business's longer-term health and sustainability.

But I want to focus here in this paper on ways to address the *faculty* barriers to raising these critical questions about business purpose, and the legitimate concerns about how to do so effectively and responsibly within a business school context. I believe that it is this sort of self-reflection on business purpose, along with the practical skill-building around acting on one's conclusions, which constitutes *education for wisdom* and Rooney, McKenna and Liesch's (2010) *social practice wisdom* in a management context.

Too often in business school contexts, education for wisdom and judgment is set up in opposition somehow to education for fact-based analysis and decision-making. A false dichotomy is set up between practical education – which sometimes implies action orientation, immediate application and even a whiff of anti-intellectualism – and education for judgment – which sometimes implies standing back and pausing for reflection, longer-term application and usefulness, and perhaps the threat of analysis paralysis. The same sort of false dichotomy is often constructed in the realm of education for ethical and values-driven leadership. The discomfort around these topics is reflected in the tendency (noted by Rooney, McKenna and Liesch, 2010) for business schools to tout their attention to 'higher purpose' and social responsibility without explicating just 'how' this emphasis and education will be addressed (ibid., p. 191).

It is precisely this sort of false dichotomy between the idea of values and the practice of values that 'giving voice to values' was designed to address. 'Giving voice to values' (GVV) is a unique pedagogy that builds on Aristotle's position that character and values-based judgment are developed through practice. GVV draws upon the analytic tools and empirical research data that underlie much of traditional management curricula, but then asks students to use those tools and that data in the service of proposed values-driven positions, in an effort to encourage students to imagine what is possible when it comes to the 'higher purpose' of business. Rather than being led by a limited view of what we think *is or must be*, as viewed through our limited and biased perceptual lenses or through the lens of an institutional bias implicit in a business curriculum, GVV invites students to develop the muscle for wise moral judgments by considering what *might be*, and then practising the scripts and the action plans that may bring those visions into existence.

GVV promotes a higher level of integrity in education and the workplace, drawing on actual experience as well as scholarship, to fill a longstanding and critical gap in the development of values-centred leaders. That is, GVV is not about persuading people to be more ethical. Rather GVV starts from the premise that most of us already want to act on our values, but that we also want to feel that we have a reasonable chance of doing so effectively and successfully – and then the curriculum goes about working to raise the odds of this kind of effectiveness and success. This premise is not necessarily provable in the abstract, but the GVV *thought experiment* is about inviting students to behave and think *as if* it were true and to see how this perspective alters their sense of what is possible.

GVV's goal is both to build a conversation across the core curriculum (not only in ethics courses) and also to provide the teaching aids and curriculum for a new way of thinking about ethics education. Rather than a focus on ethical *analysis*, the GVV curriculum focuses on ethical *implementation* and asks the question, What if I were going to act on my values? What would I say and do? How could I be most effective?

Developed with venture funding from the Aspen Institute and the Yale School of Management and now based and supported at Babson College. GVV[2] has met with rapid adoption around the world, already having been used in over 300 schools and organisations across six continents (soon to be all seven). It was piloted first in MBA programmes but now is spreading to undergraduate business education and executive education, and it is being examined and adapted for schools of engineering, law and medicine. Increasingly it is being used in companies themselves as well.

So what was the impetus for the development of GVV? Despite four decades of good-faith effort on the parts of many individual faculty (and some institutions) to teach ethics in business schools, readers of the business press are still greeted on a regular basis with headlines about egregious excess and scandal. It becomes reasonable to ask why these efforts have not been working.

Business faculty in ethics courses spend a lot of time teaching theories of ethical reasoning and analysing those big, thorny dilemmas – triggering what one professor called *ethics fatigue*. Some students find such approaches intellectually engaging; others find them tedious and irrelevant. Either way, sometimes all they learn is how to frame the case to justify virtually any position, no matter how cynical or self-serving. Utilitarianism, after all, is tailor-made for a free-market economy. In fact, this is an unfortunate example of how the primary or even exclusive emphasis upon the analytics and decision-making models of ethics, as opposed to the practice of ethics, can undermine the broader ostensible (if arguably not always entirely embraced) objective of the curriculum.

GVV, on the other hand, is not about debating the ethics of a particular decision nor about proving whether or not 'ethics pays' – the unfortunate focus of too many ethics and corporate social responsibility courses. Rather GVV starts from the premise that business ethics (and corporate social responsibility) *can* pay if pursued effectively, just as a lack of ethics and corporate irresponsibility can pay sometimes, too, at least in the near term. There is no assumption of some universal scorekeeper who doles out rewards to those who are 'good'. Rather GVV is about providing students with the opportunity to ask and answer the question, How can I pursue an ethical and responsible business agenda effectively and sustainably?

Now you might ask, What about the times when individuals may not *want* to do the right thing – times when we ourselves may be tempted, for our own self-oriented reasons, to violate ethical principles? This is a valid question, of course, but GVV starts from the premise that if we could strengthen the ability and the likelihood that more individuals would enact their values when they know what's right and want to do it, many of the problems based on any other individual's desire to violate the rules of ethics would be addressed. It simply would be a more difficult and more lonely road.

So at the heart of it, GVV is simply about asking a different question. Instead of asking, What is the right thing to do?, GVV asks, Once I know what is right, how do I get it done? But this seemingly simple shift in perspective has major implications for how we teach and what kind of impacts we can have. It allows – in fact, it requires – that students create *scripts* and action plans for getting the right thing done, and then practise delivering and refining them in a peer-coaching context. In this way, students not only generate a repertoire of strategies and tactics and arguments for effectively voicing and enacting values-based leadership, their practice serves to make the application of these approaches feel more possible and become more of a default position, if you will. The idea here is based on a growing body of research that suggests that the way to behaviour change is through action, more than simply cognitive argument, and that a kind of muscle memory accounts for many of our choices. That is, 'rehearsal' matters.[3]

Now this simple idea – practice makes perfect, if you will – may appear to be obvious (at least to Aristotle), but in an academic context, faculty resistance to a so-called 'normative' stance as well as an often personal discomfort with discussions of ethics and values has resulted in an emphasis upon an exclusively intellectual or cognitive approach to these topics. The emphasis is on difficult decisions – the 'grey areas' – where it is unclear what the right path may be. Ethical issues are presented as if the primary challenge is one of weighing consequences and duties to determine the most responsible choice, with much less attention paid to scripting arguments, planning action and practising behaviour.

In the corporate context, on the other hand, there is also little attention paid to action planning and practice when it comes to ethics, but for a different set of reasons. Rather than a fear of taking a 'normative' stance, ethics training in companies often emphasises the rules and compliance to a fault, with the objective of insuring that all employees know where the 'bright lines' are when it comes to ethical (and legal) behaviour. Once again, discussions are likely to remain in the cognitive domain, focusing on parsing the rules and the situation to determine whether we are stepping over the line or not.

Thus, for somewhat different reasons, both business education and corporate training avoid the realm of rehearsal for action – an unfortunate reality because it is in this arena of rehearsal that the false dichotomy between *practical education* and *education for judgment* (or wisdom) can be resolved. Although it may appear that rehearsal for action is somehow about devaluing critical reflection and questioning, to the contrary, GVV sets up the rehearsal as an explicitly acknowledged *thought experiment*. That is, faculty members do not require students to commit to a particular values-based position. Rather faculty ask them to reflect upon, develop and practice scripts and action plans in the service of a given values-driven position, *as if* they were going to pursue it. Thus, students are directed to create a workable approach to that particular position.

We do this because the prevailing discourse and ruling assumptions in the business education context are too often about *whether* it is possible to act in an ethical and responsible way in business, rather than upon *how* to do so. Typically, in a well-intended attempt to engage students with questions of values, questions of ethics and corporate responsibility are posed in an either/or format – often as a debate (e.g. responsibility to shareholders versus responsibility to a wider set of stakeholders). However, this approach paradoxically positions both viewpoints as equivalent and mutually exclusive, and yet frames the debate within a context where the prevailing discourse – the *go to* arguments – favours the former.

GVV, on the other hand, proffers explicitly values-based positions and invites students to work collectively to craft workable ways to enact them. The protocol of questions that students are encouraged to work through in an effort to craft these strategies, however, includes a set of questions that implicitly engages the students in a process of critical questioning, evaluating the soundness of the position even as they work to craft an implementation plan. Students must identify what is at stake for all parties involved in and affected by a particular decision and course of action. Importantly, they are asked to identify the sorts of arguments they will encounter from individuals whom they are attempting to influence, and to think through possible responses to those arguments. In this way, they are explicitly reflecting upon and reconsidering the assumed definitions and credibility of concepts like meritocracy, competitiveness, excellence, success, sustainability and so on in a business context; and when necessary, they are engaged in crafting a new discourse for discussing these foundational concepts. Thus, embedded in this 'practical education' is an explicit process for 'education for judgment'.

Now of course, the GVV approach does raise the question of just *who defines* the values-based positions for which students should be encouraged to create arguments and action plans. This is a critical question, of course, because it is at the heart of both the faculty discomfort with so-called normative positions, on the one hand, and the concern (expressed by Rooney, McKenna and Liesch, 2010, p. 194) that the business curriculum has been co-opted by the institutions within which it is embedded, on the other.

It is here that GVV has engaged in a sort of pedagogical reversal of one of the prevailing questions in education around values. In the typical discussion of business ethics education, faculty and practitioners alike will argue that the focus of this curriculum should not be on the clear-cut questions of right and wrong – the so-called 'black and white' issues – because these are 'easy'. Instead the curriculum should focus on the 'grey' areas – wrong versus wrong or one right versus another sort of right – because these are where the real challenges emerge.

I would argue to the contrary that although these 'grey' areas are indeed intellectually challenging and thorny, that is why these issues are precisely the ones where intelligent and reasonable people of good will may legitimately disagree. GVV focuses instead on those so-called clear-cut questions where most (not all) people would likely agree about what is right – often cases of clear illegality, fraud and deception. It is these questions where, despite some clarity about the ethics of the situation, individual managers are often concerned about or even convinced of the impossibility of taking effective action. 'Practical' education around values – actionable education – would therefore provide students with the opportunity to research, generate, practise and perfect the arguments and scripts as well as the strategies and tactics for an effective action plan in the service of these widely shared values-based positions.

In so doing, however, students are also enhancing their skilfulness and comfort levels with constructive and intellectually open discussion of those 'grey area' questions as well. And therefore, the practical education offered by GVV is also allowing for (even requiring) the open discussion of positions that may fall outside the implicitly valorised discourse of business education.

Finally, the question arises of just where this education for action, GVV, fits within the traditional management curriculum. Typically when business educators attempt to integrate ethics and values education into the curriculum, they tend to focus on two topics: (1) building awareness of the kinds of ethical issues that managers are likely to encounter; and (2) introducing models of ethical analysis to aid in decision-making about what the 'right' thing to do may be when ethical issues arise.

There are good reasons why the focus has been in these two areas. When it comes to analysis, we would argue that students need to see examples of just how ethical infractions emerge, present themselves and grow, so that they will recognise them when they surface and understand the potential consequences of looking the other way or succumbing to pressures to participate in illegal and/or unethical practices.

This is, of course, a valid educational objective, particularly when students are increasingly operating in a more global context where laws, norms and pressures may be quite different from those to which they are accustomed. In addition, technological advances make the concepts of privacy and even of property rights more fluid than we may have previously assumed, and our confidence in information security and intellectual property protections are less sure than many would like to presume. Consider the recording industry's forced evolution with the advent of internet music downloading; consider *WikiLeaks* and *LulzSec* and *Anonymous* and the questions these groups raise about appropriate and inappropriate corporate (and state) secrecy; consider online journalism and the questions it raises about writers' rights to the work they produce. For all these reasons, raising students' awareness of what might go wrong and how it might present itself is important.

Similarly, a focus on analysis is also critical, particularly when it comes to values and ethics. These kinds of challenges are often complex and individuals may easily fall prey to sloppy thinking and to the twin dangers of self-oriented overconfidence or of relativism: that is, assuming that just because I believe it's right, everyone will or should agree, on the one hand, or believing that context is all and that there are no fixed and common values at all, on the other. The introduction of models of ethical reasoning (typically consequentialist and duty-based) provides students with tools for becoming self-aware about their own patterns of thinking and disciplining them so as to avoid some of the typical analytic traps.

In addition to these good reasons for a focus on awareness and analysis, there are some other drivers and some limitations as well. Perhaps the greatest limitation to a focus on awareness is that although these subtle or 'new' or stealth questions of ethics do exist, the types of issues that tend to receive the most public attention in the media and in the halls of justice and in the halls of the legislators tend to be the types of issues where there was actual illegality and downright fraud involved. That is, the issues which have contributed most to the undermining of public trust in business practices often tend to be situations where awareness was not the problem. The problem really had more to do with individuals who either did not care about the ethics, or with individuals who did in fact care and were aware of the issue but who felt they had no recourse to address it. This kind of problem requires something other than awareness-building to address it.

One of the practical limitations of a focus on analysis has to do with the fact that the ethical-reasoning models that are shared here will, by design, very often lead to contradictory responses to any particular ethical conflict. That is, a utilitarian analysis is designed to allow us to see the sometimes overlooked costs of a strict adherence to duty-based reasoning, and vice versa. And while attention to these models of ethical reasoning may well lead to a more rigorous thinking process, they certainly do not prepare students to enact their decisions once made.

Although these limitations do not cancel out the benefits and even necessity of attention to awareness and analysis, they do point to a still existing need or gap: that is, a focus on *how* to enact our values, or what I would call action, as discussed below. But there are some other reasons why we tend to focus our business ethics education efforts in these two areas of awareness and analysis that bear unpacking.

As noted above, faculty are often uncomfortable with presuming to espouse that we know what the right or ethical answer is in a particular situation; and even if they have strong beliefs about these things, they are often uncomfortable or even philosophically opposed to 'imposing' their own values on their students. And although I have yet to meet a business faculty member who does not want to educate responsible business persons, faculty may sometimes wonder if it is reasonable to suggest that students behave according to certain codes of ethics, given the realities of the market; perhaps the market has an 'ethic' of its own that is beyond any individual's moral compass.

These concerns – some of them based in a sort of personal anxiety and others based in strong, intellectual and/or emotional conviction – reinforce the push to focus on awareness and analysis, as such endeavours can seem to skirt the issue of prescriptive ethics. They don't pretend to instruct students on what is right but rather on how to recognise that a question exists and ways to think about it rigorously. And as such, these two approaches also are attempts to respond to the assessment-of-learning question, an issue that has become increasingly pressing as a result of accreditation requirements. Rather than being asked to evaluate the ethics of a student, or even of a student's responses to test questions, the focus on awareness and analysis allows faculty to explain that they will be grading based on the student's depth of insight, the rigor of their analysis, the clarity of their expression and so on. The problem here, of course, is that faculty members are then sometimes faced with an extremely effective analysis that argues for a seemingly morally egregious position.

The GVV pedagogy and curriculum offers a response to the limitations described above by taking the next step. That is, once students are aware of an ethical issue and even though they may be capable of rigorously analysing it, GVV focuses them on action and asks a new question. We flip the question, What is the right thing to do?, and ask instead, Once we know what we think is right, how do we get it done? Faculty are equally engaged in this inherently dialogical practice.

In this way, GVV can focus on those issues of outright fraud and illegality that the more rarefied focus on awareness building may take for granted. GVV can use the tools of analysis (consequentialist and duty-based thinking) to understand what's at stake for all parties involved, as a means to developing the most effective and responsive action plan for addressing the issue at hand, without becoming stymied by their fundamental divergence. And in a sort of pedagogical sleight of hand (fully acknowledged, by the way), GVV can relieve faculty from the role of espousing a particular 'right answer' while still – and very importantly – allowing them to stand in a position of espousing the importance of responsible and ethical business dealings. That is, as we will describe more fully below in the discussion of '*how* we teach', GVV starts from a presumed 'right answer', if you will, to certain ubiquitous values-conflicts and invites students to craft scripts and action plans for implementing it that have the best chance of being persuasive and successful.

In this way, faculty members are also relieved from teaching a subject for which they have not been trained. The resolution of accounting GVV scenarios draws upon the language and tools of accounting, rather than the language and tools of philosophy; an effective argument to a boss or a colleague or a client will be framed in business terms, not in an appeal to John Rawls or Aristotle (even though the insights of Aristotle or Rawls may be reflected in it). And the grading problem is resolved because faculty will be assessing the clarity, depth of analysis and research, and feasibility of an action plan and script, rather than of an ethical position.

Finally, and perhaps most profoundly, this focus on action addresses the concern that some faculty may have about the appropriateness of applying a moral lens to the market. By focusing on situations that reflect the explicit laws and regulations and/or the implicit assumptions for the smooth functioning of a 'perfectly competitive' market, the grounds of debate have shifted from the questioning of the underpinnings of market efficiency to a discussion of how to achieve this objective within the Adam Smith and Milton Friedman-approved constraints of law and socially accepted ethics.

Thus, I propose that the GVV pedagogy can serve both to address the false dichotomy between practical education and education for judgment (wisdom), as well as provide an answer to the thorny question of just *how* business schools and educators can critically address issues of higher purpose in a school whose function is also very much embedded in preparing future practitioners.[4]

Notes

1. Of course, I would argue that the existing business education discourse is hardly non-normative, but here we are merely identifying the faculty discomfort around explicit discussions of ethics, higher purpose and so on.
2. For a full description of GVV, see Gentile, 2010. Visit www.marygentile.com for related articles, interviews, video, Op Eds, reviews etc.; and see the curriculum itself at www.givingvoicetovalues.org.
3. For more on these ideas, see the work of Jonathan Haidt; Max Bazerman and Anne Tenbrunsel; Antonio Damasio; Perry London; Douglas Huneke; Philip Zimbardo etc.
4. Some of the material in this chapter previously appeared in an article (Gentile, 2012) and is used by kind permission of the Eastern Academy of Management.

References

Gentile, Mary C. (2010). *Giving Voice to Values: How to Speak Your Mind When You Know What's Right*. Yale University Press, New Haven.

Gentile, Mary C. (2012). 'Values-driven Leadership Development: Where We Have Been and Where We Could Go'. *Organization Management Journal*, 9(3): 1–9.

Khurana, R., and N. Nohria (2008). 'It's Time to Make Management a True Profession'. *Harvard Business Review* (October): 70–7.

Rooney, D., B. McKenna and P. Liesch (2010). *Wisdom and Management in the Knowledge Economy*. Routledge, New York.

12
Hearing Voices: Wisdom, Responsibility and Leadership

Simon Robinson

Missing Something?

Rooney and McKenna (2007) argue convincingly that the scientific paradigm in management theory has led to a decline in the role of wisdom, leading to 'clouding judgment, degrading decision making and compromising ethical standards' (2007, p. 113). This echoes an ongoing debate about business school curricula being focused in a scientific approach to management and leadership, excluding issues of value and responsibility (Ghoshal, 2005; Schumpeter, 2009; Rayment and Smith, 2010). This has also moved into a debate about the ethical identity of management and the professions (Khurana and Nohria, 2008; Robinson, 2011; MacIntyre, 1981; Bauman, 1989).

This scientific education narrative is reinforced in UK higher education by a stress on occupational utility which views employability as skills-centred. Skills in this are seen as value-neutral and not connected to questions of purpose or to character attributes or virtues (Robinson, 2005). Hence, in terms of Aristotelian intellectual virtues, the stress is on *techne* or *episteme*, not on *phronèsis* or practical wisdom. All this reflects an ongoing tendency to fragment knowledge (Bender, 2005). This is reinforced by a stress in higher education on the development of citizenship which characterises this as a personal rather than professional response to society (Colby et al., 2003).

Much of this debate is also reflect in the 2007–08 credit crisis. Analysis of this has suggested that lack of competent regulation, narrow business organisation cultures and simple vices such as avarice or greed have led to a lack of awareness of the wider business environment (Robinson and Dowson, 2012; Rayment and Smith, 2010; Sun, Stewart and Pollard, 2011; Gregg and Stoner 2009; Visser, 2011). This was finely caught in the film *The Inside Job* (Sony Pictures, 2010), where not only were the key business players unaware of the implications of their actions, but major academics seemed equally unaware of the different narratives at play and even of the possibility of conflict of interest. This suggests that there are wider sociological and psychological elements that reinforce a so-called value-neutral view of management, something I will return to below. It is hardly surprising that ongoing research suggests that this results in confusion for students about just what responsible business practice involves (Kaul and Smith, 2011).

Plural Narratives

It would be easy to account for this stress on instrumental rationality through the thesis of MacIntyre (1981). He argues that management cannot be a true profession, because the manager operates outside ethics. By definition, the manager is not concerned with purpose or value, only with getting things done. He or she treats 'ends as given, as outside his scope; his concern is with technique, with effectiveness in transforming raw materials into final products, unskilled labour into skilled labour, investments into profits' (1981, p. 30).

MacIntyre contrasts the community of practice, based in purpose and some idea of a good outside the business, with management based in the institutional needs. The first is the domain of the professions, and the second involves a secondary set of targets which if they dominate threaten to destroy the core purposes.

There are two major problems with MacIntyre's argument. First, he characterises the situation as a polarisation: the community of practice focused on the core purpose and common good and the institution focused on survival and secondary targets. There is an assumption that such institutional targets are not based in ethical value. However, they clearly do have an ethical narrative, based in the value of sustainability, without which it would be hard for any community of practice to continue. At the very least there has to be dialogue between institution and the community of practice. Second, and connected, it is difficult to see just two value narratives in any organisation. On the contrary, any public or corporate body has many. A brief example from university life will suffice.

In moving offices professor A is asked to fill the five crates she has been allocated. The professor suggests that she needs 55, to deal with all her books. She is informed that books are not the university's responsibility and these should be housed at home. She responds that books are a key part of the academic narrative and the ongoing community of practice, and thus ownership is not the issue, but rather how they are responsibly used and shared in the practice of learning and research. It would be easy to characterise this as a simple battle between different voices of instrumentality and professional purpose. In fact, it involves several voices giving rise to different value narratives each of which generates a view of responsibility. The first voices come from the estates office of the university, but have a social context, with a strong steer from national bodies to ensure that the practice of the university is sustainable. This is a social and community narrative about how any organisation affects wider social and environmental sustainability. The organisation then becomes responsible for its core physical practice, from its carbon footprint to its use of space, and is accountable to wider society. It could be argued that this social narrative is, or should be, central to the community of practice, not simply the institution.

A second 'voice' is that of discrete organisational sustainability. The organisation has limited resources and to sustain its infrastructure has to cut back on space. Supporting that voice might be several different narratives, such as that of the accountancy profession, whose task is to provide a true picture of resources. Human resource management also has a value narrative around sustaining the workforce. There may too be a local community narrative, with long-standing desire to maintain such an institution (Scott, 2005).

A third 'voice' is that of 'academic narratives' around the meaning of learning, and the need to provide space and relationships that enable this. This voice is counter to simple sustainability narratives which advocate hot-desking and shared space. It speaks of academic community and the hospitable environment needed to help students develop the skills of critical conversation. Even this voice has different narratives from the high-flown view of Newman (1982) which sees such learning as an end in itself, transcending institutional concerns, to the view that it is central to both employability and intellectual and cultural responsibility (Robinson, 2005).

But how do such narratives relate to the twin voices of consumerism and massification? The first of these stresses that education is a commercial transaction, setting up a contract to give the student a certain form of education. This focuses, then, on the student's, and indeed employer's, views of what makes a person employable (Archer and Davison, 2008). For some the tram lines of employability are set, represented by the narratives of the different professional bodies that have a stake in higher education, from law and medicine to engineering. More generalised narratives of employability tend not to focus on the relationality of professions, and more on instrumental skills. But even instrumental skills are increasingly questioned in the debate about the identity of management, and how far it is a 'true profession' (Khurana and Nohria, 2008: Robinson, 2011).

Massification, the increased numbers of students, partly realised because of the social narrative of equality of access, sets up another complex narrative around providing customers with the best possible experience, given increasingly limited human and material resources.

Even this brief review of the different voices in the enterprise of higher education shows three things. First, there are many different narratives which members of the organisation may find it difficult to recognise and appreciate. In higher education this was underlined by the CIHE report on ethics in universities (CIHE, 2005). Second, the different narratives are all informed by significant values. This means that it is hard to ignore any one of them or to simply assert one as being more important than the others. Third, the narratives and underlying values all inform different accounts of responsibility, and indeed take on practical significance in relation to these accounts.

The consumer narrative, for instance, suggests that the teacher is directly accountable to the student, and to the institution, in maintaining standards. The institution in turn takes on responsibility for ensuring that the contract is delivered, and may in the interest of maintaining standards, seek to impose how the contract is delivered. The learning narratives may have a different kind of accountability based in the community of practice and around different values such as academic freedom. This provides an equally strong value narrative, and the question then is, How are the different narratives to relate in practice?

All this suggests that, contrary to the Rooney and McKenna thesis, there is no simple conflict between value-neutral administrative narratives and value-centred narratives, and that, contrary to the MacIntyre thesis, institutional goods are not value-free. Choice between any narrative involves the need to be aware of the underlying values and how they relate to the other narratives, and how these relate, in turn, to the purpose or purposes of the overall organisation in relation to the wider social environment. At one level this reinforces Tawney's view of social ethics, that all practice reflects underlying values, that is, that no practice or related narrative is value-free (Tawney, 1930). Nonetheless, Rooney and McKenna remain right (2007), that wisdom, and thus wise leadership, seeks critically to engage value and how its meaning is accounted for and sustained in different narratives.

Wisdom

Like all interesting concepts wisdom has a long history. I shall focus in on simply two views of *practical* wisdom from Aristotle and Aquinas, and from that suggest a view of wisdom that is based in holism, synoptic thinking and plural identity.

Aristotle's virtue of *phronèsis* (1969) is the capacity for rational deliberation that enables the wise person to reflect on her conception of the good and to embody this in practice. Aristotle sees this not as a moral virtue but one of the intellectual virtues. This virtue is often the one most tested when targets have to be met, precisely because it is about reflecting on purpose.

Practical wisdom (Latin *prudentia*) for Aquinas (1981) involves several elements, in particular: openness to the past (*memoria*), openness to the present, involving the capacity to be still and listen actively (*docilitas*), and openness to and taking responsibility for the future (*solertia*). This stresses openness and care before any hasty judgment or decision. In being open to the present and the future it also stresses an appreciation of reality and thus of both constraints and possibilities in any situation. It works against a simple utilitarian view of ethics, and against a primarily target-centred approach to leadership and management.

Taken together these views of wisdom suggest several things. First, wisdom is holistic. It involves cognitive, affective, somatic and social aspects. The first of these demands clarity about the concepts that are used, and the capacity to justify them rationally. We can hardly be said to be responsible for our thoughts if we cannot provide some account of and justification for them. Core to this is some understanding of purpose and a wider view of the good. Any account and justification of thoughts and actions also demands openness to critical intellectual challenge. The example of the credit crisis of 2007–08 showed a lack of such wisdom. The mathematical formula that provided the basis for claiming the risk-free status of CDOs was understood by few (Lanchester, 2010). The only concept that much of the leadership was clear about was profit. Perhaps more importantly, Tett (2009) notes how there was a culture amongst the financial world that worked against any questioning of practice.

The affective aspect of wisdom involves values (Cowan, 2005) and demands the capacity to appreciate values underlying thoughts and action. This is not simply testing coherence, it is also about understanding distinct meaning and value, such that one prefers one practice to others. Even at this stage, then, this involves a comparison with other practices and their values. Hence, deciding upon one's own values or the values of the organisation does not take place in social isolation, or apart from relationships to the social and physical environment. The focus on values also engages feeling because values connect to purpose and identity and thus any sense of self-worth. Affective reflection still involves critical reflection, without which it is hard to take responsibility for the related values. Both of these involve what McKenna and Rooney (2008) refer to as 'ontological acuity', a critical awareness and appreciation of the ideas and values of different narratives in the social environment, and the underlying worldviews and dynamics that may be responsible for keeping those in place. The third and fourth aspects of holism involve awareness of the social and physical environment, how we relate to these and thus what their significance is and the significance of our practice.

The broad consciousness of the environment, in the past, present and future, and our relationship to it relates wisdom directly to our identity and purpose, and our responsibility for meaning in practice. Taylor (1989) argues that such self-interpretation is key to identity. Mustakova-Possardt (2004, p. 245) sums up this responsibility for both worldviews and awareness of the social and physical environment in the idea of 'critical moral consciousness'. This involves

- a moral sense of identity;
- a sense of responsibility and agency;
- a deep sense of relatedness on all levels of living;
- a sense of 'life meaning or purpose', linking to underlying beliefs.

It is not surprising, then, that such wisdom forms the basis of what Taylor (1989) refers to as 'deep decision making'. None of this prescribes a particular response. What it does demand is awareness of what one is doing, how that fits into the purpose of the organisation and how that effects the internal and external environment. In other words there is a relational context to agency that goes beyond the individual self, demanding awareness and responsiveness.

Alongside holism is synoptic thinking, the capacity to see the connections between different aspects of experience. As Bender (2005) notes, this is often the first casualty in academic disciplines with hard boundaries. It is also one of the first casualties in the development of any institution, especially where effort is put in to defending the boundaries of the institution. Wisdom in Aquinas's view is able to make the connections over time. Indeed, it requires that such connections are made for any decision-making. This would seem almost a simplistic notion. Yet, research consistently reveals its absence in high-level business disasters. A recent survey (St Paul's Institute, 2011) notes that only 14 per cent of finance workers in the City knew what its motto was, and a majority were unaware of previous recessions in the 1980s and 1990s.

All this also involves connection between ideas, values and practice, and between the different narratives found in the individual, the organisation and outside the organisation. This presumes plurality in the social and physical environment. Hence, Taylor (1989) can speak of the 'plural person', and Ramadan (2012) of multiculturalism as a part of the social environment rather than a normative position.

Wisdom in this sense becomes more than an 'intellectual' virtue, requiring affective and somatic awareness. It connects: core intellectual values, not least the development of rational agency; ethical values, including justice and respect; spirituality, used as a generic term pointing to underlying beliefs about the world, sometimes expressed in terms of worldviews; competency values, not least professional and technical skills and values – from communication, to teamwork, to concern for excellence.

Responsibility

As noted, such wisdom relates directly to responsibility. Schweiker (1995) suggests three interrelated modes of responsibility, the first two of which originate in Aristotle's thinking: imputability, accountability to and liability for. At its most basic, imputability is about making a causal connection – the imputing of a cause that is responsible for something. A stronger view suggests that to be fully responsible for something this necessitates a rational decision-making process (McKenny, 2005). Taylor (1989) argues that this decision-making constitutes a strong valuation that connects action to deep decision-making. This owning of the thoughts and related decisions is what constitutes the moral agency and identity of the person or group. This deeper form of imputability can itself be seen as wisdom. Hence, Ladd (1991) can speak of responsibility as itself a virtue, or at least connected to virtues.

From such a level of awareness the third mode of responsibility, responsibility for people, projects or place, is directly engaged. To whom, or to what am I or my organisation responsible? Faced by the plurality of the self and the environment it is difficult to provide a simplistic answer to this question. Any answer has to take account of responsibilities that arise from different narratives. As manager I may be responsible for my institution (its success and ethos), for my professional colleagues, possibly for the integrity of my professional organisation, certainly for my customers and my work force, and possibly for the industry of which my firm is a part, and for the wider social and physical environment. This might seem overwhelming, but such plural responsibilities have to be managed. At one level this involves accepting an attitude of plural responsibility. The workers on the ill-fated *Herald of Free Enterprise* who saw the bow doors were open as the ferry left Zeebrugge could not confine responsibility to a narrow view of their job (Robinson, 1992). They were responsible for that *and* for the ship as a whole, *and* for passengers, *and* for health and safety. Once again wisdom does not prescribe which action we should take, it does demand we take action in the light of our knowledge of the social and physical environment and our relationship to it. This both/and view of responsibility takes us very close to the universal responsibility advocated by Bauman (1989), Levinas (1998), Dostoevsky (1993) and many religious writers.

Universal responsibility can have its problems. It is not clear how one can claim responsibility for everything. However, it does not have to claim moral responsibility for every action, but rather responsibility for reflection on the breadth of the social and physical environment and the implications of this for our relationship to that environment. The response is driven by the depth of consciousness, and the appreciation of the meaning and value of the different aspects of the environment. This is at the heart of much religious ethics. In the Christian Gospels this is exemplified in the parable of the rich man (Dives) and the poor man (Lazarus) (Luke 16:19–31). Dives had no awareness of the poor man at his gate, showing how consciousness of the social environment is not based in a simple objective perception but rather on the valuation of the other (Robinson, 2008). The other who is not valued, in this case the poor man, is not seen. Hence, once more, there is the need to address critically how we perceive the other, and the worldviews which hold that perception in place. This view of epistemology provides a striking alternative narrative to the scientific view of business studies.

Several things emerge from this reflection. First, while wisdom is seen by Aristotle as an intellectual virtue, as distinct from a moral virtue, it cannot be seen as value-neutral. On the contrary, consciousness is value-centred and requires an appreciation of value. Second, whilst wisdom is not prescriptively moral it does have direct moral implications.

In particular, the critical reflection on meaning and practice directly challenges any attempt at totalisation, forcing all views in one narrative (Western, 2007). Bauman (1989) argues, by extension, that it is only through hearing the critical voices in plural narratives that a repeat of the Holocaust is avoided. Third, this view of responsibility is not only universal but also social. Both/and responsibility involves sharing responsibility between individuals and groups, once more going beyond narrowly defined individual responsibility. If responsibility is shared, involving an attitude of mutual responsibility for the whole, this leads to sharing the practice of responsibility. This relates directly to all aspects and levels of decision-making. Hence, even at the level of data gathering it is critical to work together with other groups if there is to be the fullest awareness of the situation. Research in family social policy and families has noted the importance of negotiating responsibilities in developing and maintaining ethical meaning. Finch and Mason (1993) concluded that a majority of families did not work from principles or any predetermined value base, but from a negotiation of responsibility which involved three things:

1. Identifying the stakeholders in any situation.
2. Analysis of the stakeholders in terms of power and responsibility, enabling a full appreciation of constraints and resources in the situation.
3. Negotiation of responsibility. This does not simply look to the development of goods for all stakeholders. Rather, it accepts the premise of mutual responsibility and enables its embodiment in the light of shared or related values and the capacities of the stakeholders. Hence, it enables a maximisation of resources through collaboration. Far from stakeholders passively accepting benefits it involves all in the practice of responsibility.

All of this leads to a view of responsibility which is focused in creative and proactive action. The dynamic is the opposite of spending time justifying individual responsibility and looks to work through response in terms of possibilities, enabled through sharing. In one respect this relates to the Islamic concept of *hizmet*, or responsive service (Pandya and Gallagher, 2012). Focused in awareness of creation and humanity's role as co-creators this impels action. It also relates to what has been referred to as the theological virtue of hope, the capacity to creatively envision the future (Robinson, 2008). As Snyder (2000) suggests, such hope is based in some idea of shared support, goals, agency and pathways, that is, realistic possibilities. Such hope improves the more that respon-sibility for action is shared. Once more this takes us back to the synoptic thinking of wisdom, being able to see the connections between ideas, values and practice that can make such pathways possible, including different disciplines and professions, and personal and organisational resources. The focus on creativity also connects this to enterprise, ena-bling this to be viewed as essentially social. It also relates to the idea of the moral imagination (Lederach, 2005). Lederach explores imagination in terms of how we perceive the other and the self and how this moves to different possibilities in peace-building. It is not surprising that wis-dom can connect the world of business to that of conflict resolution. The South African King III (2009) report connects the two in terms of ways of developing governance, thus connecting the post-apartheid narratives to business leadership. In passing, this sense of connectivity is at the heart of Newman's view of the university (Newman, 1982).

Accountability *to*

The argument thus far suggests that wisdom generates a proactive, shared responsibility, enabling a responsible, realistic and creative response to the plurality of the social and physical environment; the creative engage-ment of difference.

However, where does the buck stop? In a sense this brings us back to earth. The creative responsibility outlined above has to be earthed in roles, functions, persons and groups so that someone or some group can be held accountable. And this brings us to the second mode of respon-sibility: accountability *to*.

Much of the contemporary management that McKenna and Rooney critique is focused on 'accounting', the process of giving an account, and a narrow view of accountability lines that does not relate the plural relationships of the social and physical environment. The stress here is on *techne*, and on ends and giving an account of how the ends are met. This explains how technical rationality can be so focused on giv-ing an account of its actions, exemplified in the record-keeping of the Third Reich (Bauman, 1989). O'Neill (2002) suggests that such technical rationality has dominated even the main professions, leading to hyper-accountability, limiting the practice of intellectual virtues to *techne* and *episteme*, and a loss of trust. In one sense the stress on scientific and technical knowledge in management is, as McKenna and Rooney sug-gest, part of justifying the lack of wisdom in management practice. Wisdom, then, can be characterised as either not rigorous or one of the soft skills, not necessary for management. However, alongside McKenna and Rooney's intellectual and epistemological narrative about modern management is a, possibly older, moral narrative (Bauman, 1989; de Woot, 2007). This suggests humankind does not naturally accept being held accountable. Accountability presumes judgment about thought and practice, and with that the implication that we might be responsible for any shortfall, and with that the imputation of guilt, and possible associated shame (Robinson, 2008). This in turn leads to what Cohen (2001) refers to as states of denial. Like Bauman (1989), in the context of knowing about atrocities, he argues that such denial inevitably follows one of four paths: (1) obedience to superiors, (2) conformity with society, (3) necessity and (4) splitting of the personality. The first two place responsibility on others. The third denies that the individual or group has a choice: we had to do it. The fourth is a different kind of denial. It denies that there are different voices within the self or the wider environment, leading to splitting of other narratives from the work narrative. The denial may be intentional or unconscious, and tends to be supported by a meta-narrative, moral or epistemological. Such denial precisely denies agency, consciousness of a complex and ambiguous social environment, and the possibility of anything other than a narrowly defined response to that environment. In other words it denies the need for wisdom, working against critical awareness of the social and physical environment, and a critical examination of one's own thoughts and motives.

Without the practice of wisdom and shared responsibility, accountability can develop several possible pathological responses, which grow from denial and collusion with denial. The first is to deny any accountability, other than for a narrow area of contractual work, at individual or organisational level. The second is to avoid giving any account. At its most extreme this involves cultic dynamics, with leaders who cannot be questioned or held to account. The most striking example of this in business was Enron (Sherman, 2002). A third response involves hyper-accountability. At one level this is the ultimate denial of responsibility, and with that the denigrating of wisdom. This is partly about making systems so perfect 'that no-one needs to be good', as T.S. Eliot (1942: 149) puts it. No one needs to exercise wisdom or creative responsibility, because the systems take care of this. The focus on activity then becomes adhering to the system and improving those systems, leading to the organisational isomorphism noted by McKenna and Rooney (2008).

The guilt attached to non-compliance confirms that there is a moral tone to this dynamic. However, it is important to note that compliance with process does not necessarily exclude the practice of wisdom or responsibility. A case in point is research-ethics protocols in universities or research firms. Effective regulation focuses judgment about issues such as low risk or possible effects on participants or other stakeholders. Each research proposal requires critical reflection and the exercise of wisdom and responsibility leading to dialogue.

An unbalanced stress on accountability suggests also the need for other aspects of wisdom, often associated with the Judeo-Christian tradition. Campbell (1984), for instance, argues for three aspects of practical wisdom: folly, simplicity and discretion. The first focuses on the person and their vulnerability, not simply targets or technical excellence. This demands awareness of limitations in the self and others, and the capacity to work with these. The second, simplicity, focuses on personal engagement. In the place of email and long email trails (as part of a possible defence against the system) this looks to phone or face-to-face communication. The third, wisdom as discretion, is about when to intervene and when not, part of decision-making that takes account of complexity.

Leadership

The implications of this for leadership are several. First, wisdom-centred leadership works against views of leadership that focus on a single- or narrow-value foundation, such as transformational leadership (Burns, 1978) or servant leadership (Greenleaf, 1977). The workforce brings to the work project many different value narratives, cultural, professional, institutional, local community and so on, all of which go to make up plural identity, and thus can contribute to any ethos. Second, transformational leadership tends to focus on conceptual consensus as the basis for organisational development. It is not clear that such a firm consensus is possible. It is more likely that there be a procedural consensus, of the kind advocated by transactional approaches to leadership (Rost, 1991), an agreement on how we go about things. Wisdom leadership, as I have tried to outline it, suggests that leadership is better focused on responsibility. Building on the core critical reflection and wider consciousness of wisdom, this is able to respond to the plural environment, internally and externally, both respecting and testing the different value narratives, and affirming plural identity and areas of shared responsibility, and negotiating creative response. This places wisdom and responsibility at the centre of professional practice at all levels of the organisation. Far from representing 'soft' or unnecessary skills, this approach is rigorous, practice-centred, holistic, able to hear and appreciate the plurality of the social environment and connect different voices to the identity of the organisation and to creative enterprise.

Such leadership is essentially dialogic, with dialogue embodying wisdom and responsibility in three interconnected aspects: critical consciousness, giving an account of thought and action, and creative action.

In the first of these, dialogue is critical to the development of consciousness of the social environment and its meaning. Dialogue further enhances relationships to the other who shares responsibility for that environment. In one respect it reveals the sameness of the other. It also focuses on difference, and with that the importance of tolerance. Such dialogue also helps the development of a realistic and truthful assessment of the data in any situation. It enables the development of agency, demanding the articulation of value and practice, which clarifies both what we think and do. Dialogue itself, though, also develops critical thinking. Even just the different perspective of the other questions can sharpen one's own account of values and core concepts.

The dialogue is not simply around ideas, and with that comes the danger of moving into the defence of ideas, exemplified by Huntington's (1998) clash of civilisations thesis. A holistic perspective, however, involves getting to know the self and other in relation to mutual plural culture, involving feelings as well as ideas, all focused in responsive action. This involves mutual challenge and mutual learning, with an output not of defence but of positive action. Hence, such dialogue primarily involves genuine engagement with the other, as person, project or place, and not the simple assertion of the organisation's location or identity in the public realm. All of these elements demand this involves not simply being responsible for critical thinking but also for the feelings that emerge around any felt sense of identity or around core values.

In the second aspect, dialogue can be seen as the key means of accountability. In one sense this involves dialogue as the major means of transparency. It embodies transparency because it requires all parties to give an account of their meaning and practice, and thus be held accountable for it, and for its subsequent development.

Such transparency enables the organisation to give an account to society in general, and this is an important development of dialogue beyond simple bilateral relationships. This is not a free flowing of meaning between participants, such as Bohm's (1996) theory of dialogue. Rather one might ask, Is the dialogue focused in shared accountability to the social and physical environment, and with that accountability to many different stakeholders? This multiple accountability, which has echoes of Bakhtin's (1981) focus on the interplay of many different voices, demands a critical awareness of the different stakeholders and their underlying values. There are also echoes of Friere's (1972) view of dialogue in which the challenge is mutual.

Dialogue also demands the development of commitment to the self and the other. It is not possible to pursue dialogue without giving space and time for it to develop, and this in turn demands a non-judgmental attitude. Commitment to the self and others is also essential if the potential critique of values and practice is to emerge from articulation and reflection. The practice of dialogue also enables listening, and with that, empathy, appreciation and responsiveness. We learn about the other as well as ourselves only if we are open to both. This deepens any sense of continued accountability to the other in the dialogue. This is partly because it sets up a contract, formal or informal, that establishes expectations that are continually tested by that dialogue.

In the third aspect of dialogue the stress is on action. We do not have to reach conceptual consensus before working through the shared issues (despite Habermas, 1992). On the contrary, these provide a shared area of concern and, along with the shared values, can be worked through regardless of differences. The stress on action strengthens the holistic framework. Action tests the accountability and commitment of those involved in the dialogue. Being accountable for actions also involves testing the actions against purpose and meaning. The actions themselves then become the basis for reflection on meaning. Such reflection then becomes the basis for the development of integrity, connecting the different voices and practice (Waples and Antes, 2011; Koehn, 2005). This also enables the development of shared responsibility, not simply the recognition of shared interests or values (cf. Porter and Kramer, 2011). The effect of all of this is to extend the imagination and develop creativity. It shows what is possible, especially where responsibility is shared, and so increases the capacity to respond. In this respect, such dialogue enables the development of hope (Robinson, 2008).

The title of this chapter is intentionally ironical; after all, 'hearing voices' is deemed by many in a therapeutic context to be pathological. This chapter has argued that health in organisations actually requires that the different voices be heard and appreciated in relation to organisational purpose, identity and relationships. Accessing these enables a view of reality that is developmental and creative. In contrast, the behaviour of large corporations can exhibit a form of madness (see *The Inside Job* and the frequency of this term) which leads to a break down in the perception of wider reality, with thinking and practice focused in a dominant narrative that is polarised, paranoid and defensive.

References

Aquinas, T. (1981). *Summa Theologica*. Resources for Christian Living, New York.
Archer, W., and J. Davison (2008). *Employability: What Do Employers Think and Want?* CIHE, London.
Aristotle (1969). *Nicomachean Ethics*. Penguin, London.
Bakhtin, M. (1981). *The Dialogic Imagination: Four Essays*. University of Texas, Austin.
Bauman, Z. (1989). *Modernity and the Holocaust*. Polity, London.
Bender, T. (2005). 'From Academic Knowledge to Democratic Knowledge'. In S. Robinson and C. Katulushi (eds), *Values in Higher Education*, pp. 51–63. Leeds University Press.
Bohm, D. (1996). *On Dialogue*. Routledge, London.
Burns, J. (1978). *Leadership*. Harper and Row, New York.
Campbell, A. (1984). *Moderated Love: A Theology of Professional Care*. SPCK, London.
CIHE (2005). *Ethics Matters: Managing Ethical Issues in Higher Education*. CIHE, London.
Cohen, S. (2001). *States of Denial*. Polity, London.
Colby, A., T. Erlich, E. Beaumont and J. Stephens (2003). *Educating Citizens*. Jossey-Bass, San Francisco.
Cowan, J. (2005). 'The Atrophy of the Affect'. In S. Robinson and C. Katulushi (eds), *Values in Higher Education*, pp. 159–79. Leeds University Press.
de Woot, P. (2007). *Should Prometheus be Bound?* Palgrave, Basingstoke.
Dostoevsky, F. (1993). *The Grand Inquisitor*. Hackett, Indianapolis.
Eliot, T.S. (1942). 'The Rock'. In idem, *The Complete Poems and Plays*, pp. 145–51. Faber and Faber, London.
Farrar, M., S. Robinson, P. Wetherly and Y. Valli (2011). *Islam and the West*. Palgrave, Basingstoke.
Finch, J., and J. Mason (1993). *Negotiating Family Responsibilities*. Routledge, London.
Friere, P. (1972). *Pedagogy of the Oppressed*. Continuum, New York.
Ghoshal, S. (2005). 'Bad Management Theories Are Destroying Good Management Practices'. *Academy of Management Learning and Education*, (4)1: 75–91.
Greenleaf, R. (1977). *The Servant as Leader: A Journey into the Nature of Legitimate Power and Greatness*. Paulist Press, New York.
Gregg, S., and J. Stoner (2009). *Profit, Prudence and Virtue*. Imprint Academic, Exeter.
Habermas, J. (1992). *Moral Consciousness and Communicative Action*. Polity, London.
Huntington, S. (1998). *The Clash of Civilizations and the Remaking of World Order*. Touchstone, New York.
Kaul, M., and J.A. Smith (2011). 'Exploring the Nature of Responsibility in Higher Education'. Unpublished research, Anglia Ruskin University.
Khurana, R., and N. Nohria (2008). 'It's Time to Make Management a True Profession'. *Harvard Business Review*, 86(10): 70–77, 140.
King III (2009). *Report on Corporate Governance*. IOD, Johannesburg.

Koehn, D. (2005). 'Integrity as a Business Asset'. *Journal of Business Ethics*, 58: 125–36.

Ladd, J. (1991). 'Bhopal: An Essay on Moral Responsibility and Civic Virtue'. *Journal of Social Philosophy*, 22: 73–91.

Lanchester, J. (2010). *Whoops!* Penguin, London.

Lederach, J.P. (2005). *The Moral Imagination*. Oxford University Press.

Levinas, E. (1998). *Entre Nous: On Thinking-of-the-Other*. Columbia University Press, New York.

MacIntyre, A. (1981). *After Virtue*. Duckworth, London.

McKenna, B., and D. Rooney (2008). 'Wise Leadership and the Capacity for Ontological Acuity'. *Management Communication Quarterly*, 21(4): 537–46.

McKenny, P. (2005). 'Responsibility'. In G. Meilaender and W. Werpehowski (eds), *Theological Ethics*, pp. 237–53. Oxford University Press.

Mustakova-Possardt, E. (2004). 'Education for Critical Moral Consciousness'. *Journal of Moral Education*, 33 (September): 245–70.

Newman, J. (1982). *The Idea of the University*. Notre Dame University Press.

O'Neill, O. (2002). *A Question of Trust*. Cambridge University Press.

Pandya, S., and N. Gallagher (eds) (2012). *The Gulen Hizmet Movement and Its Transnational Activities: Case Studies of Altruistic Activism in Contemporary Islam*. Universal Publishers, London.

Porter, M., and M.R. Kramer (2011). 'Creating Shared Value: How to Reinvent Capitalism – and Unleash a Wave of Innovation and Growth'. *Harvard Business Review* (January–February): 62–77.

Ramadan, T. (2012). 'Multiculturalism'. In P. Wetherly, S. Robinson and M. Farrar (eds), *Islam in the West*, pp. 2–11. Palgrave, Basingstoke.

Rayment, J.J., and J.A. Smith (2010). *MisLeadership*. Gower, London.

Robinson, S. (1992). *Serving Society*. Grove, Nottingham.

Robinson, S. (2005). *Ethics and Employability*. HEA, York.

Robinson, S. (2008). *Spirituality, Ethics and Care*. Jessica Kingsley, London.

Robinson, S. (2011). *Leadership Responsibility: Ethical and Organizational Considerations*. Peter Lang, Geneva.

Robinson, S., and P. Dowson (2011). 'Responsibility and Integrity in the Curriculum'. *Journal of Global Responsibility*, 2 (October): 253–69.

Robinson, S., and P. Dowson (2012). *Business Ethics in Practice*. CIPD, London.

Rooney, D., and B. Mckenna (2007). 'Wisdom in Organizations: Whence and Wither'. *Social Epistemology: A Journal of Knowledge, Culture and Policy*, 21(2): 113–38.

Rost, J. (1991). *Leadership in the Twenty-first Century*. Praeger, New York.

St Paul's Institute (2011). 'Value and Values: Perceptions of Ethics in the City Today'. Available at www.stpaulsinstitute.org.uk/assets/docs.

Schumpeter, J. (2009). 'The pedagogy of the privileged'. *Economist* (24 September).

Schweiker, W. (1995). *Responsibility and Christian Ethics*. Cambridge University Press.

Scott, P. (2005). 'The University and Civic Values'. In S. Robinson and C. Katulushi (eds), *Values in Higher Education*, pp. 8–23. Leeds University Press.

Sherman, S. (2002). 'Enron: Uncovering the Uncovered Story'. *Columbia Journalism Review*, 40: 22–8.

Snyder, C. (2000). 'The Past and Possible Futures of Hope'. *Journal of Social and Clinical Psychology*, 19(1): 11–28.

Sun, W., J. Stewart and D. Pollard (eds) (2011). *Reframing Corporate Social Responsibility*. Emerald, Bradford.

Tawney, R.H. (1930). *Equality*. Allen and Unwin, London.

Taylor, C. (1989). *Sources of the Self*. Cambridge University Press.

Tett, G. (2009). *Fool's Gold*. Little and Brown, London.

Visser, W. (2011). *The Age of Responsibility: CSR 2.0 and the New DNA of Business*. John Wiley, London.

Waples, E., and A. Antes (2011). 'Sensemaking'. In C. Wankel and A. Stachowicz-Stanusch (eds), *Management Education for Integrity*, pp. 15–48. Emerald, Bradford.

Western, S. (2007). *Leadership: A Critical Text*. Sage, London.

13
Managerial Wisdom in Corporate Governance: The (Ir)Relevance of Accountability and Responsibility at Corporate Boards

Peter Verhezen

Our capitalist market system today has been characterised by the sins of arrogance, greed, untrustworthiness and callousness. Is it possible that wise decisions – that is, making 'right' judgments that lead to good actions and beneficial results – may be able to help in addressing the daunting challenges of our corporations within the prevailing market mechanisms?

Currently, *pecuniary reward incentives* within governance *rules and regulations* are the main business motivators. Good corporate governance – the apex of power of any organisation – is being interpreted as compliance with specific rules and regulations, and to install useful pecuniary incentive systems that aim to align top management's decisions with those of shareholders.

I briefly elaborate on the generic principles and characteristics of corporate governance in part one, and in part two I seek to explicate how wise decision-making might be incorporated within a model of corporate governance. Finally, in the third part I analyse the notions of accountability and responsibility in corporate governance, and how to embed them within the notion of managerial wisdom.

1 Corporate Governance Practices: 'Comply or Explain!'

The legitimacy of the corporate board that represents the owners comes from the fact that law, customs and norms confer upon those board members both the *power* (the formal and informal authority) and the *obligation* (the 'formal' accountability and 'informal' responsibility) to manage the business and the affairs of the corporation. Corporate governance establishes the identity of the (legal) power within the organisation and how it can be used. Corporate governance is the system by which business corporations are directed and controlled.[1] Executives make decisions on a daily basis that are supposed to create value for the organisation. However, quite often those decisions may better serve top management at the expense of other parties related to the firm: those costs are known as *agency costs* which find their roots in the separation of ownership and top management. Corporate governance principles are justifiably considered as a needed check and balance system of top management of the firm, who runs the firm on behalf of the owners but who may have to necessarily maximise shareholder value, causing an *agency problem* (Huse, 2007; Wallace and Zinkin, 2005; Dimma, 2002).

The traditional agency theory of corporate governance sees the firm as a nexus of contracts between free and rational individuals optimising their own interests (Friedman, 1970; Fama and Jensen, 1983; Jensen and Meckling, 1976; Jensen, 1986; Lorsch and Clark, 2008). The incorporation of a firm leads to a nexus of *contractual relationships* in which a set of *promises* is made to investors, workers, suppliers, customers, local communities and other stakeholders. It may be argued that corporate governance is about how such promises are institutionalised or materialised, whether by legal forms or more informal arrangements.[2] In essence, corporate governance is about building trust or keeping trust, whereby the governance rules and regulations should strengthen shareholders' contracting power within the firm and control possible corporate deviance or violation from the contracts between the different participants, both investors as well as non-shareholder constituencies. Governance will therefore not prevent misconduct or misdeeds, but it can actually improve the way an organisation is managed to deploy assets and resources in the most efficient and effective way, and possibly prevent some excessive threatening risks on the downside through the application of '*best*' (*international*) *corporate governance principles* (Clarke, 2007; Charan, 2005, 2009; Chew and Gillan, 2009; Carver, 2010; Agrawal and Chadha, 2005).

From a shareholder perspective (Fama and Jensen, 1983; Jensen, 1986, 2002; Bebchuk and Fried, 2004), effective governance should aim to increase the equity value by better aligning incentives between management and equity holders and between minority and majority shareholders. From a stakeholder (Freeman, Dunham and McVea, 2010), resource-based theory (Pfeffer, 1972) or network perspective (Peng and Qi Zhou, 2005), effective governance should provide policies that produce stable and safe employment, provide an acceptable standard of living to workers, mitigate risks for debt holders, provide reliable products and services to customers, improve the community and acknowledge the importance of ethical and ecological objectives or constraints. Although those different perspectives may not completely overlap, and although they hardly can be 'maximised' at once (Jensen, 2002), it may be argued that there is no fundamental contradiction between such views in the longer term; they can be assumed to be complementary (Freeman, Dunham and McVea, 2007; Donaldson and Preston, 1995; Verhezen, Notowidigdo and Hardjapamekas, 2012).

Despite the developed forms of corporate governance and regulation prevalent in the West, excessive debt financing and the subsequent financial crisis and associated scandals were not averted (Roubini, 2011; Rajan, 2010; Shiller, 2012). Is it possible that in recent decades, the virtues of self-discipline, prudence and stewardship have been in decline in the corporate scene? Indeed, the senior management of financial institutions has been publicly accused of evading any form of formal accountability or ignored any kind of ethical responsibility. Instead of contributing to societal needs spawned by passionate commitment to timeless values, corporate boards are viewed by wider society as aiming for short-term profitability driven by pecuniary incentives, in some instances not even complying with the letter of the law, let alone following the spirit of the law. Nonetheless, pecuniary incentives are mere hygiene motivators, whereas a higher purpose uplifts people and management in a company. Rules and regulations installed by a board can hardly compete with such higher purposes; nor can pecuniary incentives really match the power of those inspirational values. However, too much emphasis on control and on complying with formalistic governance rules and regulations, and focusing on financial results and incentives, can 'crowd out' and undermine the effect of a values-driven strategy (Verhezen, 2010; Gentile, 2010). Empathetic and wise boards find a dynamic balance of *yin* and *yang*, of accountability and autonomy, being inspired by an *enlightening* organisational purpose and vision that lifts the spirit of employees and managers alike. Such visions usually go beyond the traditional trade-offs of either/or. Firms like Whole Foods, Timberland, Unilever, Google or Disney, among other visionary companies, seem to indicate that the *stakes* of shareholders and other relevant constituencies (e.g. customers, employees, communities) are not traded off against each other, but integrated and aligned as much as possible (Kanter, 2009). A number of these well-performing firms explicitly endorse and pursue the triple objectives of 'people, planet and profit', making them accountable *and* responsible for their business activities (Elkington, 1997; Kanter, 2011).

The current adage within mainstream corporate governance that as long as one follows and complies with best practices – and if not, one needs to give a valid explanation why not – one will have an effective system to direct the firm to achieve its goals, may be a gross understatement. 'Comply or explain' is a good start, but will not guarantee that firms are well *governed*, that is, properly *controlled* and effectively *directed*.

The effect of failing boards is a low-trust workplace where individuals lack the autonomy to make smart and real-time decisions between competing priorities. In a fast changing environment, and in the absence of a higher and compelling corporate purpose, only actual pain and distress will disrupt organisations and make them react to the rapidly accelerating pace of change (Kanter, 2009; Bainbridge, 2008). Crises often result in more heavy-handed control, which is usually counterproductive.

2 Does Managerial Wisdom Compel to a 'Higher' Common Purpose?

The corporate ethical debacles at Enron, Parmalat and Ahold – the result of faulty financial reporting and outright fraud – have emphasised the importance of corporate values and corporate oversight in decision-making. The more recent mortgage and Euro crises show that a system of purely pecuniary reward incentives is not functioning for the 'common good'. Moreover, erroneous assumptions – often leading to excessive risk-taking or driven by greed, hubris or plain ignorance – have aggravated the impact of the crises. Nor would any rule or regulation be able to rectify such imbalances, as Shiller (2012) has pointed out. When the leader of an organisation lacks plain 'wisdom', the system can be compromised, which results in diminished performance or outright failure. My argument in this chapter is that corporate governance mechanisms require wise decision-making at the board and subsequently executive level. Management needs to make practical choices and 'wise' informed decisions, but what is the meaning of wisdom in a management context?

Wisdom may be understood as a way of being that is fundamentally practical in a complex and uncertain world: the praxis to act rightly, depending on our ability to perceive the situation accurately, to have the appropriate intuition about such a situation or trend, to discern and reflect about what is appropriate in this particular situational context, and to act upon it (Schwartz, 2011; Hays, 2003). To a great extent, managerial wisdom is dependent on, and influenced by, experience and the moral acuity to act appropriately in particular situations (Malan and Kriger, 1998).

Some may define wisdom following a western tradition as the expertise in the conduct and meaning of life, or an expert knowledge system in fundamental life pragmatism (Baltes and Staudinger, 2000), and thus, by extension, the meaning of an organisation. Such practical intelligence – the (tacit) knowing *how* rather than the knowing *that* – requires continuous adaptation, shaping and selection in responding to make balanced judgments and decisions in different kinds of complex and ambiguous contexts (Sternberg, 1998; Kok, 2009). Others may emphasise an eastern approach to integrate the cognitive, reflective and affective elements of wisdom (Ardelt, 2003). Somehow, wisdom implies the integration of different perspectives. It encourages us to transcend self-interest into a broader integrated whole, or 'common good' issues, by balancing intrapersonal (one's own), interpersonal (others) and extrapersonal (community or larger interests) needs through the mediation of values (Sternberg, 1998; Orwoll and Perlmutter, 1990; Kessler and Bailey, 2007). Wise leadership emphasises the 'integrated whole' instead of the separated parts, and often is recognised by its exemplary moral nature. In Aristotelian tradition, wisdom is concerned with ethical judgments that are noble and worthwhile (Aristotle, 1984; Kok, 2009). Wise leadership acknowledges the importance of a more holistic 'common purpose' beyond mere short-term profitability that takes into account the concerns of the organisation and society alike (Boyatzis and McKee, 2005; Kanter, 2011; Porter and Kramer, 2006; Nonaka and Takeuchi, 2011). A wise leader makes sound and balanced judgments, acts prudently, prioritises the organisational 'common' purpose above self-interest, and communicates a far-sighted understanding of the industry, so that the organisation is provided with a sense of what needs to be done.

Managerial wisdom is indeed about appropriate practical *decision-making* that should be virtuous and well communicated. Wise decision-making usually occurs *within a certain traditional context*, fuelled by a continuous learning process that acts, re-acts and pro-acts in particular situations, guided by *integrity*, and based on the *experience* gained, the *knowledge*[3] acquired that is the result of *a logical, rational process* and/or *intuitive insights* to foresee and prepare events. Hence, McKenna, Rooney and Boal (2009) assert that (managerial) knowledge without integrity can be dangerous and dreadful, while integrity without (managerial) knowledge is rather weak and unfocused. Managerial wisdom is an ability that enables one to minimise the cognitive limitations of bounded rational capabilities by relying on (1) (cognitive and affective) knowledge, (2) long individual or organisational experience that functions as a tradition,

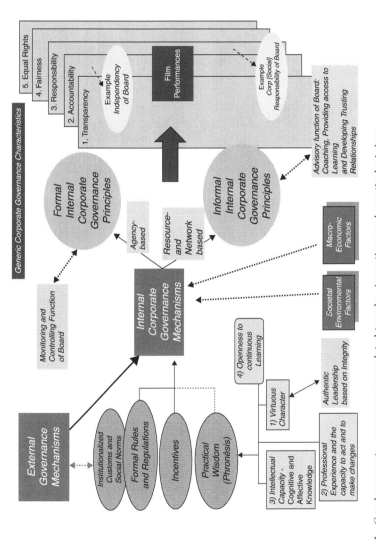

Figure 13.1 Good corporate governance correlated to rules, incentives and practical wisdom

(3) intellectual and moral virtues underpinning managerial decisions, and finally (4) an openness to continuously learn to improve (Aristotle, 1984; Kessler and Bailey, 2007; Cranton and Carusetta, 2004; Fernando and Chowdhury, 2010; Schwartz, 2011).

Wisdom embraces a certain kind of *truthfulness* that is sincere or trust-worthy, and accurate or objective (Verhezen, 2009). Wise corporate leaders are able to grasp the 'truthful essence' of the organisation through excellent communication skills and convincing power that subsequently can spur management and employees to take action in teams. Such leaders are usually committed to *authentic* behaviour, guided by the leader's true self as reflected by core values, beliefs and feelings. Authentic leadership and authentic relations are characterised by transparency and a high level of *integrity* that creates trust on the one hand, and by guidance toward worthy objectives or a higher 'common' purpose beyond a mere self on the other (Parameshwar, 2006). When people are giving their word, most people are sincere (well meaning). Only within the praxis one will be able to express *sincerity* (or trustworthiness that requires a high level of authenticity) and some rational (factual) *objectivity*.[4] Organisational integrity, in the sense of stewardship, creates and cultivates standards that can provide the cultural cohesion for continued organisational life. It reflects a certain professional respon-sibility and competence, emphasising a right attitude to approach a dilemma, rather than specified moral characteristics. Such an *attitude of integrity* may lead to behaviour which complies with what one can expect of a virtuous and trustworthy administrator or executive who is able to communicate and demonstrate these ethical values superbly (Verhezen, 2008; Simons, 2002). Most multinational organisations com-bine a compliance- and integrity-based strategy to address the issue of (un)ethical behaviour (Rose, 2007). However, there seems to be a con-sensus that integrity-based, rather than compliance-oriented, strategies may provide superior results in tackling moral dilemmas (Paine, 1994; Trevino et al., 1999; Trevinyo-Rodriguez, 2007). The force of integrity relates to the fact that individual employees feel empowered and involved in integrity-based strategies whereas they may feel as though they are being watched in the case of compliance strategies.

To be a person or leader of integrity one has to honour one's word to oneself and to other people, which means that one keeps one's word, and when one cannot or will not, one deals with the impact and com-municates the consequences and how to deal with them appropriately. This pragmatic re-interpretation of integrity allows corporate leaders to manoeuvre in an increasingly complex and ambiguous business context to honour their word, even if they cannot keep it to its fullest sense. Such an attitude will enhance personal as well as organisational reputations.

Practical wisdom (*phronèsis*) remains an ongoing, finite and fallible process, reaching out to what can be aspired to. Effective leadership understands how to embrace managerial wisdom to make choices that are consistent with the fundamental but evolving goals and objectives of the firm and to enhance the overall performance of the firm. Unless authentic leadership shapes the practices within and between organisations, and unless values constituting a higher organisational purpose are 'incorporated' into 'best' (informal) corporate governance practices, managerial wisdom will remain a distant corporate ideal at best, or be completely irrelevant to organisations, thereby possibly wasting valuable resources and/or harming external stakeholders. Relying on formalistic corporate governance rules and pecuniary corporate incentives may only 'crowd out' wise decision-making and its commitment to a higher common purpose.

3. Managerial Wisdom Creates and Preserves Corporate Value beyond Compliance

It is widely agreed that the board's fiduciary duty to optimise the shareholders' value aims to guarantee transparency, fairness, accountability, responsibility and equal-rights treatment. Mere compliance with such principles and characteristics will not have a real, substantial impact on the ruling and functioning of the organisation. It may only lead to an array of inhibiting, politically correct dictates; not necessarily ameliorating corporate governance and the performance of the firm (Sonnenfeld, 2004). Compliance with specific formal *rules and regulations* is frequently overstated by companies and can even be counterproductive as it is too focused on the *pecuniary reward system* which may endanger the long-term viability of a firm.

Managerial wisdom by board members involves the direction, monitoring and controlling of top management in order to *create corporate value in a sustainable manner at the upside* and to *preserve corporate value at the downside* (as visualised in Fig. 13.2). Corporate value is most often expressed in a decent financial return on the capital invested. However, if we agree that management is the technology and art of human accomplishments within business, such value creation and preservation focuses on more than the bottom line. Well-performing and wise executives acknowledge that great firms are often driven and motivated by

206

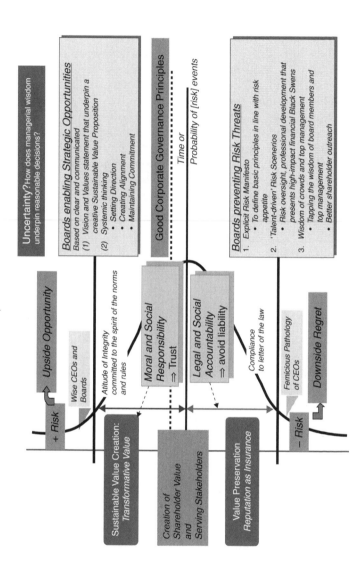

Figure 13.2 Accountable and responsible boards enabling opportunities and preventing threats

a 'higher' (common) purpose beyond complying to the financial dictate of shareholder maximisation, as Ben & Jerry's (now part of Unilever) and Whole Foods (Mackey, 2011), for instance, clearly reveal.

The *legitimacy* of the board usually arises from the demonstration of integrity and competence that provides a higher 'common purpose'. This means steering the organisation towards improved performance over extended periods of time: not just maximising quarterly profit but also emphasising sustainable corporate value that takes the protection of environment and prudent use of natural resources as well as social progress into account. Building board legitimacy requires wise, independent directors to guarantee the appropriate monitoring process of top management and to direct those executives to become more *accountable* and *responsible*.

It is widely assumed in the corporate governance literature that a majority of *independent board members* will counterbalance the power of top-management entrenchment (Brown and Caylor, 2006; Gordon, 2007; Lev, 2012). Indeed, it is assumed that boards inevitably have close contact with top management and that this proximity to management makes it harder to remain 'psychologically' distant and objective, leading to agency problems, an anchored bias or 'an inside view' (Kahneman and Lovallo, 1993; Klein, 1998; Larcker and Tayan, 2011). Independent or outside board members – assumed to have a relatively high integrity securing their reputation – are less entrenched with top management and the CEO to safeguard the implementation of governance principles in the organisation, and guarantee fair, equitable and transparent treatment of *all* shareholders. Independent boards supposedly will guarantee the legal protection of dispersed equity ownership against the actual influence and power of CEOs and their top management or safeguard minority shareholder rights against controlling majority shareholders (family or state).

The presumption of the independence of board members in securing some formal (fiduciary) *accountability* to investors and shareholders is questionable in the light of recent experience. It is well known that institutional investors and regulators call for boards of US- and UK-listed firms to have a required number, if not majority, of independent directors. Indeed, those independent directors are assumed to have the managerial wisdom to guarantee appropriate monitoring and directing of the top-management activities. However, firms with more independent boards – proxied by the fraction of independent or outside directors minus the fraction of inside directors – have not necessarily achieved substantial and sustainable improved profitability, and in some instances they even underperform compared to other firms (Bhagat and Black, 2002; Bhagat and Bolton, 2008). Studies in Australia, Singapore and the United Kingdom reveal facts that counter the conventional wisdom of favouring independent boards (Faccio et al., 1999; Lawrence et al., 1999; Mak et al., 2001; all quoted in Bhagat and Black, 2002).

Wise leadership – both on the regulatory and on the corporate side – emphasises independency as *a state of mind*, while acknowledging that some minimum legal requirements may be helpful. However, believing that legalising a human board's behaviour through rules and incentives could achieve more *accountability* and *responsibility* may result in badly spent organisational resources, and can even harm the organisation and its environment. Creating and preserving long-term organisational value implies that a board and top management are accountable for financial performance to shareholders and investors, while they also need to take full responsibility to serve stakeholders where appropriate and viable. A corporation displays social responsibility when it engages itself in processes that appear to advance a general or contextual social and/or ecological agenda beyond mandatory legal requirements. Those CSR processes are predominantly of an intangible nature, aiming to generate reputational capital, improved corporate culture, and legitimacy or loyalty within the business community.

The notion of independence and oversight as the main proxy for high-quality corporate governance may be misguided and even unrealistic. Most 'independent' boards can hardly resist being 'captured' by top-management influence in one way or another. Moreover, simultaneously serving a monitoring and a management coaching function in the same company is a high expectation for anyone, even the most professional expert (Macey, 2008). The Enron board, for instance, with 11 independent directors on its 14-member board, was not only a model of professionalism (of board and management), it was also a model of board capture by management. There are numerous anecdotes, and even studies, where a highly independent board has not prevented large-scale wealth destruction.

Some scholars argue that only real dissident outside directors, initiated and proposed by hedge funds or other institutional investors, can be perceived as genuine independent mavericks to change a board's functioning, and not liable in any way to the management they are supposed to monitor (Macey, 2008). Such an independent attitude may also be found among *wise* leaders at corporate boards who are not just motivated by pecuniary incentives but also by a compelling vision and a higher 'common' purpose.

Indeed, boards that are genuinely guided by practical wisdom perceive *independence as a state of mind*, not as a legal compliance issue. The reliance on the integrity of all those board members – either insider or outsider directors – will most likely produce superior results than mere *tickbox* compliance to a legal status of independency. One cannot ignore the fact that a board remains a collegial decision-making body and that boards are often 'captured' by the interests of top management, especially under a single-tier board structure as in an Anglo-Saxon context (Charan, 2009; Macey, 2008). Perhaps 'independent' directors are not independent enough. The suggested driving force of re-interpreting independency of the board is not a legal rule, nor ignoring human organisational board behaviour, but emphasising the importance of a virtuous leadership behaviour which underpins managerial or practical wisdom. *Integrity of mind* here implies that board members are aiming to adhere to financial objectives that are aligned to non-financial goals, and to objectively monitor top management while walking a fine line in remaining collegial (i.e. being proximate) with other fellow board members and with management, whom they advise and supervise. There is some evidence that a moderate number of insider non-executive directors of an average-sized board tend to be more profitable than firms with hardly any insider on the board (Bhagat and Black, 2002; Bhagat and Bolton, 2008). A collaborative board with a small but committed minority group of inside directors improves board decision-making due to their superior information. Although inside board members may lack legal independence, they have their human capital, and often most of their financial capital, committed to the firm, making them formidable contributors and committed advisors to the firm. Insiders may outperform outside directors in terms of strategic planning decisions because of their intimate expertise and specific knowledge of the firm. Affiliated and inside directors seem to have a positive effect on the return on investment and stock market performance (Klein, 1998; Bhagat and Black, 2002; Lev, 2012).

With the rise to power of institutional investors – shifting corporate control back to owners from managers –the demand for more accountability and responsibility of and within firms is growing. This is perhaps a too-tall request or expectation?

Concluding Remarks

Pecuniary reward incentives within certain regulatory boundaries and formal governance rules have been the main motivators to incite innovative and efficient corporate behaviour that supposedly results in a fair return to the investment made by shareholders. However, managerial wisdom has hardly been perceived as a constitutive, and thus relevant, factor in creating and preserving corporate organisational value. A re-interpretation of the notions of accountability and responsibility may be needed, shifting away from verifying which formal governance features are in place at boards to evaluating the success of various functions of good corporate governance to steer the organisation to sustainable corporate value. The independency of board members, for example, is not an exercise in mere legal compliance but rather a state of mind that implies that board members adhere to the notion of integrity required to honour their fiduciary duty to optimise sustainable corporate value.

The hypothesis here is that the notions of *being accountable* for legal and fiduciary contract to the shareholders and *being responsive and responsible* to the demands of a broader constituency will need to be reinterpreted and inspired by the constituting characteristics and features of practical wisdom. Managerial wisdom or *phronèsis* has been defined as an amalgam of (1) integrity, values reflection and a compelling purpose; (2) cognitive and affective tacit knowledge; (3) professional experience; and (4) fuelled by a continuous process of learning.

Authentic leaders are most often quite true to themselves and deploy high levels of integrity that are incorporated in their decision-making, acknowledging the importance of continuously learning how to address ethical and environmental challenges while preserving or enhancing the economic value of the firm. Nonetheless, wise and integrative leadership transcends the conventional trade-offs between an economic reality and the different increasing ethical and environmental demands.

Profitability does matter, but judging solely on outcomes is a serious deterrent to taking risks that may be necessary to make wise judgment calls. Wise leaders are aware that the way decisions are evaluated affect the way decisions are made. Wise boards set clear ethical standards, and use rewards and punishments to ensure standards are followed. Indeed, corporate governance mechanisms and corporate leadership in charge of supervising strategic choices should integrate ethical and environmental values – or a higher 'common' purpose – with commercial value, encouraging a *crowding-in* effect of integrity rather than emphasising the usual *crowding-out* effect of purely pecuniary rewards to top management for taking risks that allegedly pay off. An effective leader does not necessarily lead by control only, but rather by vision and conviction and a willingness to be accountable for his or her management decisions to the board while also taking full responsibility for the consequences of the firm's activities to relevant stakeholders. Unless wise leadership shapes the practices within and between organisations, and unless new re-interpreted notions of accountability and responsibility are incorporated into 'best' corporate governance practices, managerial wisdom will remain a distant corporate ideal.

Is it not 'true' that wise leaders look toward the past with gratitude, try to be of service for their organisation in the present and consider the future with responsibility? Practising such a state of mind may lead to organisations steered by wise boards that can be trusted again.

Notes

1. According to the Organisation for Economic Co-operation and Development (OECD), 'Corporate governance is the system by which business corporations are directed and controlled. The corporate governance structure specifies the distribution of rights and responsibilities among different participants in the company, such as, the board, managers, shareholders and other stakeholders, and spells out the rules and procedures for making decisions on corporate affairs. By doing this, it also provides the structure through which the company objectives and strategy are set, and the means of attaining these objectives and monitoring performance' (www.oecd.org/daf/corporate affairs/corporategovernanceprinciples). The OECD set for good corporate governance contains the following basic principles: (1) *Ensuring the basis for an effective corporate governance framework* – the corporate governance framework should promote transparent and efficient markets, be consistent with the rule of law and clearly articulate the division of responsibilities among different supervisory, regulatory and enforcement authorities; (2) *The rights of shareholders and key ownership functions* – the corporate governance framework should protect and facilitate the exercise of shareholders' rights; (3) *The equitable treatment of shareholders* – the corporate governance framework should ensure the equitable treatment of all shareholders, including minority and foreign shareholders. All shareholders should have the opportunity to obtain effective redress for violation of their rights; (4) *The role of stakeholders in corporate governance* – the corporate governance framework should recognise the rights of stakeholders established by law or through mutual agreements and encourage active cooperation between corporations and stakeholders in creating wealth, jobs and the sustainability of financially sound enterprises; (5) *Disclosure and transparency* – the corporate governance framework should ensure that timely and accurate disclosure is made on all material matters regarding the corporation, including the financial situation, performance, ownership and governance of the company; and lastly, (6) *The responsibilities of the board* – the corporate governance framework should ensure the strategic guidance of the company, the effective monitoring of management by the board and the board's accountability to the company and the shareholders. It is quite obvious that this definition is quite consistent with the one presented by Adrian Cadbury, which is quite influential among UK and increasingly other national corporations and followed as a guideline by quite a number of their boards (http://ecgi.org/codes/documents/cadbury.pdf).

2. See Macey, 2008; Hermes Pensions Management Ltd, Dec. (www.hermes.co.uk/corporate_governance). Corporate governance refers to corporate decision-making and control, particularly the structure of the board and its working procedures. However, the term 'corporate governance' is sometimes used very widely, embracing a company's relations with a wide range of stakeholders or very narrowly referring to a company's compliance with the provisions of best-practices codes.

3. See Kessler and Bailey, 2007. Socrates' belief that wisdom is knowing what one does not know represents a fundamental characteristic of humility and prudence. Wisdom can therefore be perceived as an attitude that balances knowledge and human fallibility or ignorance. Wisdom involves a recognition of, and a response to, human limitations. To be a wise person lies not in what one knows but rather in the manner in which that knowledge is held and how that person puts the knowledge to use. The essence of wisdom is in knowing that one does not know, in the appreciation that knowledge is fallible, that wise persons can be fallible, in the balance between knowing and doubting.

4. See Williams, 2002; Stout, 1993, 2003; Grayling, 2007; Verhezen, 2009. Intentional sincerity or trustworthiness in fact refers to a more operational notion of integrity, honouring one's word; and professional accuracy refers to experience, expertise and specific knowledge in the organisation. The combination of integrity and professional experience unfolds to truthfulness. Truthfulness is the activity or process that possibly results in wisdom. The notion of *truthfulness* or *Wahrhaftigkeit* has an objective status – as well as a normative one. The criteria of ethical worth – such as integrity – remain fallible and dependent on (1) our *intentional* sincerity and (2) *professional* accuracy in using our moral vocabulary. Indeed, truthful moral reasoning requires the 'virtues' of (1) *sincerity* ('what you say reveals what you believe') – or trustworthiness – and (2) *accuracy* ('you do your utmost best to acquire true beliefs') – or 'objectivity'-acquiring abilities. While sincerity is no proof against error, it is just the disposition so say what you think is true without wanting to mislead, but intentionally looking towards the truth of the matter. Sincerity involves a certain kind of spontaneity when one tries to 'tell the truth'; it refers to a normative pragmatics or a matter of deontic attitude centred on the notions of commitment and entitlement. Being sincere implies a self-reflective attitude of authenticity. One is authentic when one is true to oneself. Authenticity requires having the will you want to have – identifying what you care about with the 'desires' (of integrity) that guide your action. The notion of accuracy includes resistance to self-deception and wishful thinking, which implies the acknowledgment of traditions and (scientific) authority. Accuracy implicitly refers to (a semantics explaining) a conceptual content or relevant *semantic* adequacy.

References

Agrawal, A., and S. Chadha (2005). 'Corporate Governance and Accounting Scandals'. *Journal of Law and Economics*, 48: 371–85.

Ardelt, M. (2003). 'Empirical Assessment of a Three-dimensional Wisdom Scale'. *Research on Aging*, 25(3): 275–324.

Aristotle (1984). *The Nicomachean Ethics.* Oxford University Press, New York.

Aristotle (1992). *The Politics.* Penguin Books, London.

Bainbridge, S.M. (2008). *The New Corporate Governance in Theory and Practice.* Oxford University Press.

Baltes, P.H., and U.M. Staudinger (2000). 'Wisdom: A Metaheuristic (Pragmatic) to Orchestrate Mind and Virtue toward Excellence'. *American Psychologist*, 55: 122–36.

Banks, Erik (2004). *Corporate Governance: Financial Responsibility, Controls and Ethics.* Palgrave Macmillan, Basingstoke.

Bebchuk, L., and J. Fried (2004). *Pay without Performance. The Unfulfilled Promise of Executive Compensation.* Harvard University Press, Cambridge, MA.

Bhagat, S., and B. Black (2002). 'The Non-correlation between Board Independence and Long-term Firm Performance'. *Journal of Corporation Law* (Winter): 231–73.

Bhagat, S., and B. Bolton (2008). 'Corporate Governance and Firm Performance'. *Journal of Corporate Finance*, 14: 257–73.

Boyatzis, R., and A. McKee (2005). *Resonant Leadership: Renewing Yourself and Connecting with Others through Mindfulness, Hope, and Compassion.* Harvard Business School Press, Cambridge, MA.

Brown, L.D., and M.L. Caylor (2006). 'Corporate Governance and Firm Valuation'. *Journal of Accounting and Public Policy*, 25: 409–34.

Carver, J. (2010). 'A Case for Global Governance Theory: Practitioners Avoid It, Academics Narrow It, the World Needs It'. *Corporate Governance: An International Review*, 18(2): 149–57.

Charan, R. (2005). *Boards That Deliver: Advantages Corporate Governance from Compliance to Competitive Advantage.* Jossey-Bass, San Francisco.

Charan, R. (2009). *Owning Up: The 14 Questions Every Board Member Needs to Ask.* Jossey-Bass, San Francisco.

Chew, D.H., and S.L. Gillan (eds) (2009). *Global Corporate Governance.* Columbia Business School Press, New York.

Clarke, T. (2007). *Corporate Governance.* Routledge, New York.

Cranton, P., and E. Carusetta (2004). 'Developing Authenticity as a Transformative Process'. *Journal of Transformative Education*, 2(4): 276–93.

Dimma, W. (2002). *Excellence in the Boardroom: Best Practices in Corporate Directorship.* Wiley & Sons, Ontario.

Donaldson, T.L., and L.E. Preston (1995). 'The Stakeholder Theory of the Corporation: Concepts, Evidence, and Implications'. *Academy of Management Review*, 20(1): 65–91.

Elkington, J. (1997). *Cannibals with Forks: The Triple Bottom Line of 21st Century Business.* Capstone, Oxford.

Fama, E., and M. Jensen (1983). 'Separation of Ownership and Control'. *Journal of Law and Economics*, 26: 310–25.

Fernando, M., and R.M.M.I. Chowdhury (2010). 'The Relationship between Spiritual Well-being and Ethical Orientations in Decision-making: An Empirical Study with Business Executives in Australia'. *Journal of Business Ethics*, 95 (3): 211–25.

Freeman, E. (ed.) (2010). *Stakeholder Theory.* Cambridge University Press.

Freeman, E., L. Dunham and J. McVea (2007). 'Strategic Ethics – Strategy, Wisdom, and Stakeholder Theory: A Pragmatic and Entrepreneurial View of Stakeholder Strategy'. In E.H. Kessler and J.R. Bailey (eds), *Handbook of Organisational and Managerial Wisdom*, pp. 151–80. Sage, London.

Friedman, M. (1970). 'The social responsibility of business is to increase its profits'. *New York Times Magazine* (13 September): 32–3, 122, 126.

Gardner, W.L., B.J. Avolio, F. Luthans, D.R. May and F. Walumbwa (2005). 'Can You See the Real Me? A Self-based Model of Authentic Leader and Follower Development'. *Leadership Quarterly*, 16: 343–72.

Gelter, M. (2009). 'The Dark Side of Shareholder Influence: Managerial Autonomy and Stakeholder Orientation in Comparative Corporate Governance'. *Harvard International Law Journal*, 50(1): 129–94.

Gentile, M.C. (2010). 'Keeping Your Colleagues Honest'. *Harvard Business Review* (March): 114–17.

Gordon, J.N. (2007). 'The Rise of Independent Directors in the United States, 1950–2005: Of Shareholder Value and Stock Market Prices'. *Stanford Law Review*, 59: 1465–1568.

Grayling, A.C. (2007). *Truth, Meaning and Realism*. Continuum, New York.

Hamel, G. (2012). *What Matters Now: How to Win in a World of Relentless Change, Ferocious Competition, and Unstoppable Innovation*. Jossey-Bass, San Francisco.

Hays, J.M. (2003). 'Dynamics or Organizational Wisdom'. Working paper, Australian National University.

Huse, M. (2007). *Boards, Governance and Value Creation*. Cambridge University Press, New York.

Jensen, M. (1986). 'Agency Cost of Free Cash Flow, Corporate Finance, and Takeovers'. *American Economic Review*, 76: 323–9.

Jensen, M. (2002). 'Value Maximization, Stakeholder Theory, and the Corporate Objective Function'. *Business Ethics Quarterly*, 12(2): 235–56.

Jensen, M., and W.H. Meckling (1976). 'Theory of the Firm: Managerial Behavior, Agency Costs and Ownership Structure'. *Journal of Financial Economics*. Repr. in Clarke (ed.) (2004), *Theories of Corporate Governance: The Philosophical Foundations of Corporate Governance*, pp. 58–63. Routledge, London.

Kahneman, D., and D. Lovallo (1993). 'Timid Choices and Bold Forecasts: Perspectives of Risk Taking'. *Management Science*, 39: 24–7.

Kanter, R.M. (2009). *Supercorp: How Vanguard Companies Create Innovation, Profits, Growth, and Social Good*. Random House, New York.

Kanter, R.M. (2011). 'How Great Companies Think Differently'. *Harvard Business Review* (November): 66–78.

Kessler, E.H., and J.R. Bailey (eds) (2007). *Handbook of Organisational and Managerial Wisdom*. Sage, Los Angeles.

Klein, A. (1998). 'Firm Performance and Board Committee Structure'. *Journal of Law and Economics*, 20: 493–502.

Kok, A. (2009). 'Realizing Wisdom Theory in Complex Learning Networks'. *e-Learning*, 7(1): 53–60.

Larcker, D., and B. Tayan (2011). *Corporate Governance Matters: A Closer Look at Organisational Choice and Their Consequences*. Financial Times Press, New Jersey.

Lev, B. (2012). *Winning Investors Over. Surprising Truths about Honesty, Earnings, Guidance, and Other Ways to Boost Your Stock Price*. Harvard Business School Press, Boston, MA.

Lorsch, J.W., and R.C. Clark (2008). 'Leading from the Boardroom'. *Harvard Business Review* (April): 104–11.

Macey, J.R. (2008). *Corporate Governance: Promises Kept, Promises Broken*. Princeton University Press.

Mackey, J. (2011). 'What Conscious Capitalism Really Is'. *California Management Review*, 53(3): 83–90.

Malan, L.-C., and M.P. Kriger (1998). 'Making Sense of Managerial Wisdom'. *Journal of Management Inquiry*, 7 (3): 242–51.

McKenna, B., D. Rooney and K.B. Boal (2009). 'Wisdom Principles as a Meta-theoretical Basis for Evaluating Leadership'. *Leadership Quarterly*, 20: 177–90.

Nonaka, I., and H. Takeuchi (2011). 'The Wise Leader'. *Harvard Business Review* (May): 59–67.

Orwoll, L., and M. Perlmutter (1990). 'The Study of Wise Persons: Integrating a Personality Perspective'. In R.J. Sternberg (ed.), *Wisdom: Its Nature, Origins and Development*, pp. 160–77. Cambridge University Press.

Paine, L.S. (1994). 'Managing for Organisational Integrity'. *Harvard Business Review*, 72: 106–17.

Parameshwar, S. (2006). 'Inventing Higher Purpose through Suffering: The Transformation of the Transformational Leader'. *Leadership Quarterly*, 17: 454–574.

Peng, M.W. (2003). 'Institutional Transitions and Strategic Choices'. *Academy of Management Review*, 28(2): 275–96.

Peng, M.W., and J. Qi Zhou (2005). 'How Network Strategies and Institutional Transitions Evolve in Asia'. *Asia Pacific Journal of Management*, 22: 321–36.

Pfeffer, J. (1972). 'Size and Composition of Corporate Boards of Directors: The Organisation and Its Environment'. *Administrative Science Quarterly*, 17: 218–29.

Pfeffer, J., and G.R. Salancik (1978). *The External Control of Organisations: A Resource Dependence Perspective*. Harper and Row, New York.

Porter, M.E., and M. Kramer (2006). 'Strategy and Society: The Link between Competitive Advantage and Corporate Social Responsibility'. *Harvard Business Review* (December): 78–93.

Porter, M., and M. Kramer (2011). 'Creating Shared Value'. *Harvard Business Review* (January–February): 62–77.

Rajan, R.G. (2010). *Fault Lines: How Hidden Fractures Still Threaten the World Economy*. Princeton University Press.

Rose, J. (2007). 'Corporate Directors and Social Responsibility: Ethics versus Shareholder Value'. *Journal of Business Ethics*, 73: 319–31.

Roubini, N. (2011). *Crisis Economics: A Crash Course in the Future of Finance*. Penguin, London.

Schwartz, B. (2011). 'Practical Wisdom and Organisations'. *Research in Organisational Behavior*, 31: 3–23.

Shiller, R.J. (2012). *Finance and the Good Society*. Princeton University Press, Oxford.

Simons, S. (2002). 'Behavioral Integrity: The Perceived Alignment between Manager's Words and Deeds as a Researcher Focus'. *Organisational Science*, 13 (1): 18–35.

Sonnenfeld, J. (2004). 'Good Governance and the Misleading Myths of Bad Metrics'. *Academy of Management Education*, 9 (1): 108–13.

Sternberg, R.J. (1998). 'A Balance Theory of Wisdom'. *Review of General Psychology*, 2(4): 347–65.

Stout, J. (1993). 'On Having a Morality in Common'. In G. Outka and J.R. Reeder (eds), *Prospects for a Common Morality*, pp. 215–35. Princeton University Press.

Stout, J. (2003). *Ethics beyond Babel*. Princeton University Press.

Trevino, L., G. Weaver, D. Gibson and B. Toffler (1999). 'Managing Ethics and Legal Compliance: What Works and What Hurts'. *California Management Review*, 42(2): 128–42.

Trevinyo-Rodriguez, R. (2007). Integrity: a systems theory classification. Journal of Management History, 13(1) 74–93.

Verhezen, P. (2008). '(Ir)Relevance of Integrity in Organisations'. *Public Integrity*, 10(2): 135–52.

Verhezen, P. (2009). *Gifts, Corruption and Philanthropy: The Ambiguity of Gift Practices in Business*. Peter Lang, Oxford.

Verhezen, P. (2010). 'Giving Voice to a Culture of Silence: From a Culture of Compliance to a Culture of Integrity'. *Journal of Business Ethics*, 96(2): 187–206.

Verhezen, P., P. Notowidigdo and E. Riyana Hardjapamekas (eds) (2012). *Is Corporate Governance Relevant? How Good Corporate Governance Practices Affect Indonesian Organizations*. University of Indonesia Press, Jakarta.

Wallace, P., and J. Zinkin (2005). *Corporate Governance: Mastering Business in Asia*. John Wiley & Sons, Singapore.

Williams, B. (1996). 'Truth in Ethics'. In B. Hooker (ed.), *Truth in Ethics*, pp. 19–34. Blackwell, Oxford.

Williams, B. (2002). *Truth and Truthfulness*. Princeton University Press.

Index

Page numbers in **bold** refer to figures.

Printed and bound in the United States of America